Laughing All the Way

Laughing All the Way

Barbara Howar

STEIN AND DAY/*Publishers*/New York

for my sisters,
Puddin and Charlsie,
who are also
my friends

looking forward into the past
or backward into the future
i walk along the highest hills
and i laugh about it all the way
e e cummings

1

Laughing at myself is what I do best. Lord knows I have had practice, there being no city like Washington for laughable situations, but it appears to me that I have outdistanced even politicians in my race toward the ridiculous. I wanted to make my mistakes at the top and I have. You may think it simple to play the fool in a town that pursues the activity with unrestrained zeal, but my success was no lucky accident. I have had to work making my blunders count against strong contenders through four administrations.

Before you dismiss me as deranged for taking lightly all the trouble I have caused or found in Washington, you had best understand that only somewhat unusual people choose to live in the nation's capital in the first place, and that those of us who know the city and still love it were probably certifiable to begin with. It is not that the U. S. government is an entirely comic matter; but to deal in power, ambition, and the people driven by both, a fine madness and sense of humor are handy things to have. My problem was that I was seldom able to distinguish between reasonable and unreasonable merriment, and the chances are good that I never will.

This story, however, is neither a comedy nor a memoir. It is a report on a life lived in Washington; on a time, a town, and a heroine, all equally foolish. I came looking for glorious recognition, a seat in History. I was not equipped to play the power game but have spent part of a lifetime muddling through it anyhow. Of course, this makes me the rule rather than the exception.

I am not of the right sex to wield great political influence, but my gender has permitted me to consort with those who do. I have an eye for nonsense and hypocrisy and the sheer physical stamina needed to endure total exposure to Washington. This qualifies me as much as anyone to judge local character or point out the absence of it. I level the incriminating finger at my own follies too: I am responsible for my shortcomings, evil deeds, and ignoble thoughts. While these simple admissions set me aside as a Washington oddity, you must bear in mind that, given the chance, I would likely make the same mistakes all over again. I am that much one of the crowd.

I know it was sagely written that each life must get some rain, and though I seem to log more time with an umbrella than the girl on the Morton Salt box, I have loved practically every minute in Washington. I have few complaints and intend no apologies. Living among politicians has had an enormous effect on me and, while I am not prepared to think the reverse is true, I believe the city and I were well met. It is right that I should recount Washington in the bizarre period of the 1960s. We somehow deserved one another.

I have to begin with Mama, a spirited, courageous woman. She survived a disturbing Southern girlhood, an unfulfilling marriage, and alcoholism. She was the strongest, sanest influence on me in the story I am about to tell.

Her father was a rich, whisky-drinking Irishman of high color and humor who liked to cook and gamble when he was not indulging his own children or other men's women. His wife was a serious beauty of German descent, refined and intellectual. She was a fanatical Catholic convert who bore five living children and, at the age of twenty-four, underwent three operations to remove the body of a sixth child that died in the seventh month of pregnancy. In the hospital, she developed uremic poisoning that went straight to her brain, leaving her a madwoman for her remaining sixty-three years. She was never sent to an institution. Mama passed her childhood with an insane mother who only emerged from her room to brandish a butcher knife at my mother's girl friends who she thought had come to seduce her husband. Mama was forced to play and socialize in someone else's home, someone else's world. It was the pattern of her life, a life full of needs, that would have a profound effect on my own.

She was the oldest of five children, raised by whatever servants could be hired to take on a bunch of wild children in an enormous house terrorized by a hopelessly insane woman. When things were particularly bad at home, Mama would take her younger brothers and sisters to board in a Catholic convent, feeding, dressing, and bathing them while the good Sisters clucked over the tragic situation and prayed for a miracle that would improve it. Then and throughout her life, she was her family's source of strength, an unwanted responsibility that she dreamed of exchanging for freedom.

At sixteen Mama accidentally killed a woman who stepped in front of her automobile; at seventeen, she ordered her father's mistress out of town; at eighteen, she pawned a diamond ring and ran away to the adventures of waiting tables in Atlanta. Her Papa adored her and encouraged her spirit, while harnessing it wherever he might. He supported the dead woman's family for twenty years, financed his mistress to Memphis, redeemed the diamond and brought Mama back from Atlanta, and, though he never laid a hand to her, I am told he damned near killed the pawnbroker.

She could only leave home as a bride, but Papa refused to allow her to marry a man she loved because he was a Yankee and divorced. She married my father who was neither, reasoning, she told me later, that it would be nice to have her own apartment, to come and go as she liked. In fact, she and my father lived in Papa's house until his death; and for the remaining forty-five years of their marriage, my father kept close control over her every move.

When her Papa died at the age of forty-six of fast living, Mama gave in to despair for the first and only time in her life. She grieved for nearly two years, then pulled herself together one day and never looked back. She left Nashville, moved to Raleigh, North Carolina, with her husband and daughters, and settled into the lethargic alcoholism peculiar to unfulfilled southern women with the time and money to indulge it: not wild and delirious drunkenness, just a day-to-day use of liquor to keep going until my sisters and I were interesting enough to share our lives with her.

She suffered her last twelve years with a bone disease that disintegrated her spine. Rather than "live out life with a morphine needle in my brain," she elected in 1971 to have a spinal fusion in St. Luke's Hospital in New York City. The operation was a success, but she died ten days later because a congenital tendency of her blood to clot was not noted on her chart and was not treated. Sixty-five years old, she faced

[4]

surgery and death surrounded by the three people she loved best, the three people she had lived for, her daughters. Of us all, she loved me most and lived the last half of her life through me, so much so that it is still difficult to separate the things I did for myself from the things I did for her.

I need nothing to remember her by. The only tangible things I have are an enormous three-foot scrapbook with BARBARA HOWAR embossed on the front and four cardboard boxes of assorted newspaper clippings, invitations, magazines, and letters. These are the sum of an exciting fifteen years I lived in Washington among powerful politicians. We both had wanted this for me: I for living, she for savoring. For Mama, that scrapbook was something she could pore over when she was not actually living out those clippings with me. She kept it with pride, as living proof to her equally frustrated friends that something in *her* life was gay, glamorous, and out of the ordinary.

It is overwhelming to sort through those clippings, to see part of my life yellowing in a memory book and not to feel proud of much of it. I can thumb through the book now only because I understand what Mama and I were looking for during those silly, vacant years. My regret is that I do not have that wise, ambitious, and funny woman standing by me any more showing me where I made a fool of myself.

That was the case. There is no getting around it. It is all right there in the scrapbook, simpering feature stories showing me as a determined young socialite, chairing events for equally wealthy and aimless people. Glued into those pages are hundreds of printed quotes, irreverent and caustic, directed at powerful political figures and their hypocritical lives. Mostly I succeed in exposing my own weaknesses and questionable values. There are stories from *Life, Newsweek,*

[5]

and *Time*. I see myself in full color, a directionless girl, a reckless jester at Washington's political court, but sometimes adept at elbowing her way to power, always using and being used by publicity, and absorbing it all. Some of my remarks and opinions struck close to the nerve, but they were little more than a combination of intolerance for sanctimonious farce and lucky guessing. I was no moral rebel; I simply had no stomach for other people's political or social charades. I did not disapprove of anything, I only demanded that the people distributing the nonsense not insult my intelligence by asking me to buy their motives. I wanted Washington to confess its silly deeds so that I could enjoy myself playing the game in an honest way. The rest could be as good or evil as they liked as long as they had the courage to be counted for precisely what they were. I was unwilling to suffer fools other than myself.

I used people to get attention and they used me, a nice enough girl, good company, good copy, certainly not averse to playing whatever game necessary to escape the Washington horror of being bored or ignored. It was a fair exchange and damned good fun. That power was not a game for women did not daunt me then or now. My concern is that I cannot speak of those Washington days from the lofty standpoint of someone who knew all along that we were pretty ridiculous.

There I am in 1964, on the cover of the *Saturday Evening Post*, posing from the back of the Lady Bird Special Train, showing teeth, legs, and enthusiasm for the candidacy of Lyndon Johnson. Unlined and smug, there is the face of a girl in her twenties who neither knew nor cared what Lyndon Johnson stood for, who knew only that he was the best available bet to save the country from Goldwater conserva-

[6]

tism and me from domestic boredom. I was riding a train south to campaign for a man after the presidency instead of being trapped at home doing all the dull, dreary things that my childhood friends were doing.

There is a color photograph of me in *Time* in a six-hundred-dollar dress dancing cheek to cheek with a man I helped elect President of the United States. For me, happiness was national exposure: being in front of the network television cameras at the Johnson-Humphrey Inaugural while I danced with Lyndon Baines Johnson in full view of millions of people, enjoying the Walter Mitty dream of Washington women. I was *that* woman dancing with *the* President. Those fifteen minutes in Lyndon Johnson's arms elevated me from obscurity. For, whatever else the old Commander-in-Chief may have been, he was highly skilled at wrapping a leg around a dancing partner. I did not go unnoticed.

I loved every minute of that January night in 1964. Aware of being a source of curiosity and jealousy, I brazenly mugged in front with the First Family. I was as vainglorious as any politician in the national spotlight, which is to say I was a gluttonous pig for attention. I also knew that whatever heady pleasures I felt, the same would be true for Mama, riveted to her television set in Raleigh, both of us vindicated at last in our tacit agreement that I was too good to marry the home-town boy and drown in hometown boredom. Not for me, the suffocating southern life—I was "making it" and was as determined to stay in the public eye for four years as was Lyndon Johnson. We only differed in our approach to glory: I did not share the President's mania for approval. I did not give a damn what anyone thought of me just so long as they talked about me.

[7]

The four boxes of newspaper clippings attest to my success: Barbara Howar, arbiter of taste to Texans; Barbara Howar doling out juicy tidbits and clever remarks about Washington; Barbara Howar, the only Johnson "insider" at an anniversary dance given by the Ted Kennedys for the Robert Kennedys; Barbara Howar in New York discothèques with Luci Baines Johnson; Barbara Howar redoing Lynda Bird Johnson with George Hamilton; Barbara Howar throwing swinging parties bringing together Johnson and Kennedy people under one roof; Barbara Howar hostessing, jetting, spending, gossiping, pacesetting, dancing with a lampshade on her head if necessary; Barbara Howar first with the bizarre new fads cropping up in the sixties; Barbara Howar, in inch-long eyelashes and three hairpieces, demanding the spotlight, making friends and enemies envious while she made an ass of herself.

I was hopelessly enamored of my escapades. I was the first to agree when *The New York Times* said I was the best thing to happen to Washington since Jackie Kennedy, and the fastest on my feet for *Women's Wear Daily*, who followed me everywhere but the Ladies' Room. *Life*, suggesting I was too good to be real, probably wrote my epitaph. Good or bad, they could not write enough about me. I would have come from the dead to give an interview, probably with a clever quip about how "with it" we were in Hell.

That all the world did not share my devotion to Barbara Howar was lost on me. It never crossed my mind that I was not adorable or that Lyndon Johnson and his family might become disenchanted with my charms. There simply was no shutting me up. I had to tell every newspaper and magazine that Mrs. Johnson, a lady who spent every waking minute planting trees in ghettos and sprinkling tulip bulbs around settlement houses that had no plumbing, was "off base" with her Beautification Program, that it was "like buying a wig when your teeth are rotting." I had to say in print that Mrs. Johnson's rich New York friends "would be better advised to donate their money to couthless endeavors like fighting street crime, and that to celebrate their philanthropy I would gladly wear a bronze plaque saying: "TODAY I WAS NOT RAPED OR MUGGED THROUGH THE KIND GENEROSITY OF THE LASKER/LOEB FOUNDATIONS." I had to tell the world often that I had a three-year-old son born during "a war that is twice his age."

I never dreamed of barring the press from covering a "small, intimate" gathering we gave in a hired hall for E. William Henry, appointed Chairman of the Federal Communications Commission by John F. Kennedy and curiously retired under Lyndon Baines Johnson, past President and Chairman of the Board of Johnson-owned KTBC in Austin, Texas. It was a party reported in the minutest detail, complete with pictures showing Kennedy-era ladies in short vinyl dresses looking down their east-coast noses at Johnson aides in wide western belts and narrow ties when the reverse was fashionable; Arthur Schlesinger, bellied up to the bar with a Johnson advisor, Arthur wearing a pink shirt, dotted bow tie, and a vaguely stricken look of "should I know you from somewhere?"; Joan Kennedy, shimmering in a silver foil dress, politely oblivious that she was meeting for the dozenth time the ladies of the Great Society. There were pictures where I—the touted fashion advisor to Lady Bird Johnson, constant lady-in-waiting to her daughters, dispenser of White House taste and decorum—am shown dancing on top of the bar in a short white dress barely held up by the fourteen-karat gold chains I told gossip columnist Maxine Cheshire "were cutting into my tender young flesh . . . just a little number the Marquis de Sade whipped up for me."

I suppose I should have asked the wife of the Spanish ambassador not to pretend she was the hatcheck girl or, at the very least, to refuse tips. On reflection, it would have been wiser if actor Robert Vaughn had not picked that party as the place to announce his candidacy for President. But it was all grand good times in 1966. Washington was still cloaking fear and confusion over John Kennedy's assassination behind a facade of supersophistication. Lyndon Johnson did not yet have an iron grip on the city, and we were still vague about Vietnam, still determined to maintain the gaiety of recent years. It was the height of the Batman craze and my guest of honor, Bill Henry, and writer Philip Stern were still enjoying a recent social triumph where they regaled official Washington in a skit where they were costumed as Batman and Robin, who, in turn, posed as LBJ and Jack Valenti talking long distance to Ho Chi Minh about stopping the war. Clark Clifford laughed; Stuart Symington found it funny; why not Lyndon Johnson? And so we danced and gyrated to the ear-splitting music of the mid-sixties, whooping it up until three in the morning while the New Frontier and Great Society were served by Batman waiters in a room dominated by a fifteen-foot papier-mâché model of the Caped Crusader. No one questioned the frenzied celebrating; we assumed it would last forever.

But as newspaper wire services dispatched the message of sin and debauchery in the nation's capital, the White House image-makers began curtailing the frivolity that had seemed acceptable in the Kennedy years, declaring piously that politics and pleasure were no longer compatible pursuits. The Baths of Caracalla were to be closed while Washington officials got religion or, at least, some honorable mentions in the nation's press.

It was an unaccustomed damper in a town renowned for fully enjoying itself in time of crisis, a town conditioned to export reforms rather than live them. There would be, the Johnson White House decreed, no more Arabian Nights in the embassies of underdeveloped countries, no more stories of Mrs. Henry Ford's dress falling off while she did a wild dance with a couple of the fellows from the Cabinet at a White House party for England's Princess Margaret, no more press accounts of our President dancing long, late, and close with the shapely wife of the visiting Prime Minister of Denmark, no front page pictures of Treasury Secretary Henry Fowler shaking a leg with movie star Carol Channing, of the Reverend Billy Don Moyers dancing at the Smithsonian with a girl in a see-through dress. Positively there would be no more Barbara Howar in full color in *Newsweek* and *Time* dancing the frug with Sander Vanocur at the Algerian Embassy, with presidential aide Douglass Cater at the Moroccan Embassy. It was the wildest burst of the sixties, but LBJ was running scared. "Yawl come" changed overnight to "yawl cool it." His private polls showed the country disapproved of exuberant political night life and, though it was highly irregular for Lyndon Johnson to concern himself with the wishes of the electorate, the word came down that gaiety was out. So was I.

I had somehow become synonymous with outrageous merrymaking, and the reasoning went that unloading me was Johnson's ticket to sobriety. I was the most visible and dispensable of the chandelier-swingers, and my demise would serve as a warning to other ambitious Johnson followers who might harbor irreverent feelings about his administration.

[11]

The first of the Great Society to be recycled for oblivion, I was a dandy guinea pig to perfect the technique later known as "the Johnson Treatment." I would have preferred being dropped in the used bin at the Salvation Army.

A highly publicized prewedding party Ed Howar and I were to give for Luci Baines and Patrick Nugent on the roof of the Washington Hotel was abruptly called off by the White House. According to a *Life* writer: "Once Lyndon decided to purge her, Luci's party was canceled . . . and the Greek chorus started in on Barbara. It was like watching jungle cats on the trail of a wounded doe. I've never seen such a job done on anyone in Washington." I fancied myself less a "wounded doe" than a splendid tigress. Certainly I belonged somewhere in the cat family. That same *Life* writer quoted LBJ as saying, "I like that girl, but she talks too much." Never were *Life* and Lyndon so credible.

There was nothing the "wounded doe" could fight back with. She took herself home, back to North Carolina, back to the red clay of reality, pained and humiliated, home to Mama, splattered like a bug on a windshield. It began for me a long period where I rightly disliked myself but for all the wrong reasons. I felt my public disgrace put me back into life's humdrummery in worse shape than I had begun. It never occurred to me that I could distinguish myself in more admirable fashion. I assumed that I was only to have one chance in this life to be special and I had blown it. Overnight, I had gone from an arrogant girl who fancied herself so special even her grocery selections looked more interesting than anyone else's, to a social outcast, forever stripped of celebrity.

During that time in North Carolina I never received a card or call from any but two of my friends. The only thing in the mail that vaguely resembled an invitation was an advance notice of a summer clearance sale at Saks Fifth Avenue. There was nothing but time to question values, time to rummage for inner resources, and take a close look at myself. I was having trouble finding anything that appealed to me.

Everything fell apart. My marriage went with it. I had led Ed Howar a merry chase, kept him busy opening doors and lighting cigarettes, using him as window dressing for my ego trip, someone to pick up the check, someone I knew about as well as a hired gigolo. He was just as much a product of his background as I; our understanding and tolerance of each other were equally limited, our rapport was broken by my ambition. We neither knew nor liked the people we had become. As things got worse, we stopped trying to communicate. Six months later we were divorced.

That summer of 1966 was passed in funereal calm, in a rented house on the North Carolina coast. All conversations were discussions of whether or not Ed and I should withdraw our six-year-old daughter, Bader, from Luci's wedding, where she was to be the flower girl. It was a touchy protocol decision, a child care problem that would have boggled Dr. Spock.

Bader's name was spread over newspapers and magazines, and she would trace her finger over the columns till she found it. White House press releases had transposed Bader to Bedar, resulting in much indignation from her and feeble excuses from me as to why I was not in a position to inform the White House of their error. Nor was I able to explain to Bader that we were *voluntarily* withdrawing her from the wedding, or soften the eventual blow of facing her playmates when they found out—as they always do in Washington—that she was not to be the flower-strewing little princess in one of the most celebrated weddings since the Marriage Feast at Cana.

It was Mama who finally reasoned that Bader would be better off as the unwanted member of the wedding than as the center of further publicity that would ensue if she were withdrawn. "Just start packing your bags. Those sons-of-bitches used you and dropped you when you learned how to play their game. Well, maybe they don't know any better, but we do. We're going back to Washington and give them a run for their money. If I have to rent a nanny's costume and take her myself, Bader is going to walk down that aisle, and you, Barbara Howar, are going to stand up there and show them you have some guts. They've disposed of you one time too often for my money. They couldn't break your spirit before, and they won't do it this time. I've had about enough of those tacky Johnsons. Who do they think they are? They aren't even *real* southerners."

And so, by God, we packed up and came back to Washington to face what was not our first tangle with the Johnsons, only the last. It was a nightmarish ordeal. Mama was at my side, taking little Bader's hand and telling me to hold my shoulders up, nodding a cool "Good morning, Mrs. Johnson" here and a correct "How well you look, Mr. President" there. Sweetness and light, fire and ice, we showed more class than the Johnson White House was accustomed to. Mama had occasion to walk with Bader past the vast army of TV cameras and reporters that choked off the endless steps to the gaudy Shrine of the Immaculate Conception at Catholic University, the scene of the wedding. Everything was overdone and overreported, in the Johnson-Texas style I came to regard as the Early Hog Calling Period. Desperate for the inside news, a television correspondent stopped Bader and asked, "Would you like to grow up to be a pretty bride like Luci?" Before she could answer, Mrs. Johnson's social sergeant-at-arms, Bess Abel, grabbed the child by the upper arm and jerked her away. Mama, never enamored by brides or Mrs. Abel, took the child back with a delicate, gloved hand, saying into the microphone, "Bess honey, don't you worry yourself about Bader. I'm sure you must have a thousand little duties to do." The newsman repeated his question to Bader who answered: "I want to be like my mommy." The statement perhaps moved television audiences to nausea, but it touched me. I was flattered it had crossed her mind to emulate me and more than a little fearful that she might.

Later, Mama and I could regale each other with wedding stories, her experiences before the ceremony in the private room for the bridal party, and my ordeal and observations as a guest. When Ed and I walked into the vestibule of the church, we were singled out quickly by a strange young usher whom I would have thought unable to recognize us in a police lineup. I took his arm and a deep breath, preparatory, I thought, to the long, agonizing walk down the main aisle, only to take the ten or so steps necessary to reach a back pew where Ed and I were quite unceremoniously deposited, some dozen or so empty pews from the other guests.

It was actually a splendid vantage point from which to view the grand entrances of the women—most of whom could have passed as "mother of the bride"—clad in gentle, modest gowns of pastel colors, with hats, shoes, bags, and gloves in almost matching shades. Certainly I saw a number of things not reported in the wedding stories: a hefty Texas couple who took turns snapping flash pictures of each other in their pew with a camera the lady eventually returned to her bulging beaded purse; the impressive display offered by

[15]

one of Mrs. Johnson's lady friends who, in the best tradition of Nieman-Marcus gimmickry, cooled her sizeable self with a battery-operated fan.

I would gladly relive the entire drama to see once more the pageant of a florid Hale Boggs, the late Louisiana congressman and Johnson sidekick, who ceremoniously ascended the priest's pulpit before the wedding and read aloud from the Old Testament:

> "May your wife be like a fertile vine and may your children spring around the table like olive trees. . . ."

I had seen Hale Boggs in many poses during those years, but I was not expecting him in the role of lay preacher. Most certainly I was not prepared for the spectacle of the largest choir and loudest organ east of Salt Lake City which answered Mr. Boggs. Sopranos shrieked back the text in song: "fertile vine, fertile vine, fertile vine"; followed on cue by bass voices chanting: "may your children spring around the table like olive trees", sopranos again: "olive trees, olive trees, olive trees." Over and over, a hundred strong voices boomed into the heavy, sultry air and echoed off the marble walls. They shattered the pious quiet of the cavernous cathedral and moved me to tears of laughter that I hid behind a handkerchief—leaving, I hope, the impression that I had at last found God.

At the White House, where we were watered down in a pink and white tent before the ordeal of an official receiving line in the Blue Room, I found myself jowled up with Perle Mesta whom I had mentioned in an article *Life* had done on me some weeks prior to Luci's wedding. I had told the reporter that "following in Mrs. Mesta's footsteps" as a Washington hostess "was my idea of nothing to do. . . ." Actually my idea of nothing to do was having to face Mrs. Mesta and all those people, rubbing up against what seemed like every Johnson in the world with still another *Life* quote ringing in my ears: "The Johnsons . . . are not my speed nor I theirs. . . ." However, Madame Mesta only swelled like a toad when she encountered me. Like Alice, I would not have been surprised to hear her shout, "Off with her head." It was our first televised wedding together since Mrs. Mesta had hosted a reception for the mock TV wedding of the stars of the Washington-based comedy series, "The Farmer's Daughter," where Inger Stevens as the Swedish maid married her congressman-employer. That Mesta wedding reception, like the television show, was obviously sponsored by the Clairol Company, for, as the famous Washington guests went through the receiving line they were given free lipstick samples. While no cosmetics were passed out at the Johnson-Nugent wedding, I was struck by the similarity of the guest list.

Inside the White House, as I stepped up to the military aide to give him my name, I was frozen with apprehension at facing the most powerful man in the world—a situation made worse by the knowledge that my remaining bond with the Johnsons was the mutual wish that I could vanish into thin air. I petitioned the Good Lord: "Get me out of this one, Sweet Jesus, and I'll never do another bad thing as long as I live," a promise so empty it should have occasioned thunder and lightning.

Moving woodenly, smiling plastically, "Yes, Mr. President. Thank you, I'm very proud of Bader too."—"Such a lovely wedding, Mrs. Johnson."—"Luci, how beautiful you look." Mumbling congratulations to Pat Nugent who, to the great surprise of everyone, leaned over and kissed me. Done, I walked away from my final audience with the Johnson family, and was relieved beyond belief to be halfway through my public penance. Hands trembling from strain, I went through my paces like a robot listening to a voice in my head that sounded like Mama: "Walk now, don't run. . . . Move toward the State Dining Room . . . smile . . . look calm. . . . Head straight for the bar . . . just one glass of champagne. . . . Now get the hell out of here."

In the State Dining Room that sweltering August day, shoe-horned full of Johnson kin and friends, I was greeted by hostility and silence somewhat like that the thirteenth fairy must have encountered when she popped in on Sleeping Beauty's christening party. There were two spontaneously gracious gestures that afternoon. First, Helen Williams, the Johnsons' longtime maid, gave me a guarded hug and tearfully told me "not to hold anything against Luci. She didn't want to do this to you, Barbara, they made her . . . that baby just did what she was told. She loves you. You know that." Then, Alice Roosevelt Longworth, splendid in her big picture hat, walked the length of the mammoth East Room, slowly and deliberately. She gave me a warm greeting, her eyes sparkling mischievously, daring anyone to challenge her attention to me, and flashed me a smile that said "Forget this . . . it's just a silly interlude." I would have fallen on a sword for either lady.

My final exit from the White House was not made laughing but smiling bravely, painfully aware that I would not soon be traipsing through that mansion that gave me such pride, such a sense of instant history and swelling patriotism. As I walked with my husband, child, and mother past the Catlin paintings of American Indians, I remembered other White House visits. Times when Mama and I would drive in through the Southwest Gate, park the car under the canopy to the Diplomatic Entrance, and sashay ourselves and our awestruck Raleighite guests past guards and guides, to take a private tour of the public rooms, and when we really wanted to lay it on, go right into the family quarters. Times when Ed Howar and I would stand at the foot of the grand staircase, formally at attention and swallowing back tears of pride and excitement, while the First Family descended, the President always a little to the front, as the Marine Band played "Hail to the Chief"—still the most moving music I ever heard in Washington.

2

I am a sixth generation southerner, a fact in which I take inordinate pride, but to be perfectly frank I have never been certain whether my ancestors chose to remain in the South because they loved it or because they were too lazy to leave. Still, I have never avoided being southern nor have I made a cult of it; I just am. Except for those irritating instances when the stereotype of the dumb southern belle has been applied to me, my southernness has served me well. Since I can remember I have oversalted my food and vocabulary, eaten meat fried, stood up for "Dixie," and preferred country music when I was not tuned to the sound of my own voice— which, you may as well know, falls somewhere between the decibel levels of Minnie Pearl and Scarlett O'Hara. While I am not entirely certain my tendency to act from emotion rather than intelligence is a desirable trait, a southern accent does come in handy, and I am not above dropping a few extra vowels when it suits my purpose, saying "you all" to kings, presidents, and traffic cops. Fluttering an imaginary magnolia leaf helps cover gaffes, blunders, and poisonous asides. I am also very handy with the barnyard language of an agricultural area when my southern temper is aroused.

From my mother's blood lines I drew black Irish moods, a reckless bent for excitement, a need to traffic in danger and feel the delicious prickle of daring. My father's people were a conservative and careful lot, law-abiding, God-fearing patriots who would have floundered without rules and regulations: honest town-folk with more determination than flare, conscientious, upstanding, and a trifle dull. They are wholesome, treelined, wall-to-wall, middle-class people with abiding caution and controlled emotions, all laudatory virtues not wildly apparent in my personality. From my father I inherited an almost neurotic need for honesty. From him I learned the benefits of an orderly mind; but whatever intellectual merits I have often appear to be in such short supply that I hesitate tracing them to my father. I have learned a lot of dumb things on my own.

Neither family tree produced any soaring talent, but we have survived with our sense of humor intact. Six generations of southern blood bred me into an understanding that I am special—an understanding fortunately accompanied by the good sense not to question it too closely. I go home often because it is the only place I can still distinguish the throwbacks from the rest of the folks.

I grew up in Raleigh, the middle child of mismatched parents acting out a Strindbergian marriage that was kept together by fear of God and social censure, and made tolerable by alcohol and a peculiar need for one another that I am neither disposed nor equipped to explain. We pussyfooted around my father, never using his fountain pen or fingernail scissors or touching the newspaper till he had finished. We ate when he was hungry, took accurate telephone messages, and learned rather early that he would stand by us in the face of financial or criminal disaster, but that he could be a tyrant if we failed to return his car keys to the proper bowl on the table in the hall.

Rather than defy Daddy, we worked around him, gave lip service to his demands, courted his idiosyncrasies and soft-pedaled our political differences. Like all southern conservatives, my father was the product of a culture that valued smart dogs more highly than smart women, and smart Negroes not at all. It was easier for us to accept the premises that whites are better than blacks, and men superior to women. Quite frankly, I doubt it ever crossed our minds that he was not correct in his assumptions. Certainly we girls accepted with sympathy and understanding Daddy's disappointment that not one of us was a boy and tried very hard to help him make the best of a bad situation. My sisters and I avoided him and worked through Mama, who thoroughly enjoyed her role as power broker.

We were all seasoned at fluffing up Daddy. He was a basically dear and likeable man surrounded by a pack of female Uncle Toms who pandered to his masculinity and allowed him to rule unchallenged, to assert himself right out of the picture. He was a good provider, with more energy for success than for his family, a willing victim of the social system that traditionally robs a man of truly knowing his children or enjoying them. It was a system that forced my mother into the tragedy of having nothing more to do with her life than be all things to her children, keeping us for herself to live out her personal frustrations, devouring us in a less known version of the Jewish mother. It was a good life complicated only by the lack of warmth such a patriarchy produces and by the alcoholism necessary, I suppose, for my parents to forget their personal unhappiness.

We were a class-conscious, small-town, southern family with an unmortgaged house filled with the symbols of status. We were driven by the need to keep up appearances, hiding our problems behind a cheery facade of neighborhood conformity. All calamities were judged by how they would look to the people next door, who undoubtedly viewed their tragedies in much the same way. The first priority in the case of the pregnant girl was how to marry her off without embarrassment; the boy expelled from prep school for cheating was protected by pretending illness; the man arrested for drunk driving, wife beating, or dipping into company funds was equally adroit at packaging his deed for public consumption. The cause of the problem was ignored in the shuffle to cloak it in propriety; any lie or trick was acceptable as long as it was tidily bundled in face-saving hypocrisy.

I have a friend in Raleigh, the daughter of old money, a lonely girl who married properly and had two children before she became an alcoholic and moved on to the hard drugs that wrecked her life. She is now back home, alone, on the third floor of a large mansion, living out her time on morphine supplied by church-going parents who still refuse to acknowledge her problem and who continue to ignore the available help that might salvage their only child. Her father remains on the board of all the state hospitals, still an ardent prohibitionist, still too concerned with his image to let the world know something is amiss under his roof. For those who bother to inquire, these good, upstanding parents will tell you their daughter has back trouble. They drop her personal calling card into silver platters at wakes, weddings, and debuts as though she had actually been present instead of spaced out in the family attic like some grotesque creature from a Brontë novel. To a greater or lesser degree, depending on the family coffers, this is how tragedy is handled down home.

I was taught not to take my pants down in someone's garage; not to gang up on smaller children; to be respectful of elders; never lie, cheat, steal, or damage other people's property; and to be home before dark. I was forbidden to swear or interrupt conversations or say "nigger"—no respect for the Negro, just a subtle caste distinction for upper-class southern children. I was guilty of all of these, which was actually all right as long as nobody caught me at them. I was also warned to avoid adopted children because "one never knows what they come from."

Every adult of my childhood either drank most of the time or sermonized those who did. I confess to being nearly grown before realizing that not everyone's parents dressed for the day accessorized by a brown paper bag with a bottle of bourbon. My favorite friends had parents who fought and drank behind lace curtains and were so busy keeping the Baptists and bootleggers in business that we kids were free to grow up with less of the hypocritical priggishness church-going abstainers visited upon their children. Drinking parents afforded us brief spells of running wild.

In the same way, I accepted the Saturday night "cuttings" of the household help, drunk on "white lightning" or "Sneaky Pete" at Fat Daddy's Danceland in the Negro section of Raleigh. I took in stride the black-eyed, bruised ladies of quality who had suffered similar brutality in a nicer section of town at the hands of white gentlemen filled with a higher-quality whisky. I accepted my father's gout when he shuffled around on a cane, even though I knew perfectly well that gout is a southern euphemism for "jake leg," an affliction peculiar to those who develop a taste for locally distilled gin. I understood that "hunting trips" and "card parties" were genteel excuses for out-of-town drinking bouts and that, for a few days, I would be left to my own not altogether honorable devices. While they were often sad and depressing times, I was given a sense of freedom I came to love.

Like all small southern towns, we had our share of neighborhood weirdos. There were two widowed sisters who lived in something less than sororal bliss in a mammoth house down the street. They became quite commonplace in their shrieking, violent battles, which we watched through the windows. We were fascinated but nonplussed when the larger of the sisters would come to the porch shouting: "Hear ye! Hear ye! There will be no fight today. We are going to the Flower Show!" Just as casually, we accepted the village pervert who could throw his voice and make us think his dog could talk. We knew to avoid him in the kiddie matinée where he followed us every Saturday and was seemingly unoffended when we moved to another seat, lest he "hypnotize us and sell us into white slavery." We were blasé about old Faytie, the town's "confessed homosexual" who, we were certain, wore a yellow tie on Thursdays as a secret signal to other homosexuals, and poor Black Woodrow who pushed an ancient perambulator down the main street shaking a big Mason jar full of corns and toenails while he begged for his deformed offspring, singing: "Help the little cripple children, can't half walk. Help the little cripple children, can't half talk." There were two lesbian ladies we called the "Big Hats" owing to their elaborate millinery tastes. We kids would follow them for a block or two, speculating on the clinical side of their relationship, but we ultimately absorbed them calmly, considering them just a couple of ladies in the passing small-town parade.

I was a Depression baby with no memory of bread lines, save those state-protected ducks that queued up at Pullen Park Lake for the crumbled biscuits and cornbread we would save from Sunday lunch at the Dixie Inn. Deprived of nothing tangible, we played in the street, skating or hopscotching between violent games of Kick the Can, hung from trees that lined the road, and played Witch in the Ditch (or Nigger on the Griddle) when we were not riding Flexie Flyers on the few existing sidewalks. There was at least one bicycle in every garage and Tarzan rope-swings in the woods out back where we built elaborate forts, played doctor, and stalked each other with Red Ryder BB Guns. Adult recreation consisted of sporadic golfing at the country club, football and basketball games at the four local colleges, and, always, heavy drinking in the kitchen.

I was reared by a succession of Negro women who worked twelve hours a day and slept on an army cot in a room off the back. These women were not the old family retainers Faulkner romanticized, but third- and fourth-generation Negroes far removed from the Civil War era of the grand plantation that my father was so fond of recalling. They reared white people's children for fifteen dollars a week and all they could "tote" home to a house full of their own kids whose fathers they had lost track of. Theirs was a life of survival, void of militancy. Their main concern was getting from one payday to the next without being knocked up or knifed, and they seldom avoided either for long. Sometimes they would leave to work in the tobacco factories in Durham or Richmond where they made five dollars more a week and did not have to sleep in. Generally they returned and, if they had left behind a reasonable record of sobriety and honesty, and were willing to take the salary cut and work Sundays, they got their jobs back.

Daddy gave his old tuxedo coats to the headwaiter at the country club, smiling as he clapped his back and called him a "lazy nigger." If his own Saturday night had not been bad, my father would go bond Sunday morning for his jailed help. On more than one occasion I knew him to pick up the tab for a set of store-bought teeth, with the understanding, of course, that when the help got "lippy" or "uppity" enough to prefer the tobacco factory to rearing his children, the teeth remained with him.

These women were used up and disposed of very much the way we run through paper plates and napkins today. There always seemed to be a Loujeania, Cleddie, Hattie, even a Pearly Mae, shuffling around the house in worn mules, an old silk stocking on her head, vanilla extract behind her ears. She knew how to keep a civil tongue in her mouth alongside the ever-present wad of Sweetpeach Snuff.

I shelled peas, helped her bring in the wash, never ate cookies in the living room, my way, I guess, of showing her the same subservience she endured in other parts of the house. Hers was the only voice of authority I recognized, so much so that later I would listen to a Shirley Chisholm with a Pavlovian attention I do not hold for a Margaret Chase Smith.

I loved each of those women, surrogates for my absent parents, and a great part of whatever sense of morality I have came, I think, from whatever they had time to impart. Eloise, a strong and proud woman with more than a little white blood in her past, was the first adult to caution me not to go through life "as a hellion-hearted girl making trouble for folks"—advice I managed to put out of mind for the next twenty years. When I was eleven, Eloise left to have a baby, and I was told that she had done something very bad, that I was to forget her and everything she had ever told me. Indeed, she had already briefed me on the pleasures of sex and instructed me on the body's functions. I missed her desperately and wanted more of her clumsy affection. During lonely evenings she would sing me all the verses to "Birmingham Jail" and illustrate the facts of life with colorful anecdotes I could not get from my parents, for the simple reason that we did not know each other that well. She dragged me to Negro churches where I learned to fear God, sitting up front with her in an unaccustomed state of starch and polish, squirming and chewing on the wooden handles of paper funeral parlor fans for hours of sermons and moaning repentance. I was terrified of fire and brimstone, enthralled by visions of salvation for those who could endure life patiently, do God's will, be His humble servant in this world, and get a better deal in the next. It was pretty much the same line handed me later in Catholic churches.

Raleigh was a small town in those days, a suburb in itself. Civil War carpetbaggers had encouraged black squatters to settle around the nicer white neighborhoods, a measure of Reconstruction particularly galling to a city whose ancestors had not wholly put themselves out to fight Yankees. In my old neighborhood, one-story clapboard houses of blacks were sprinkled among the two-story brick dwellings of the whites. After the Supreme Court decision on integration, most whites moved to outlying housing developments dotted with tacky shopping centers that do not cater to Negroes, except for the occasional black couple in a movie house or a handful of dark children holding numbers to be served in a franchised ice cream parlor.

Twenty-five years ago, black and white played together constantly, we whites taking our superiority for granted. I was the undisputed leader of an integrated gang, wore fly-front pants before they were fashionable, smoked, swore, and shoplifted better than any boy of either color. I could climb trees higher, throw rocks farther, shoot strips of rubber innertubing from wooden guns three times the distance of anyone else. I could interrupt telephone conversations on the party line with the most shocking words.

There was a rotting wooden bridge that spanned the muddy river at Lassiter's Mill where we swam in our underwear and took turns daring each other to leap the thirty feet from the bridge rail to the water. It was a measure of courage or cowardice. I can recall the exhilaration of being the only girl fool enough to take the chance and the wonderful feeling of being one of the boys when I came up alive and gasping for air. I could, and in fact did, do anything the boys could do, except go to the bathroom standing up, which always struck me as an act more convenient than superior.

Under my command, we started the brush fire that burned out the old Negro cemetery up the hill from our block. The graves were marked with wooden tombstones that bore only one name along with highly questionable dates of birth and death: "Lonnie . . . Come in 1846, Gone in 1916." They all went in 1943 amidst smoke and chaos. Negroes, screaming to God for help, frantically passed buckets of water to keep the fire from spreading to their wooden shanties nearby. Fire trucks seldom came in Raleigh unless white sections were in danger. Even without them, it was the most exciting event of my youth. I still recall an old Negro woman who sometimes did fancy ironing for my Mama, wringing her hands and wailing, "Andrew, poor Andrew, they done devil him in his rest."

It never occurred to me I had committed an egregious crime against human beings, nor did it cross my mind that I would be punished for it, because, in truth, I had heard many a grown white man say that the whole of nigger town ought to have been burned out long ago. If anything, I was a source of sly amusement among my elders, a spirited nine-year-old girl, white and not responsible. A twelve-year-old black boy named George Washington House was supposed to be watching out for me. That is what he got paid twenty-five cents a week for.

Growing up with Negro children, however lacking in balance, gave me a feel for their language and a sense of natural harmony with them. Years later I would entertain bigoted friends with "nigger stories" told in perfect dialect; and, much later, when I came to understand racism, the camaraderie of those days gave me a comfortable rapport with the black people who let me be their friend.

We did not think about color then, any of us. We were just kids together who came from the same red clay, united in our hatred of Germans and Japs, happy to be the right age to enjoy the drama World War II afforded. We played at war for four years and it never got gory enough for us. I have long suspected the Confederate armies fought so bravely during the Civil War as much to satisfy their violent women as to avenge national honor, an outlet, perhaps, for so much sexual suppression. Certainly my thirst for blood was never thwarted.

The big treat in my war-mongering days was to stand on the main highway that links New York and Miami and watch convoys coming or going between Quantico and Fort Bragg. Solemn, in a WAC suit my mother brought me from her annual New York trip, I sometimes stood rigidly at attention, my rifle over my shoulder and my hand over my heart. Other times I would hold up a water canteen in comradely salute to the truckloads of soldiers, drinking them so many toasts I would have to waste precious moments going to the bathroom behind the bushes. My friends and I would jump around shouting "Sieg Heil!" or "Banzai!" We would roll over and play dead when we shot one another, then leap up to yell "V for Victory!" and call out obscene suggestions to the cattled-up soldiers as to which part of Hitler's or Hirohito's anatomy they should shoot off first. A photographer took my picture in full uniform saluting a convoy. The day it ran in the *Raleigh Times* was one of my proudest moments and probably the beginning of a deep and abiding love for personal recognition. The American Legion, ever alert for patriotism, asked Mama if I could stand at attention beside the card table set up to sell War Bonds in front of the Ambassador Theatre every Meatless Tuesday. Tuesday was the day my mother's friends played cards while they did their drinking, and it was not convenient.

My most treasured possession was a captured swastika flag, for which I exchanged all my Katzenjammer Kids comics and my entire collection of playing card jokers, including the wooden Kraft cheese box I kept them in. I nailed the flag on my bedroom wall surrounded by the V-mail letters Mama's youngest brother sent from Europe, where, to my great pride, he served with General Patton. Sometimes he remembered me with Nazi medals from a German corpse; but my souvenirs were nothing compared to the boy down the block whose collection of hand grenades, swords, and Japanese helmets were sent him by two uncles before they died at the end of the Pacific campaign. I so envied him those treasures I was moved to steal a helmet from his trophy room, but had to march it right back after dinner and make a sullen confession.

Daddy was bitterly disappointed when he was refused an army commission, owing to an old tubercular lung scar. So, in fact, were we all, each for different and not altogether loyal reasons. He became a crack hoarder, supplying us with whisky, sugar, mayonnaise, and a Zenith floor-model radio that transmitted the overseas war news I monitored nightly, eyes wide, jaws working over an enormous wad of black-market bubble gum.

Daddy smoked Lucky Strike Greens when tin foil went to war, and Mama wore a gray uniform and a jaunty cap to drive the Red Cross Bloodmobile—up until 1942 when she had an accident backing out of the College Inn parking lot where it was her habit to take a beer break. She was reassigned to the switchboard at the Filter Center, but she changed quickly to another job less essential to the war effort. She and her best friend, Bette Poole, became nurses' aides and learned to make beds while the patients were in them and empty bedpans while the patients were off them: tasks not to their tastes, because they soon switched to bandage rolling and brought home huge bundles of splints, tapes, and slings, which Grey Poole and I would apply to his baby sister, Boopie, trussing her up from head to toe and racing out to terrorize the neighborhood, while our mothers drowned their war worries in bourbon and Boopie screamed and flailed about the playroom like the tortured little mummy she was.

My older sister wore angora sweaters and somebody's silver bombardier wings while she passed out coffee and donuts. She was less concerned with the war, I recall, than with the soldiers she danced with at the USO who were home on leave, or the "pen pal" correspondence she maintained with the boys still at the front. My personal war efforts consisted of turning off Henry Aldrich during mock blackouts and dogging the steps of the air raid warden on his neighborhood rounds. I was also charged with squeezing yellow food coloring into white margarine and squashing and stringing tin cans which we stored in the garage for weekly pickups, alongside stacks of newspapers and every wire coat hanger I could smuggle out of the house.

There was meat every day, and occasionally a couple of pullet hens from those wrung and plucked for the Carolina Freezerlocker Plant on Glenwood Avenue, where all the town richies hoarded their meat in numbered vaults that were mechanically hauled up by an awesome gentleman with rumored "German connections." On rainy days I played grocery store in the basement, stacked with canned goods, gas tins, retread tires, and country hams curing themselves on hooks. I removed the can labels so early in the war that for most of rationing, we never knew whether we would be eating peaches or peas with our bootlegged meat.

To avoid the summer polio epidemic, we drove over the mountain in a high priority "A" stickered car to visit our own German relatives in Tennessee. My Great-Great-Aunt Nadinia Hess adored me and Adolf Hitler, and I was farmed out to her three afternoons a week on the off chance that her vast real estate holdings in Berlin might survive the war and need an heir. A frail, sharp-featured old woman, given to poking her cane at you when expounding Prussian superiority and the efficiency of the Third Reich, she wore a crocheted Bavarian shawl and sat queenlike in a Victorian bed, alongside an ill-tempered Spitz dog called Cripple because he was. She ruled the poorer branch of Hesses, two quite mad spinster ladies always in conversation with Blessed Mary—"Now Blessed Mary, you move over on the divan and let Barbara sit down"—in a malodorous old mansion in downtown Nashville that, quite appropriately, has been turned into a funeral parlor.

Great-Great-Aunt "Dini" instructed me in German lore, extolling the greatness of her distant cousin Rudolf Hess, celebrated until he parachuted behind British lines, crazy as a loon and babbling for peace. She disavowed the kinship after that, but given the general lunacy of the American Hesses, I have never been sure. I passed those afternoons in sullen agony, stuffing up on éclairs and tea sandwiches, indulging in wild fantasies where I blew up the house, singlehandedly wiping out the old ladies, who along with Blessed Mary, were fronts for an international spy ring. I would be ceremoniously decorated by the President and presented with a rolled document containing indisputable evidence that we were not related to that pack of geriatric fascists or any other Hess with Nazi leanings.

I was enthralled by war movies, especially the newsreels and the "Time Marches On" short subjects of our boys overseas. The colored maid would take a friend and me every Saturday to the Ambassador Theatre where she could sit in the third balcony if accompanied by a white child. We stayed for the main feature twice to see the news again, wolfing giant Captain Tootsies and Guess Whats that would drool down our chins when we booed FDR the way we learned to do at home. Afterward we would go to the ice house for half-smoked frankfurters and cold RC Colas or Orange Crushes, the maid fanning flies and swapping gossip with other maids while my friends and I reenacted the movie. I was always John Hodiak until I saw the Fighting Seabees, then I was Dennis O'Keefe for the duration. The war ended considerably sooner than my fascination with violence, a fact that would amuse me later when I found myself in the middle of an antiwar demonstration.

I went on to play Nyoka the Jungle Girl or Mary Marvel, passing the rest of adolescence doing nothing more exciting than making crank calls: "Madam, is your refrigerator running?"—"Sir, do you have Prince Albert in the can?" It was never the good, clean fun of World War II.

In 1946, Mama had the poor taste to have my younger sister Charlsie in a hospital corridor crowded with war brides who looked like Jeanne Crain, their long wavy hair held back by pink or blue ribbons depending on the sex of the baby. Mama was silver-haired and forty-two. Both of us were embarrassed by Charlsie's birth and probably for the same reasons. I was more than a little annoyed at the prospect of becoming an unsalaried babysitter, an inconvenience I made up for by experimenting on Charlsie with Toni Home Permanents until her hair fell out, and later by signing her name in big, block letters to my lunch tab at the country club. I blossomed into my teens accompanied by a toddler on an imaginary horse named Red Dust whose highly visible and untidy rider addressed me as "Blah Blah." The equine interest and nickname have survived the years, as has my aversion to both.

Charlsie, masculinely named because she was the last blunder in Daddy's quest for a son, was eleven years my junior, which may explain in part my devotion to her and my continuing need to protect her from all the aspects of life I found painful. Since my parents were away often and drank away the time they spent at home, Charlsie was left in my dubious care. I bought her clothes, arranged birthday parties, and dragged her with me everywhere. I loved and resented her every step of the way. I carted her on my dates, subjected her to the boredom of afternoons in Hobson Gattis' Drug Store consuming grilled pimento-cheese sandwiches, and filled her with sufficient junk food to dwarf a less sturdy child. She was tolerant of my moods, fetching me Cokes from the kitchen, hanging up my clothes, and trying not to put her finger in her nose when we would slow down to flirt with the college boys on our endless drives past the fraternity houses at the state college.

She went to summer camp with me, to school, and on most Sunday afternoons she indulged my passion for horror shows in the old rat-filled Wake Theatre, a movie house about twenty feet wide, with sprung seats and an air-cooling system that blew your hair straight back off the face. In turn, I took her to every dog and horse film made, and once sat like a galumph in a bleacher filled with screaming kiddies and flying objects, so that she could wave at Howdy Doody for the television camera. She became expert at lying about my fast driving and smoking vices. We became habit with one another and stuck together during the drinking battles Mama and Daddy would begin in the kitchen and move upstairs to us, where we were expected to choose which parent we would side with on their frequent attempts to separate.

Daddy was given to insulting his peers and superiors in midnight telephone calls where it was his wont to go into great detail concerning their birth origins, habits, intelligence, and manhood. We came to call this nocturnal pursuit "telephonitis." To curb the habit, Mama would cut the phone wires, requiring a weekly visit from the repair man whom she greeted with: "Well, Barbara has done it again!" It was with great relief that I passed the blame to Charlsie when she got big enough to look handy with a pair of scissors.

Our older sister, the only one of us with a double southern

name or a taste for collard greens, was eighteen when Charlsie was born, and delighted by a baby sister strangers thought her own. Named Ann-Frances and called Puddin, she was seven years my senior and cared little for my company. We fought constantly. I drew mustaches on the movie stars in her *Photoplay* magazines, feigned nausea over her Frank Sinatra records, and screamed "hubba-hubba" into the extension when boy friends phoned. In turn, she cut the heads off my Dionne Quintuplet paper dolls, painted my Scotty dog's paw-nails with Ultra Violet polish, and complained dramatically about sharing a room with someone whose aversion to soap and water was neighborhood legend. Our sole conversations, I recall, consisted of arriving at the price she would pay me to go downstairs during cocktail parties and pantomime a bootblack while she entertained company with a snappy rendition of "Chattanooga Shoe Shine Boy." I charged higher to shuffle along playing Margaret O'Brien to her Judy Garland while she sang "If You Like-a Me Like I Like-a You" from *Meet Me in St. Louis,* a movie she saw seven times.

She had a black velvet cape like Snow White's and an ivory-colored bedside radio that I was not allowed to touch until she went away to dramatic school in New York. I spent the first six weeks she was gone wrapped in her cape, listening to "A Date with Judy" on her radio, and playing horseshoes with her forty-three sterling silver bangle bracelets, which Mama wouldn't let her take north because, she said, "It wasn't a good idea to trust Yankees with your valuables." This advice Puddin later forgot when she ended her promising dramatic career to marry a Connecticut boy whose only apparent talent was fathering a baby born seven months later and five others that followed in rapid succession.

"Premature babies," charitably accepted in those days,

were sometimes run through an incubator for an hour to lend credence to the myth. My first nephew weighed in at over ten pounds and there was not an incubator in the county large enough to accommodate him. His mother is quite open about the subject of his early birth and her honesty earned his respect. Certainly she has mine. Many of Puddin's friends, and later my own, were forced to marry for the wrong reasons. Generally, like my own sister, the unions ended in divorce; but, at the time, shotgun ceremonies were so common in the South that the bride was often more concerned with shopping for a layette than for a trousseau.

My sister's unfortunate marriage and eventual struggle with the six children she dutifully bore on religious dictates, combined with my grandmother's illness from having "all the babies God sends," were sufficient evidence for me to question the teachings of the family's Catholicism. Certainly these grotesque events made me less than the ideal recipient for the theological lessons suffered during the twelve years I spent in a Catholic school. I was subjected to a substandard parochial education, not because of my Catholic mother's religious devotion, but because my Protestant father had been required to sign a pledge to that effect before he and my mother could marry.

Many years later I asked Lillian Hellman what it was like to be a Jewish girl in the South of her day. She never felt any exclusion, she told me, because she was, after all, neither black nor Catholic. The same was true in Raleigh. The few Jews living there pretended they were not, leaving Catholics as the most disliked, feared, and avoided minority group in the city. However genteelly disguised, this prejudice, ever-present throughout my adolescence, left me with a nagging sense of inadequacy and a need to prove myself acceptable, even desirable. I was also filled with envy for the several wealthy Catholic children in town whose parents had the good sense to marry into Protestant families and send them to public schools.

There is a glorious courage attached to those who suffer indignities for something they believe, but I believed in no part of the Catholic doctrine and was bored into active rebellion. I passionately hated Catholic school and suffered the nuns' and priests' ministrations to my soul with little grace. So, I might add, did they. Our mutual disregard for each other was our one thing in common. But for twelve years we lasted it out, each doing God's will grudgingly.

I attended class with all the first and second generation Greeks, Syrians, and Italians whose families cooked with garlic and sold most of the fresh produce and all the legal beer in the county. Even so, they were poor and to them I was rich, driving to and from school in my own car, wearing different cashmere sweaters every day, a string of graduated pearls, and genuine Spaulding saddle oxfords that I purchased on my own charge account at Taylor's Department Store. My duck's tail hair style was neatly clipped every other Tuesday at the Cozy Cat Beauty Parlor, and I never bought secondhand books. I also had a complete collection of Nat Cole on 45 rpm records, and owned all the published Classic Comics which, like Lady Bountiful, I loaned out for book reports.

Mine was a lonely position, worsened by my blatant heathenism. But somehow we managed and I came to accept my classmates and be accepted by them, as much as it is possible to be within the bitter confines of a church school. The ending, however happy, left me with an unshakable distrust for organized religion.

We were taught by Dominican nuns and secular priests in a valuable downtown real estate compound consisting of the church, rectory, convent, and a school building that housed all twelve grades with two classes in each room. There was a dusty playground for community recess. We went to mass every morning, assembled in the front courtyard to salute the flag, then followed behind an older boy carrying a large bronze cross on a six-foot staff into the school building, marching, grade by grade, singing hymns. Each day an old green bus would disgorge orphans from the Nazareth Catholic Home. Some of them were actually parentless, others just farmed out while their fathers served a prison sentence. Each had a haunted expression. They were decent, nice kids but full of a fear that verged upon religious fanaticism. They had few personal belongings and showed up faithfully each day with completed homework and a single peanut butter sandwich wrapped in a brown paper hand towel. They worked carefully and stayed to themselves until the bus picked them up in the afternoon.

I took lunch down the street with Peggy Lou Cooper at one of her mother's two Victorian boarding houses where, for thirty-five cents, you sat at big tables with boarders and traveling salesmen, and helped yourself to all the fried chicken and stewed corn you could hold. After lunch Peggy Lou and I would lounge around the bedroom she shared with two girls who came from farming communities to take commercial courses at Hardbarger's Business College or to clerk in Woolworth's and Montgomery Ward's. We would devour love comics, experiment with Angel Face powder and Fatal Apple lipstick, or ransack her roommate's leatherette jewelry boxes, reading letters from boys in neighboring towns named Shotwell, Apex, or Lizzard's Lick.

Peggy Lou was my best friend, and I loved and envied her communal living so much that I would have gladly traded all the advantages of my world to live in hers, to truly belong there. Her father lived in Garner, a little town outside Raleigh, where he slept in an apartment over his gas station and let Peggy Lou keep a Tennessee walking horse in a field behind the junk-car lot. We spent wonderful afternoons riding double along the dusty highway pretending we were Jane Arden solving mysteries and having high adventures. At five o'clock Mr. Cooper would open the drink machine with one of the keys he wore clipped to his coveralls, and we would settle into the broken glider to wait for my bus to Raleigh.

Peggy Lou could never understand why she was not invited to my house, and I was never able to explain that my father's vow to educate me with Catholics did not include my socializing with them. Many years later she was the attending nurse in the operating room at Rex Hospital where I was having minor surgery. I was genuinely happy to see her, but by that time I had been away to a fancy finishing school and survived a widely publicized debut. She had come to understand why she was never permitted inside my house.

There were others I loved too: the Kledaras twins, Constantine and Harry George, whose parents ran the Brite-Spot, a grill near the state college. They wore matching peasant costumes to school on Greek holidays and had shoulder-length brown sausage curls until the third grade when the parish priest marched them to the front of the class and took it upon himself to make them into "real boys," clipping the ringlets off with little rounded scissors. Their cousin Bertha had long braids of hair that had never been cut, wore mud-brown oxfords with a matching man's brief case, and threw up the half pint of milk the nuns made her drink every day. She smelled of vomit and was taunted for her gastric weakness by both the sisters and the students until she became withdrawn and weepy, often wetting her pants at her desk. One day she never came back to school.

There was also Georgia Ann, who stayed with a family that ran the all-night café across from the train station. She talked constantly of her father in Washington, D. C., who would surely send for her any day, a fantasy she lived for the twelve years I knew her. Especially I remember a boy named Fred Shedan, one of many children of the Syrian couple who cleaned and blocked hats in a shop off Fayetteville Street. He played the trombone and later formed a band that provided music for a posh party during my debutante season. He yelled to me from the bandstand but before I could return the greeting, my dance partner, a wealthy SAE from Chapel Hill, spoke up, calling him a "dirty Syrian . . . they aren't quite white, you know." I did not know, but the vignette would return to haunt me five years later when I brought a Syrian home to be my husband.

School hours were filled with ritual, the boys practicing to serve mass as altar boys, we girls drilling to become Little Sacristy Sisters. We folded vestments, changed candles, polished chalices, and emptied flower vases between church services with a skill equaled only at pit stops during the Indianapolis Five Hundred. Choir was mandatory and most of the school day was spent in church singing for funerals, weddings, and the endless Holy Days of Obligation. Though I was twenty-five years old before I learned that Beowulf was not a fast-acting aspirin, I can still chant the entire mass in Latin and remember all my catechism answers: "Why did

God make me?" "God made me to know Him, to love Him, and serve Him in this life so that I may be happy with Him in the next." I know by heart all the Ten Commandments and with the exceptions of six and nine, I still manage to conduct myself according to Moses. I recall every response for Lenten services, especially benediction chants where I changed "Ora pro Nobis" to "ole rotten donuts" and "liberamus Domine" to "leave her on a stormy day." My best number was a fast-mumbled "meet you in the back of the church and beat you at a game of dominoes," to which the good Father would intone a long "Amen."

I once put a painted turtle in the baptismal font, which, unfortunately, had BARBARA painted on the shell. I stuffed an alley cat in the choir organ where it was supposed to howl during the novena hour, but the poor creature passed away and the church stank for nearly a week. For this type of behavior I was made to clap the blackboard erasers after school and was sent to confession two or three times a week. The priest kept me so long in the small dark booth that I would eat a bag of lunch before he sent me out to do my penance, generally the Stations of the Cross. They were best executed on a full stomach.

In the seventh grade I edited an underground paper called the *Epar News*, which was "rape" spelled backward. It dealt in graphic descriptions of what I felt certain would have transpired in a secret tunnel between the convent and the rectory. From there I moved on to being the school phantom who chalked large hearts on the principal's door proclaiming "Sister Grace Electra loves Monsignor Federal." I was forever having to read *The Life of Saint Theresa: Our Little Flower* whose patience with her lot appalled and bored me almost as much as the nuns' subservient and regimented convent life.

Their lack of freedom became so depressing to me that the threat of being sent away to a convent boarding school was sufficient to shape me up for months. The sisters lived a Spartan existence, cooking, cleaning, teaching, and praying. Pleasure, they said, came from serving God and His unquestioned emissary on earth, the parish priest. This feminine religious role they foisted on those who seemed likely candidates for convent life. The rest of us were acquainted with the secondary rewards of serving a husband and propagating right and left to swell the ranks and coffers of Catholicism.

Whispering and laughing were forbidden in the pale green Lysoled classrooms, each of which was dominated by a large crucifix of the dead Christ and a color reproduction of a suffering Jesus wearing a bloody crown of thorns and pointing to his exposed and bleeding heart. There were other pictures of saints being stoned, chewed by lions, or enduring the sundry forms of persecution common to their day. There was never any recognition of the happier saints like St. Joseph, whose special appeal to me came from a secret association I made between him and Nancy Drew's father, both quiet, unobtrusive men who never complained or interfered with their offspring's activities. There was a life-sized statue of Mary in the hall where we gathered each day in May to sing "Hail Virgin, Dearest Mary, Our Lovely Queen of May . . . Oh Spotless Blessed Lady . . . We Haste to Crown Thee Now. . . ." Often I made the floral crown and placed it on Mary's head, an honor awarded according to height rather than piety, but a reward I felt I had earned by volunteering to play Mary Magdalene in the Easter passion plays, hence sparing Sister Mary Joseph the embarrassing agony of choosing from among us.

Had it been their jurisdiction, I think the nuns and priests would gladly have released my father from his pledge to educate me in Catholic schools. In truth, I was a torment to them and more than enough to try the patience of saints, which they indeed were not. I could sometimes push the sisters beyond control and one would grab me by the hair, shaking me and telling me that God would punish me by striking me dead. I would clutch my heart, rolling my eyes up in my head and crumple in a frozen heap at her feet. The cooler nuns would lift their robes and long rosary beads, tsk-tsk, and sweep over me, affording a unique opportunity which established me as the playground authority on what nuns do or do not wear under their habits.

With my acceptable non-Catholic peers, I invented unusual stories about religious rites and human sacrifice that supplemented their own extravagant ideas of what went on in the Catholic Church. When I go home today, most of my friends are still emphatically anti-Catholic, and I like to feel I played some small part in their continuing prejudices.

All the way through grammar and high school I was told every day that "God will punish you," and when He neglected to do so by my senior year, I was a heretic who could disrupt religious discussions with valid theological arguments and exchange sophistries with any lady or gentleman of the cloth. There was not a damp clerical eye when I graduated, earning after twelve years a place in heaven for them and a diploma for me that said I had satisfactorily completed my education and was qualified for college. I hope those good sisters had better luck getting into heaven than I did with college. I was unable to pass an entrance examination, which was no real crisis, because, in addition to being a man of his word, my father was a man of his time and did not believe in higher education for women.

Instead, I was given name-tagged sheets with color coordinated towels and sent away to a Washington finishing school. I went secure in the knowledge that nothing in life is to be avoided so carefully as well-intentioned people on the side of Right who think they know what is best for you. Actually, it was invaluable wisdom for someone who would eventually live among politicians.

I fell in love with Washington in 1952, a romance, however unrequited, that would survive for twenty years. Holton-Arms, the school chosen for me, coupled with the solicitous and comfortable tone set by Eisenhower's presidency, encouraged my feeling for the city that would become my home. Then situated in the heart of Washington's diplomatic residential section, the school boasted an elite student body of girls whose fathers ran the country or footed the bills for those who did.

We were given no opportunity to fall in with evil companions, to have anything to do with the taboos of the times: Jews, Negroes, communists, homosexuals, intellectuals, or "have nots" of any description. Instead, we were nestled into a cozy womb away from home where a lot of money bought a little culture, which was actually the only exchange I was qualified for or interested in. We languished through thirty-minute classes in renovated townhouses, dished up tea in Chippendale drawing rooms, and competed with one another to see who got the most mail from boys less insulated at Princeton and Yale. I spent study halls reading about lesbianism in The Well of Loneliness behind The Age of Innocence book jacket, or ordering exotic foods to be delivered from the Empire Drug Store. Free afternoons were passed in movie houses on F Street when I had the money and in terrorizing all floors of Julius Garfinckel's Department Store when I did not. For exercise, we window-shopped on Connecticut Avenue, sneaking forbidden beers in the Admiral Ben-Bow Bar, and played field hockey with rival chic schools.

Finishing schools in the fifties were a good place to store girls for a few years before marrying them off, a satisfactory rest stop between college weekends spent husband hunting. It was a haven for those of us adept at styling each other's hair, playing canasta, and chain smoking Pall Mall extra-long cigarettes. I felt secure, unworried, unashamed, neither challenged nor threatened. Nothing was expected of me and it was just as well.

The food and laundry service were good, and we passed weekdays gossiping about whose father was richest and whose future honeymoon would be the most romantic. We took turns describing a trousseau of white nylon nightgowns with matching peignoirs and satin scuffs, how we would look, and what we would say when faceless husbands in dressing gowns with silk ascots would sweep us into king-sized beds and ravish us into ecstasy, daydreams far removed from the dangerous and generally unsatisfactory grappling in the back seat of parked cars that we were accustomed to. My personal "first night dream" had me fresh from the bathtub like Botticelli's Venus, smelling of Johnson's Baby Powder and generously lubricated with Johnson's Baby Oil—a physical state I now find more suggestive of channel swimming. My intelligence extended itself to writing clever letters to fraternity boys or placing collect calls to Marlon Brando anywhere in Hollywood.

Every girl seemed to be the daughter, cousin, or niece of someone with high government connections; we moved blithely about the city as a matter of course, attending diplomatic receptions, congressional open houses, and rigid military functions heavy with protocol and alcohol. Everyone of us was, at one time or another, a Cherry Blossom Princess or a member of her court.

I roomed with the only other Catholic in school, a Mobile girl who was the niece of the colorful Congressman from Alabama, Frank Boykin. Uncle Frank's reputation included a penchant for sweet young girls who liked riding to tea dances in chauffeured limousines and who thought an occasional pinch on the bottom a fair exchange for a fancy meal in the rooftop dining room of the Washington Hotel. From the hotel roof we could see all of Washington, the monuments to Lincoln and Jefferson, the Capitol Dome, and on clear nights, we would look right into the family quarters of the White House. Our alternative pastime was to hang over the roof terrace and drop written pleas for rescue to the pedestrians many floors below. We drank whiskey sours with maraschino cherries and ordered second helpings of anything we liked, for in addition to being extremely generous to young girls, Uncle Frank owned the hotel. This interest of the Congressman was not as commonly known as was his personal slogan, "Everything Is Made for Love"—everything except his wife, Miss Ossler, who appeared to keep herself above that occupation and was vigilant to see that we retained the virginal state in which she was certain we had come. Her chaperonage, if anything, added excitement.

Uncle Frank took us to Eisenhower's Inaugural Ball at the Mayflower Hotel in 1953. My roommate Lee and I were splendid in red velvet ballgowns trimmed in bunny fur, with bunches of ermine tails on each shoulder. With hair short and flatly curled, lips and nails the crimson of the period, we were nothing if not children of the fifties, dancing with our shoes off in the Chinese Ballroom when we were not upstairs drinking expensive Scotch in lobbyists' suites. Neither of us would have recognized Richard Nixon had he cut in during the Mexican Hat Dance.

The fifties were a splendid time for Washington. Influence peddling was an accepted if not admitted fact, and everyone's father seemed to have some access to power, the source and direction of which it was not popular to question; you just went along. School limousines took us to tea at the White House where we were properly chaperoned by elderly ladies from good families fallen on hard times. We were hauled and shuffled through the National, Corcoran, and Phillips Galleries. We ate seafood at Harvey's or the Occidental Restaurant with someone's visiting parents. We danced with Georgetown boys on the Shoreham Terrace or cajoled out-of-town dates into paying inflated prices to hear Elvis Presley or Billy Eckstine at the Casino Royale, an extravagance we repaid by rolling up in blankets to neck and drink beer on Sunday canoe excursions to Teddy Roosevelt Island. It was a time when we responded as sentimentally to the "Star-Spangled Banner" as to Jo Stafford's "You Belong to Me," when Korea was as good a place as any for another romantic war, and when we thought Senator McCarthy was a fine American when we thought about him at all.

I would like to tell you I was disgusted by the shallow Washington of the silent fifties, but I loved the town with an enthusiasm other small-town girls reserve for Hollywood or New York. I developed a fascination for politics and politicians that proximity would not dull. There was never any question but that Washington was the town for me. I determined from the start that I would live there after I finished school, after I went home and performed the final tribal rite of a nice southern girl: the debut.

In North Carolina as in other southern places, girl babies born of the good and near-good families are brought up from the delivery room to be debutantes. Teeth are straightened, tastes are polished in six-week tours of Europe's cultural capitals, and sexual appetites are constantly dulled in the hope that at least the appearance of virginity will last until they, as debutantes, are ready for the marriage market.

Considerable money went into making a girl marriageable, and it was neither good politics nor good bookkeeping to have a questionable reputation or get knocked up. However, in the event of either, you were expected to be rendered thus by an acceptable young gentleman whose blood and credit lines were honored anywhere. It was the mark of true filial courtesy to schedule weddings, shotgun or otherwise, to take place only after the debutante year. Nowhere is the myth of the chaste debutante more honored than in the South. She is expected to be a pure maiden, an accomplished domestic with good teeth, offered on a pedestal like an ante-bellum vestal virgin. Few of us qualified.

In the weeks before our debuts we drank, smoked, and petted our way through mounds of tuna salad sandwiches and chopped pork barbeque. We drank Orange Nehi mixed with grain alcohol from the Duke University medical laboratory and referred to each other as "teenie weenies" at Coke parties, while we lounged on screened side porches in Bermuda shorts, tearing simultaneously into platters of cheese straws and missing members of the group. The week before the actual presentation was spent in intense social activity:

tea parties, luncheons, and dinners. There were dances followed by boisterous private parties spent snake dancing or doing the Bunny Hop through the halls of the Sir Walter Raleigh Hotel until fatigue or house detectives forced us home.

I actually "came out" twice, once in my parents' garden with hard liquor and a combo; again in the Raleigh Memorial Auditorium at the Terpsichorean Ball, featuring Les Elgart's Band and fruit punch, both laced with bootlegged bourbon. The Ball was an "invitation only" arrangement with girls from all over North Carolina selected by secret committees. For three months we moved up and down the state to attend frenzied parties with orchid corsages pinned to strapless peau de soie cocktail dresses, and wearing satin ballet shoes, dyed-to-match at no extra charge.

Each debutante was permitted as many young escorts as she or her mother could scare up. Any white male with a decent family, fraternity, and set of tails was acceptable: the plainer the deb, the laxer the requirements. My own escorts, called marshals, were lodged in connecting hotel rooms at a cost of six hundred dollars which included continental breakfast, the replacement of fourteen goosedown pillows that were thrown into the ceiling fans, and the dry cleaning of the twenty-eight dress suits of the boys who were pushed in the shower and rolled in the feathers.

We debutantes, more than a hundred strong, were presented alphabetically to curtsey to an auditorium of relatives, houseguests, family retainers, and seamstresses. Obediently, we moved on to form spokes in a wheel that slowly revolved to the music of 1954. Clutching bouquets of long-stemmed red roses, we were like the era, not very spectacular—a bit of intelligence lost on us at the time. But whatever it was, it was not a joke. I took the event and myself quite seriously, smiling toothily while trying to keep my lower lip sexily moist, and feeling very grand in a hoop-skirted white satin-and-rhinestone dress that weighed thirty-five pounds and left me with a lifetime of recurring back ailments.

Once brought out, we were expected to do nothing more than find a husband with a listing in Dun and Bradstreet, join the Junior League for a few good works, and settle down to the business of having the babies necessary to perpetuate the system. It seemed I was somebody's bridesmaid nearly every Saturday night for the year following my debut, helping the bride unpack presents that were numbered and catalogued for display on satin-covered sawhorse tables decorated with artificial bunches of lilies of the valley. Sometimes we helped serve iced tea and crescent-shaped pimento-cheese sandwiches to the bride's visitors who came to inspect the gifts and often to mention, unsubtly, that they had been invited to the church service but not to the reception. The wedding itself was a glittering production where, for at least one time in her life, the bride was the featured attraction, the princess with a court, given a super send-off into oblivion by delighted parents henceforth relieved of responsibility for her.

I was never interested in being the bride but as a bridesmaid I performed well, showed the proper glee over the dated and engraved sterling silver compacts at my plate during the bride's luncheons, and leapt about for the bride's bouquet and the groom's best man at the reception. I stuffed many a set of matched, monogrammed luggage with sex manuals, Midols, Modess, and Trojans, and filled the bride's contraceptive equipment with Uncle Ben's Rice—smugly determined that none of these bourgeois atrocities would ever be committed against me.

While waiting to get married, several forms of employment were acceptable. Teaching kindergarten was for those girls who stayed in school four years. The rest were secretaries, typists, file clerks, or receptionists in insurance firms or banks, preferably those owned or run by the family, but respectable enough if the boss was an upstanding Christian member of the community.

I went to work on the *Raleigh Times* as assistant to its liberal young editor Mark Ethridge, Jr., a southern journalist in the best tradition of the *Atlanta Constitution*'s Ralph McGill; both men were a scourge to southern conservatives. Socially the job was somewhat on a par with the calling of a Miss Katy Mae whose house at Number Eleven Star Street offered the only other interesting jobs for women in the city. I loved it. Furthermore I was totally unconcerned by the outraged gentry who found it unforgivable that a decent young white woman could associate in any way with a liberal paper, even if it was owned by the morning *News and Observer* that was, in turn, owned by the "nigger-loving" but gallingly powerful and acceptable descendants of old Josephus Daniels.

I corrected Mark's copy for the composing room, wrote obituaries, and did the layouts for the society pages, when I was not running out for coffee. The all-male newsroom was generally filled with activity, cigar smoke, and profanity. Working with these men may not have prepared me for the Pulitzer Prize, but certainly they schooled me in the pleasures of ribald humor, ruining me forever for the safe world of bankers and lawyers.

My cub reporting days did little to boost my social or professional standing. I recall vividly the hot furor that followed my big, stop-the-press story announcing a profound secret: the name of the local girl who was to be the ball leader for the current debutante season. Not only was that a social slip but very much the prior right of the competitive morning *News and Observer* whose newsroom, across the corridor from ours, made communication convenient if somewhat incestuous. For my scoop I was nearly stripped of my asbestos sleeves and green eye-shade during the in-house journalistic flap that followed. The whole episode was as overblown as the leaking of the Pentagon Papers would prove to be many years later, and every bit as unimportant.

Mostly, I dealt with the irate telephone callers who objected loudly but anonymously to the paper's editorial endorsement of the Supreme Court Decision of 1954, a task that earned me cauliflower ears and a reputation of being extremely culpable in the plot to integrate and mongrelize the South. My Saturday nights at the country club invariably ended in bitter arguments with members of the Junior Chamber of Commerce with whom I had spent a good many girlhood summers harassing Negro golf caddies on sweltering days when there was nothing more exciting to do. I was never a very articulate champion of the black cause, not really certain what I believed, and not well enough informed to shout down the biases of the white southern male from whom I was conditioned since birth to get my views. To this day, I go home and am immediately surrounded by aging, balding Jaycees who hold me personally responsible for everything that goes on in Washington. This is a delicious illusion I am loath to shatter.

I had to leave the South to learn to handle myself there. The longer I am gone the more I love it and the more I understand that it is in some measure the last American frontier, that those same people I grew up with and away from are beginning to mellow, to feel less threatened by black Americans. They are the ones who stayed in the South these last fifteen years, the ones who truly understand the blacks we sprang up with, and who will achieve honest integration if it is to come. I do not think they know this yet and I do not think I will mention it my next trip home.

After two years, Mark Ethridge had sufficiently enraged the community and thought it expedient to resign before he was fired. He moved his family to Detroit, leaving me a tattered copy of *The Revolt of Mamie Stover* and a letter of introduction praising my efficiency with the journalistic coffee break. He gave me a sage bit of advice: "Get out of town while you can, kid." It was my first experience with that invidious need to be moving on that would bedevil me the rest of my life.

Actually, there was not much left for me in Raleigh as a twenty-one-year-old spinster of liberal leanings, and although I was not precisely ridden-out-of-town, there were few objections to my leaving. Certainly there were none from Mama who heaved a sigh in relief that I had avoided making a suitable marriage for even that long.

I said good-by to a stuffy and politically ambitious young banker, who could never leap the hurdle of my Catholicism to marry me, and set out to conquer Washington. This was a wild fantasy considering that my qualifications consisted of a vague but cosmetically encouraged resemblance to Grace Kelly and six years of elocution lessons at Miss Bootsie MacDonald's School of Tap and Toe. I rode the midnight Silver Meteor north on New Year's Day of 1957, peacefully squeezed into an upper berth with a squirrel jacket and an enormous teddy bear with one shoe-button eye. I had two hundred dollars in traveler's checks and all the confidence in the world that I would need nothing more to be the finest thing to hit Washington since Eleanor Roosevelt. My optimism lasted all the way to Union Station.

3

The reunion with Washington was less than spectacular. It was not an easy town for women seeking employment other than typing or stripping. Not being skilled or built for either, I had trouble finding a glamorous, high-paying position with short hours, long vacations, and all the benefits I thought a girl with a nice, classic face deserved. I presented my journalistic credentials to Alfred Friendly, editor of the *Washington Post*. He was not impressed with my resumé or my Grace Kelly profile. There were, he told the top of his desk, "no places for women with experience, much less you kids who can't do anything." His policy, and probably the only one, was shared with several slightly more polite men named Noyes whom I saw at the *Evening Star*. I was never able to get an appointment at the *Daily News*, which wiped out my journalistic aspirations and left me curious as to where the cartoonist found his prototype for Brenda Starr.

Washington, it seemed, was not to be the hot-time-in-the-ole-town I had envisioned. My money and confidence ran out as fast as my welcome from an old schoolmate, upon whom I had descended, in her third-floor walk-up apartment over a Georgetown bar-and-grill. When I passed the point of no-money-for-a-return-ticket-home, I presented myself, in a manner of speaking, to Uncle Frank Boykin, whose years in Congress had dulled his interest in women but accrued to him a certain seniority which entitled him to patronage, Capitol Hill slang for welfare. He had won enough elections to enable him to place relatives and constituents on the government payroll as doorkeepers, pages, guards, and elevator operators. Though I was neither kissing kin nor a loyal voter, he was willing to extend his patronage to me; but I was, and still am, the wrong sex to avail myself of congressional handouts.

His younger friend and colleague, Oren Harris of Arkansas, had just become Chairman of the House Committee on Interstate and Foreign Commerce, a coveted position but one that constitutionally stripped him of his patronage. His secretary was married to a man crippled during World War II who lost his appointment as House Doorman when Harris became Chairman; they planned to move back to Arkansas if he did not find a new slot immediately. After much southern haggling it was agreed that Frank Boykin would use his patronage to return Harris' man to his old job, in return for which Harris would hire me on a trial basis to fill a vacant committee job—a transaction which later earned me the Capitol Hill description of "the kid Frank Boykin traded Oren Harris for the one-legged doorman." That exchange of influential favors remains my single soft spot for the existing system of congressional seniority.

Mr. Harris must have had one fine secretary to be willing to go to the extreme of hiring me to keep her, because I was not only a disinterested public servant, but a lousy secretary. Naturally, I was ecstatic. The job paid far beyond my qualifications which, of course, would have been true at any salary. I immediately went out and charged an extensive working-girl's wardrobe and busied myself stalking the halls of Congress looking for the right kind of "gay young men" to spend my evenings with.

This was the 89th Congress, Eisenhower's last, and women who worked on Capitol Hill were aging war horses, sometimes more knowledgeable than the Members they served. They were tough, shrewd, and dowagerlike ladies, most of whom swelled the statistics list that showed women outnumbering men in the nation's capital. Most were maiden ladies content to stay in nights with the cat and a cup of hot Serutan. Others were swingers in the old political sense, seasoned and responsible women by day; by night they were something else altogether. These women knew precisely what they were about, and one was ill-advised to get in their way. It also did not do to have a fancy social background, and I was fast finding that good family connections guaranteed one all the status and welcome of the town hooker at a quilting bee. I became unaffectionately known as the "Hill Debutante," which in truth had been my single qualification for the job in the first place. Later the congressional offices would be as full of pretty girls as a Hollywood sound stage, but then they were as scarce as dedicated politicians.

For a long time I was the only female on the committee staff, my duties being similar to those of the only Negro, Leroy, a splendid man with whom I established an instant and lasting friendship. He and I ate together most days and stayed late nights to run the mimeograph machine or hand deliver bills and committee notices to Members scattered about the two mammoth House Office Buildings. We took turns fetching coffee and running errands, and quickly arrived at the understanding that I was young enough to manage the leg work and that he, though elderly, could do the heavy tasks. He had a knack for knowing where to lay his hands on any Member of Congress during an unexpected roll call vote, and it was some months before I understood that the secret of his clairvoyance lay in his access to the House gymnasium where most congressmen passed their terms. With no more than a third-grade education, Leroy was the canniest politician in the lot. He taught me more about legislating than many political science majors learn in a lifetime. He also showed me a thing or two about feeding the extraordinary egos of politicians that helped take the edge off my brazen candor and left me with an abiding disrespect for the street parlance about Uncle Toms.

My typing and spelling were atrocious, my shorthand nothing more than an ability to write fast. I committed whole paragraphs to memory, and later learned to rephrase correspondence, sometimes more lucidly than it had been dictated. I once wrote a fifteen-page letter to President Eisenhower on the Committee's findings about the International Geophysical Year, a task made impossible by the Chief Clerk's insistence that no White House correspondence leave his office with a single erasure. That letter took ten work days to complete and as many nights to smuggle home the reams of used stationery for secret disposal. It was all a prodigious waste, for it was common knowledge that Mr. Eisenhower never read that sort of report, however well it was typed.

It became an open question between the Clerk of the Committee and myself as to which of us would be fired first. More than seventy and inherited from a previous Republican chairman, he was a nervous, cranky perfectionist who would have fired me outright except that he suspected I was the chairman's doxy when I was not otherwise vamping the entire Democratic membership—lewd suspicions I did not discourage.

The truth was that I never received one undue advance from any congressman of either party in the two years I worked there, an innocence probably believed at the time by no one but myself, who took it as more of a blow to the pride than a star to the crown. During the scandal that followed the Committee hearings on the Oil and Gas Lobby of 1957, Drew Pearson wrote a column alleging that Chairman Harris had so "profanely berated" a colleague who failed to appear for an important vote that "one young lady on the staff had to cover her ears and flee the Committee Chamber." This was an extravagant charge considering I was the only female employee of any vintage and one, moreover, who had never displayed an aversion to any kind of profanity. I also did not know Drew Pearson from a sack of salt, but no one bothered to question my guilt; it was assumed that I was the "leak," a tough charge back in the days when "leakers" were not held in today's high esteem.

I was not fired, I think because it was feared I had strong press connections. It was a power position I shored up with casual references to "Drew," actually getting so good at dropping his name that I took to alluding to him as "ole Droopy"—a nomenclature that worked more effectively at the time than it did years later when I had Mr. Pearson as a dinner partner and titillated only myself by addressing him as such.

I came, after a time, to accept working on the Hill, and made myself indispensable by establishing an elaborate filing system, putting railroad legislation under "T" for Trains, and Committee expense vouchers for congressional summer junkets under "F" for Freeloads. I took care of all the back-log correspondence that accumulated by simply dropping it in the burn-basket when it got ahead of me.

Sam Rayburn had been the Committee's chairman before becoming Speaker of the House, which may have prompted his loyalty in assigning a new Special Subcommittee on Legislative Oversight to us. The subcommittee was established ostensibly to police Congress, to rummage in government closets and then announce to the gullible public that all dealings in high office were above suspicion. A clever, fanatically industrious academician named Bernard Schwartz from Columbia University was hired as chief investigator. Poor Dr. Schwartz, the embodiment of the humorless, political neophyte with an ivory-tower integrity, was no match for wily congressmen whose dedication to the country rarely extended itself beyond the quest for reelection. He did not grasp that he was supposed to be nothing more than an impressively educated front man for the congressional candy store. He settled down to investigating the hands that hired him, found malpractice and influence peddling and promptly took the charges over the heads of his astonished superiors and presented his findings to the press.

Overnight there ensued a tempest so far-reaching that it commanded the front page of every publication in the country. Once begun, the investigations reached into Eisenhower's White House, exposing Sherman Adams, surrogate President of the United States, and his dealings with industrialist Bernard Goldfine. Before Dr. Schwartz was cast back into academe, he had cost Sherman Adams his career, indicted Goldfine, shadowed Republican chances in the coming 1958 elections, and set the vicuña coat industry back a hundred years.

There was the usual angry cry for scalps. Influence peddling came to a grinding, if temporary, halt. Angry exchanges of corruption charges sent politicians running for cover, and there was a brief scare-period when congressmen avoided lobbyists and picked up their own lunch tabs. Republicans and Democrats work together quite congenially when they have something to hide or protect, and Sherman Adams—an overworked, underpaid presidential assistant with the burdens of high office placed on his shoulders by a seemingly indifferent Dwight Eisenhower—was the public sacrifice. Few people in high office spoke in his behalf, although his deeds were often less reprehensible than those of the men who tossed him to the wolves. Dr. Schwartz was dismissed by congressmen of both parties, who knew they had a tiger by the tail, which if not silenced, would turn and devour them all.

These were exciting weeks on Capitol Hill. The committee office was filled with scoop-happy journalists who thought my desk a convenient place to plant their half-soled shoes, my coffee cup a proper receptacle for cigar butts. While the committee met nervously in secret sessions, I passed endless hours in smoke-filled confusion playing the tricky word game of Botticelli with sassy reporters, and developed a passion for both.

It was during the investigation that I first met Lyndon Johnson, then Senate Majority Leader, friend, protégé, and lackey of Sam Rayburn. He came over from the Senate to deliver a few well-chosen words on behalf of the Speaker, who was infuriated by the Adams hearing. LBJ was the most impressive caller we ever had, leaving not one doubt in anybody's mind that here was a personage to be reckoned with —not only for his personal force, but because he represented the awesomely combined powers of himself and Sam Rayburn, the most powerful twosome in contemporary congressional history.

I had seen LBJ from afar at Rayburn's massive birthday parties, where Johnson was fond of shoving any woman under forty into the grumpy Speaker's arms to march around the room with him singing "Deep in the Heart of Texas" and "For He's a Jolly Good Fellow," the latter tribute being questionable. Later, I would watch LBJ at cocktail and garden parties given by staff members of Johnson's Texas colleagues. LBJ would arrive by limousine in the manner of a Middle-Eastern potentate, parting the crowd as he swept by and gathering around him admiring young congressional secretaries. Lyndon Johnson was never a social lion. Rather, he preferred small groups of worshipful Capitol Hill workers whom he frequently treated to an evening on the town in the Shoreham Hotel's Palladium Room. It was to be years before I analyzed his aversion to social and political peers, or made any connection between him and the cocky, ubiquitous Bobby Baker, or for that matter, any of the other men Johnson anointed during his reign.

I once had lunch with Mr. Baker. For reasons I forget, he announced to the group of Hill people with us that I was "a prissy little snob" who would do well "to stay on his better side." The reference to his better nature eludes me still, but he was prophetic on that day about my burgeoning snobbery. I never liked Bobby Baker, a negative reaction I could not ascribe to discriminating ethical standards, but it suggested much about my indifference to bragging fools. In the tawdry game of politics I came to know, the only thing that counted was to be a winner, and Bobby Baker was never that.

I sensed in those congressional days that every public figure had some clay about the feet and ankles. Not then and rarely since would I encounter a politician who was not forced to leave a part of his soul in escrow somewhere on his climb to the top. With a few exceptions, there are no skeletonless congressional closets. Those days lulled me into accepting as calmly as everyone else the simple pragmatic attitude that it did not matter how one acquired power, only that one used it. I developed the awareness of the necessities of this pragmatism from seeing daily in my neophyte days on the Hill that nobody was perfect. It was a comforting rationalization then, and it would be later, ironically, when I turned up as one of Washington's skeletons. But it sure blew a hole in my youthful idealization of the United States Congress.

After two years, it became apparent that if fate had some splendid scheme to set me aside from all the other girls, some cosmic encounter with destiny, it would not be consummated within the gray dreariness of Congress. The plodding pace of legislative government was not for me. I was bored, and boredom would ever be my path to destruction.

I never tired of wild parties, the quest for more wine and louder music. I never wearied of flying on private planes to the Kentucky Derby with groups that included Aly Khan, of first nights of Broadway musicals, or the less exotic satisfactions of the Army-Navy football game. But the tedium of clerical work dulled the excitement of my social life. I started doing bizarre things—my personal indicator of unrest—painting mail boxes shocking pink, leaping fully clothed into the Supreme Court fountain. One day I woke up disposed to do the only thing I had not tried: marriage. It was just that uncomplicated. My mind was made up. All I had to do was choose a man from among the available crowd who was going places, and move on to something new and more fulfilling.

I have always had a taste for men who scorn the all-American goal of amassing fortunes: journalists, artists, actors, or dreamers—uncalculating preferences that spare me as a fortune huntress, but hardly choices for a girl whose domestic sciences did not include cooking, cleaning, or economizing. In fact, my wifely qualifications extended only to hiring minions to run a house while I looked for the Good Housekeeping Seal of Approval as a super-consumer. The limitations of my privileged southern grooming went a long way in paring the list of available mates.

I had met a swarthy young man five or six years older than I at a cocktail party given by an old school friend with whom I had shared equal punishment for equally unladylike behavior when we were both at Holton-Arms. Nancy Ames, later a well-known singer, was then a bride. I met Ed Howar at her Georgetown apartment, and from that evening on, he pursued me with uncharacteristic vigor, driving me to and from the airport on my sojourns into the sophisticated world and tolerantly accepting my antics and the excuses I offered for them. He waited me out. After weeks of avoiding him and changing plans at the last minute, I felt obliged to join him for an evening on the town, despite a dreadful hangover from the previous evening. To the accompaniment of two black gentlemen playing Cole Porter on twin white baby grand pianos in a fashionable Washington restaurant, I took a couple of codeine tablets, which I thought to be aspirin, and recall little of the bleary gaiety before I passed out in a plate of Chateaubriand for two. Of this, Ed Howar showed a stoic's tolerance, which was all I thought a husband should possess anyhow.

I was then living at one of my uncountable Georgetown addresses, and my apartment was on the second floor above the quite mad couple who rented to me. The landlady was a blowsy woman whose passion for maternity clothes was not dimmed by the fact that she was childless, and at fifty, far past doing anything about it. Her husband held no job other than handyman, a full-time occupation considering the time it took to install all the gimmicks his wife ordered from Hammacher-Schlemmer and the back pages of *House Beautiful*. There were tape-recorded devices to answer the door, mechanical equipment to start coffee, ovens, showers, and music automatically, two-way mirrors, mirrors to see around corners, and intercom systems everywhere there was not some gadget designed to uncomplicate housekeeping but did not.

They had a cat named Betsy who entered and left the house, with less scrutiny than I was ever afforded, by means of a trap panel in the front door. Cats and I have never fully made it together, and, for obvious reasons, the landlady thought me culpable when Betsy disappeared into the streets. She told me that unless I returned Betsy, I would be evicted —which would not do at all considering I had acquired a deserved reputation for causing poor tenant-landlord relations, and the chances were slim that anyone in their right mind would rent me another apartment.

I spent a drunken evening peregrinating through Georgetown collecting stray cats and stuffing them through the trap door until the howls and screeches were heard for several blocks. The hysterical landlords greeted me with two policemen as I made my final deposit at around four in the morning. Never your typical country girl frightened by the big city, I managed to kick three shins, challenged everyone's sanity but my own, and only narrowly avoided arrest for disturbing the peace, drunk and disorderly conduct, assault of police officers, slander, and catnapping. I was, needless to add, promptly evicted and slapped with a lawsuit for the rest of the rent. None of this dissuaded Ed Howar from the notion that I had the incipient qualities of a good, docile wife. He paid the rent, packed my belongings, and married me. He was everything the movies said I should have: rich, handsome, educated, quiet, and possessed of the patience I knew was required of a husband for me. I also loved him. Marriage to Ed meant living in Washington forever, in style, the social existence I envisioned, the children I assumed I should have.

We spent months buying furniture for an apartment in one of his father's luxury buildings, selecting china, linen, and all the standard equipment for married American bliss. At night I was the central figure at dozens of engagement parties, flashing new gold fillings in my teeth, and a five-carat diamond ring on my finger, secure, smug that all would end well.

We married in Raleigh in a civil ceremony as a compromise between his Arab-Moslem religion and my abandoned Catholicism. There was an expensive wedding reception afterward in the grand ballroom of the best hotel. Mama was not happy to see me marry, but we were not yet close enough for me to accept her objections as more than expected distaste for a strange "foreigner" whom she was summoned from Europe to meet and embrace.

The local Catholic hierarchy was piously indignant that I was to marry out of the church, going so far on several Sundays as to sermonize from the pulpit about "our children who take up with false gods" and cautioning the faithful "to remove yourself from the near occasion of sin by staying away from heathen ceremonies."

It really did not matter, for there were precious few I chose to share my false gods with anyhow. Mama, however, was superstitious, never walked under ladders, or put hats on beds; she trifled neither with black cats nor irate priests. She thought marriage would be difficult for me under ideal circumstances and was more than a little concerned that I should start out by incurring the Catholic wrath. But she was outraged at the audacity of the clergy daring to mind her business in public. My sister Charlsie, twelve at the time, was cautioned by the nuns at school not to attend her sister's wedding. This proved to be the fatal indignity to Mama's shaky religion.

On the final visit to our house by a righteous priest who had already come before to acquaint my parents with the "folly of this marriage," Mama turned on the celibate gentleman and told him heatedly: "The only thing you priests know about children is how to tell other people to have them. You never even raised a cat, Father, and you don't know a damn thing about being a parent. If I have to choose between you and Barbara, it's an easy choice." She showed the good father to the door and settled down to the business of becoming the best friend I ever had.

The Howars were a clannish family, and, however un-Christian were my beliefs, I can never believe they were happy to welcome the first and only gentile female into the fold.

Old man Howar was twenty years older than his wife, a self-made millionaire who at fourteen had come from Jordan to America in steerage with nineteen dollars sewed into his tunic and a neckerchief full of canned sardines. He made and lost several fortunes before he learned English. Starting as a lace peddler, progressing through café cook and dress salesman, he finally became one of Washington's most prominent builders and America's richest resident Arab. He built himself the only air-conditioned mosque in the Western World on Washington's Massachusetts Avenue so that he could keep comfortably in touch with Allah between trips to Mecca.

I loved that old man; he was a peculiar, gnome-like counterpart to my mother—a strong, opinionated fox who never let his wife's desire to refine him get in his way of being a splendid human being. He was never dull, and at ninety remains alert to most of the things that others miss. I take every opportunity to expose my children to him, to remind them of his qualities in the hope that some of them have been passed on.

Mrs. Howar, a kind but arrogant woman, was extravagant and loving with her own but hard on those who were not. She was the daughter of a wealthy Palestinian, and her notions of grandeur were inherent. She spared no expense in seeing them to fruition. She was a lovely and stately woman who never drove an automobile nor entered a supermarket. Life in America removed her from her archaic culture but she clung doggedly to the Arab belief that a woman should keep herself entirely subservient to the world of men. This life had never dealt her blows more severe than me and Golda Meir. She accepted me in her "Imshah Allah" fashion, and took me as though I were one of Allah's burdens she must endure.

Tall, elegant, laden with more diamonds than Raleigh could collect in a passed hat, she moved majestically through the wedding celebrations like a glazed figure on an Egyptian vase. Her three dark, plump daughters and Syrian daughter-in-law followed behind her in abject obedience, giving nods, smiles, bows, and little more. They made a striking entourage and, I suspect, wholly disappointed Raleigh by not arriving on camel-back demanding a few good rugs as my dowry. They were generous to me, indulging me with jewelry and an autumn haze mink stole, the supreme status symbol of 1958. None of it was lost on me or anyone else in town.

We settled into a nice life after a nice honeymoon and although I nearly did not survive the complicated birth of each baby, we managed two nice children. It was a convenient existence; there was nowhere else I particularly wanted to be. My main concern was how to spend money but not show it, to be cautious, never to overdo anything for fear we would alienate the gentle, well-born bores we inherited as friends from Ed Howar's childhood. It was a ridiculous charade considering they were equally rich but obsessed with an upper-class stinginess which they disguised by pretending that money-spending was in bad taste. These young couples had been seduced by those conservative bourgeois values that devolve from too much private schooling, WASPs married to WASPs. They were young fogies who followed their families into the Chevy Chase Country Club and swore allegiance to the Junior League and the Metropolitan Club. They thought the best servants were black; Jesus Christ the only acceptable Jew; the Howars tolerable Arabs, providing, of course, all of us kept in our place.

The senior Howars gave lavish parties for visiting Eastern rulers, with huge stuffed lambs and exotic delicacies spread before the swells in the Washington Arab community. The champagne would be the finest, and, although the Moslem religion dictates forgoing alcohol, I found it unwise to get caught in the crowd when they headed for the bar. Despite the pretense of making the Howar parties look like simple little gatherings to our conservative friends, I would become very excited when Mrs. Howar would lead all us girls into a department store and outfit us in a style suitable for visiting royalty. I loved the visits from Jordan's King Hussein or the Brothers Faisal and Saud of Saudi Arabia. Mama would come up from Raleigh for the fun and champagne, trying vainly to play the role of the sober mother-in-law. We fell into a pattern; both of us butchered Arab protocol and had a fine time doing it.

During a party for King Hussein, Mama summoned me from the dance floor to have my picture taken with him. It is written that a Moslem king, however Westernized, does not light a woman's cigarette and although I had been rehearsed in these traditions by Chief of Protocol Wiley Buchanan, I was so flustered by the popping of flash bulbs that when Hussein offered me a Camel from his case, I helped myself, leaned down for a light, and came up to shocked silence as I tried unsuccessfully to disengage my stuck lip from the tip of the unfiltered cigarette. I succeeded only in spitting blood, skin, and Carolina tobacco into the face of Jordan's "Little King," all in full view of in-laws, guests, and the nation's press. Mama, full of French champagne and southern good will, breezed in between the King and I, draping one bare arm about Hussein's shoulder and the other around my waist, pulled us together and smiled jauntily into the camera, saying: "King honey, let's us have a picture for old times' sake."

On another occasion I took Mama to a dinner for ladies only in honor of the wife of the King of Saudi Arabia, a command performance of unrelieved boredom. Many of the ladies at the dinner were barely out of the veil, and the language of the evening was French or Arabic, sometimes an ineffable combination of both. None of it was comprehensible to me or Mama. We sat against the walls of the grand salon of the Saudi Arabian Embassy sipping orange juice, the surroundings looking like a doctor's waiting room filled with overdressed, brocaded women in overstuffed tapestry chairs.

Mama's Rubenesque figure was compressed into the medieval undergarment of the fifties, the Merry Widow. She excused herself to remove her corset and returned in shapeless comfort to consume the better part of an entire stuffed lamb. When the guests rose by supreme command to end the evening, Mama was the first on her feet, pumping the hostess' hand with relief, her ungartered stocking down around her ankles. Then she stumbled and fell on top of the stunned guest of honor who could scarcely comprehend English, let alone a southerner's version of it.

I was certain Mama's girdle was the first ever found stuffed under a French settee in the powder room of an embassy. I would never know what the reaction was, for we did not call to collect it. We referred to it as Underwear Caper Number I, which was superseded by Underwear Caper Number II. The latter included a similar assemblage of characters, but took place in the Mosque where Mama and I had gone on an impromptu tour with friends from out-of-town. Tradition demands that shoes be removed upon entering a Mosque, and, as Mama bent down to comply, the elastic in her underwear gave way. With a pained expression, she saw her pants fall to the carpet. Quite casually she stuffed them under a loose prayer rug and continued her tour.

While we were not always busy stashing undergarments in Arab shrines, we were seldom the picture of Western respectability. My mother-in-law was very tolerant despite the considerable embarrassment we must have caused her among her countrymen. Never once did she suggest it might be appropriate for Mama and me to restrain our howling laughter lest some king or queen believe we were making sport of someone other than ourselves.

Eventually I tired of Arab royalty. I was also weary of social games in non-Arab circles, bored with appearing understated in order to fit myself into an old Washington society that would never accept me completely. I blew the whole thing by getting blackballed by the Junior League, a not unpleasant way to exit. At a luncheon to look over the prospective members, I was seated next to the League President. I took more than the expected ration of sherry and was suffused by a feeling I would come to dread, a roaring voice in the back of my head which said: "Get me out of here." When the matronly Junior League president finished a twenty-minute disquisition on her golf handicap, she turned to me, "My dear, I do love the North Carolina golf courses, especially Pinehurst. The darkies are so well behaved. It's a perfect spot in spite of all those Yankee Jews you southerners have let in." I had no known distaste for bigots at that time, but the lady seemed less preferable than most minority groups. Feeling certain no one would ever do it for her, I suggested she go screw herself, an incautious remark that made the afternoon the only ladies' luncheon I ever enjoyed.

After that we withdrew our hopeless nomination for membership in the Chevy Chase and Metropolitan Clubs, ceased pressing the children into Episcopal Sunday School, and moved on—a move I never regretted.

4

1960 was an auspicious year for making the transition from one Washington world to another, from the petty old-line society to the larger and more exciting life of the politicians who run the country. Eisenhower's colorless White House had been taken over by John Kennedy, and the town, as it always does, followed the tempo of the new President; he was unusually youthful, witty, and straightforward for a politician. Not all the people surrounding the Kennedys had these traits as fully as the man they served, but in making the effort to emulate him they definitely improved the Washington climate.

Politics for the first time in the recollection of many Washington people was becoming chic, and, at long last, open to younger men with zest and contemporary ideas on governing. Catholics, if not unqualifiedly in demand, were becoming acceptable in societies outside their own; Jewish intellectuals were sprinkled around at dinner parties, and although they hardly made Washington a hotbed of radicalism, they added immeasurably to the character of the city. Pressure was applied to admit Negroes to the Cosmos and Metropolitan Clubs. When that failed, some of the members broke away to form The Federal City Club, a commendable endeavor but hardly a sign of anything more than token equality considering their ridiculous convenant against women members. The Press Club remained resolutely segregated and the Gridiron Club continued to exclude women and blacks, despite the fact that both were starting to qualify as journalists deserving of the exposure to the important speakers and guests the powerful Gridiron members traditionally attracted.

Jack Kennedy was a Gridiron favorite, but it was becoming increasingly apparent that he cared little for old Washington society, and that the disaffection was returned. Old Washington remained conservative. The New Frontier avoided their country clubs, and the Kennedy women snubbed the suburban activities of the Junior League, both delighting me and discouraging any lingering need I had to rejoin the older society. The final brick was put into the wall between the old-guard native Washingtonians and the political itinerants.

Despite the strong impetus toward filling government jobs with bright, energetic minds, the Kennedy years seemed lacking in something truly substantial. More than just the inevitable result of being taken over by a new crowd, the town suffered a particular type of fragmentation under President Kennedy. Socially, Washington was not a congenial place for those not close to the White House or to Hickory Hill, the suburban estate of Robert Kennedy. I never belonged in those early days of the 1960s to either set but was close enough to those who did to see the insecurity and uncertainty that cliquish power engenders. I think of those years as the Beautique Era, with the women in the two separate Kennedy groups often overlapping but always indiscernible from one another because of their determination to be exactly alike.

The Kennedy family had an impressive faculty for using

people and making them happy servants. They were notorious for excluding the office staff from their personal lives and for pressing personal friends to perform menial tasks. Friends were only too glad to be of service; to love the Kennedys was to serve them even in the most domestic capacity. Their reward was to be permitted Kennedy company.

Similar to the later rock band groupies, the Kennedy camp followers paid court to both branches of the Kennedy family, but especially to Robert Kennedy's wife, Ethel. They emulated each gesture and expression, dressed alike, thought alike, accepted or rejected each new face or fashion in the manner of their idol, and as if by some secret signal from above, would gobble you up or ignore you, fold you to their bosoms or cut you dead.

They employed a deliberate form of social exclusion, leaving out a few people here and there in order to provide an audience of envious onlookers. By inviting the celebrated and the talented from all walks of life to their parties, frequently without benefit of prior introduction, Kennedy era hostesses were written about in the nation's press, giving the often erroneous impression that all the bright and creative people were in accord with the Kennedys. I am respectful of the press, but in many instances their relationship with the Kennedys was so incestuous that some credibility must have been lost. Society reporters with irreverent attitudes were banned from the Kennedy scenes, and those privileged to cover the New Frontier knew their presence depended on respect rather than accuracy in their reporting. One played according to Kennedy rules, or one did not get back into the game again—a sad truth in any administration but blatant in the early sixties. The country, starved for glamour, was fascinated by the Kennedys and demanded to be informed at all costs. Given the curiosity of the public and the might of the Kennedys, it was not the best time for domestic journalism. Considering the ever-powerful pull of the Kennedy charisma and the continuing concern for social image, the situation is only slightly changed today.

At the time, magazines and newspapers abounded with glamorous descriptions of life among the Kennedy set, but even when I learned to distinguish one New Frontier lady from the next, I never dreamed myself worthy of moving among them. It would also have been too demanding to keep abreast of who was in and who was out, too confusing to stay current on the constantly changing standards that judged them the one or the other. It was fun merely to watch everyone dashing about frenetically shopping where Jackie did; ordering from Ethel's seamstress those sleeveless little gabardine dresses in the right shade of pink at just the right height above the knees; placing multi-jeweled pins at the exact same spot on the chest; watching the women of Washington, myself included, trying to garb themselves exactly alike in what eventually became a national craze for women to have the "Kennedy look."

As quickly as the rest of us caught up, the Kennedy crowd moved on to newer things: antique furniture courses in Jackie's favorite period; redecorating in breezy Ethel Kennedy fabrics; shopping at the same French Market and patronizing the same French hairdresser; using floor-length floral cloths on identical round caterer's tables; filling the same gold bamboo chairs with the same guests night after night; eating the same food from the same china under the same vermeil candlesticks; making the same conversation; and worshiping one another in the hallowed way reserved for anyone with Kennedy somewhere in their signature. Nothing was more enviable than vacationing in Palm Beach, Hyannis, Aspen, or on the Onassis yacht. The very "in" had babies the same time Ethel did, in the same hospital, with the same obstetrician—something that required true planning, even though Mrs. Kennedy gave everyone ample opportunity to follow her example.

It required enormous energy to keep in Ethel's good graces, to qualify for a "hi, kid" greeting and to survive the rigors of working for her charities, running her errands, organizing her household, and paying the cheerful, wholesome homage demanded of those dexadrinedlike ladies who were permitted to dance constant attendance on the perpetually pregnant mistress of Hickory Hill. The level of style demanded that dinner often be served in flower-lined tents. Consciousness-raising conversations were juxtaposed with the gay ritual of pushing fully-clothed folks into swimming pools or dancing to snappy music with planeloads of movie stars and beautiful people who were instantly elevated from the world of political do-nothings by simply breaking bread in the Kennedy households.

Reigning among the Washington diplomats were England's Lord and Lady Harlech, old friends of the Kennedys summoned to power at the start of the New Frontier. They turned the staid British Embassy into an eminently hot and popular spot, the scene of frequent revelry for those on the inside, and a source of envy for those who were not. A British invitation ranked next after the White House and Hickory Hill, even though the halls were drafty, the food mediocre, and the portraits of British Royalty intimidating.

Next on the list was the French Embassy, a Norman monstrosity ruled carefully by Nicole Alphand whose husband, food, and decor were far superior in quality to the

British, but whose connection with the Kennedys was somewhat less concrete. Madame Alphand was a sleek, clever woman with the body for French fashions and the mind for being the ranking Washington hostess. She was a glamorous woman who handled men and publicity with equal ease and dispensed meals and wine with a warmth not generally credited the French.

My invitations to both embassies left me feeling that something was lacking in sincerity, either in them or me and probably both. Newspapers and magazines repeatedly informed me that these evenings were memorable and I was not there to argue. One night at the British Embassy, boned to the teeth on current events, I was standing between Ambassador Harlech and Illinois Senator Charles Percy, listening to a protracted discussion on motor cars and jazz, a conversation so banal that I retreated to Rex Harrison and his more challenging argument as to whether grown men should wear undershirts.

However unlofty the dialogue in their salons, both Madame Alphand and Lady Harlech drew impressive crowds, and there were few complaints when Nicole Alphand lit her perfumed incense candles and filled her ballroom with the penultimate of official Washington seated on hard, gilt chairs to pass several hours watching skinny Paris models parade bizarre French fashions.

Ambassador Alphand needed little encouragement to do his impersonation of a chicken. Shorter than I and solemnly distinguished, the Ambassador would crouch low in his tuxedo jacket, making wings of his bent arms, a beak with his puckered mouth. Flapping and pecking, he scratched his little black patent leather dancing pumps into the faded Aubusson carpet. He would then thrash around like a proper piece of poultry, cackling loudly as he laid his egg while some of the most important men in the world sat enthralled, applauding his act. Hervé Alphand was also talented at fanny patting, prompting me to call him Harvey All-Hands, which he did not find as amusing as his chicken act.

I would be the first to admit that had I been an integral part of the Kennedy years, I would have warmer recollections of the administration's social side. My opinions of the latter, however, do not affect my respect for John Kennedy as a fine President—one, moreover, who appeared to become increasingly capable of governing and drawing around him a caliber of men not often equaled in Washington. When he died, something vital went out of the town and out of the country. Whatever the circus sidelights of his administration, it was endurable and enchanting because of John Kennedy, his worldliness, his vitality and courage. He went further than any political figure of recent times to prove, however historically questionable, that it is the quality of the man, not the powerful office he holds, that commands the respect that can eventually make a great leader.

That November day in 1963 was a turning point for many people and for me; politics would never again be a funny spectator sport. John Kennedy's death changed my attitude about Washington and the men who come to it. More than the plea to "ask what I can do for my country", more than the blazing drama Kennedy created with his bright cadre of new leaders, his death stirred in me a respect for the presidency that later questioning of Kennedy policy and wisdom could not diminish. Jack Kennedy paid the price to give the country its vicarious experience in Camelot.

If, after Dallas, the rest of the world was shocked by American barbarism, Washington was paralyzed. Traffic snarled, stores closed, telephone systems broke down under the drain of thousands of calls that glutted official wires and those of ordinary citizens. Washington is blasé about its celebrities, especially the political ones, but there is a strange aura of possessiveness toward the family in the White House. The President is the country's leader, but he is something more in Washington. Banal as it may seem, the First Family are neighbors; we see them come and go, and we are generally more involved in the President's actions, more directly affected by them, than the rest of the country. We ride by his house several times a day, know his friends and enemies, and keep up with the unpublished gossip on both. We see his family in stores and restaurants, and read about them in our newspapers that carry more details of their work and play than other publications. In some strange and lovely way, the First Family belongs to Washington more than we care to admit. If the President of the United States is a son-of-a-bitch, he is our son-of-a-bitch. There may be no essential justification for this proprietary attitude; I only know it exists.

When John Kennedy died the citizens of Washington were more closely involved than New Yorkers, Chicagoans, or the people of Dallas. I saw friend after friend on television walk deathlike into the White House or St. Matthew's Cathedral for the memorial service. I marveled at their dignity, understood and forgave them the cliquishness they had shown when Kennedy was alive and an integral part of their dreams and aspirations. I envied their right to greater grief, and not for the first time in those three years, I was jealous—jealous of their closeness to John Kennedy, jealous of their experiences with him, their memories of that glamorous era.

The bereaved family and close friends comported themselves in a manner befitting John Kennedy; others behaved less attractively. There was a sick, insensitive scramble of hangers-on and fringe associates to be in on the action to the bitter end. People pushed their way into the funeral, the cortège, and if they could impose on the survivors, right into the bosom of the family. It was the cheapest display of the Washington need to be close to power, even in sorrow. People who had earned no right to mourn at close proximity insinuated themselves into John Kennedy's death, fought ruthlessly for a mention in history. They became unsolicited authorities on events inside Kennedy households, and talked of the death as though it were an MGM Technicolor production staged entirely for their narrative pleasures. New details of the murder, burial arrangements, Mrs. Kennedy's courage, her future plans, behavior, thoughts, actions, and expressions were reported daily over lunches in public restaurants, the only social gatherings permitted the sensitive during Washington's official month of mourning.

Unlikely people became instant experts on the personality and politics of any Kennedy, dead or alive. Women, united in their cursory friendships with the President, huddled in the Rive Gauche Restaurant expressing grief, morbid curiosity, and often a good deal of inside information: "Jackie is so guilt-ridden" or "Poor Jackie, she had just come to realize how much she loved Jack." As bad as the rest, I could not hear enough and never once questioned the source, absorbing every new episode as shamelessly as the average addict of the soap opera. Then came whispered confessions from woman after woman who confided pridefully that she had been "closer than most to Jack." President Kennedy had a wholesome, widely discussed, and largely deserved reputation for his interest in women, one I hope he managed to indulge often during his life. But no President, however young and energetic, could possibly have gotten around to all the ladies in Washington, New York, and Hollywood who made claim to his affections after he died.

Such was the force of Jack Kennedy and the manner of his death that anyone associated with him, even the pretenders, assumed added glamour and interest. The list of those close to him grew larger every day, and it was not uncommon to have unlikely women pointed out in a crowded room as "one of the late President's girl friends." Such is the nature of the city that each became a minor celebrity. For every school, airport, highway, or building that was renamed for John Fitzgerald Kennedy, there was a female American who basked in the warmth of a fabricated romance with him. The same macabre claims were made at Robert Kennedy's death, but this was my first encounter with name-dropping at the time of grief. Those same people continued feverishly to chase the ghost of Jack Kennedy in his brothers, his widow, his children, in a way that poorly served the man. He deserved better.

Certainly Jackie Kennedy was entitled to mourn in privacy. She was given little. When she left the White House and moved into the home of Averell Harriman, the streets of Georgetown swarmed with tourists. They came in cars, sightseeing buses, on foot. They patrolled her street, loitering in front of the Harriman house, Mrs. Kennedy's mother's nearby house, and later, in front of Jackie's home on N Street. They waited all day to see her, gawking, watching for her children, her dogs, her car, her garbage. They dropped gum, cans, bottles, and candy wrappers, and on one afternoon, I saw a couple with small children huddled on the curb across from her house eating a picnic lunch. It was not possible to think them all well-wishers.

Before Mrs. Kennedy was forced to leave Washington by these curiosity seekers, I sat with her one long May afternoon on the front steps of a mutual friend's house, drinking a gin and tonic, our skirts pulled up to sun our legs while our children attended a birthday party inside. There were many things I wanted to say to her, but I could not. We sat chatting inanely about children, laughing over her recollections of the days when she and Ed Howar had been in the same group at Miss Shippen's Dancing Class—days, she said, when she was shy and gangling, and jealous of the "class siren" who wore see-through blouses and had "things to see" that Jackie had not yet acquired. Our only intimate exchange was a lengthy discussion of leg hair, whether it grew back faster if removed with a straight razor or an electric one. It was not a moving conversation, but probably it was the only chat with the hounded wife of John F. Kennedy that has heretofore gone unreported in the press.

This same devouring scrutiny was directed at Robert Kennedy but he, though equally vulnerable, seemed somehow more able to cope with public curiosity than with his own grief. His was a sorrow I never wish to see again. Bobby came one night months after the tragedy to a good-by party for the Donald Wilsons, Kennedy friends who were leaving town. Every person I had met or read about during the New Frontier days was there, and though muted, it was a pleasant evening in David Brinkley's home in the Washington suburbs. People were seated outside at small gay tables making efforts at their old jokes and games, catcalling irreverently during the sad farewell toasts to the Wilsons: Averell Harriman, Arthur Schlesinger, McGeorge Bundy—the faithful—all trying to recall the old flippant camaraderie while saying the first of many good-bys that were to follow.

It was a poignant evening, but overriding the group's sorrow was the deep grief of Bobby Kennedy who was there, I think, because he was expected to be, and because his desperation left him no other place where he could be at peace. A haunted creature, he belonged there and he belonged nowhere.

I talked with him for a while, but I could not reach him, and it seemed somehow crude to try. Despite feeling threatened because I did not know how to deal with him, I began that night to acquire a respect that would grow into admiration for Robert Kennedy as the man I came to believe in more than any other political figure of my day. Yet even at his height, at his most certain, strong, and humorous self, I would remember that night in 1964 when he gave off nothing but despair.

For me the evening marked the end of an era and clearly suggested the changing times. As though marking the climax of the Kennedy years, U.S.I.A.'s George Stevens threw Arthur Schlesinger fully clothed into the Brinkleys' swimming pool. Rather than the amusing prank of yesterday, it seemed an insensitive act, one that was greeted by stony silence. As further indication of things to come, Lyndon Johnson's aide Jack Valenti rose to his feet to deliver the final toast—to have, in some measure, the last word.

5

Changing presidents is confusing even under the orderly process of election, but the circumstances of Johnson's thrust into the White House brought chaos at all levels of government and society. Even the lobbyists, skilled at fitting themselves into new regimes, were disordered by the accelerated transition from one President to the next. No one knew who was still in, who was on his way out. Johnson's people were not yet sufficiently organized for the outsider to tell who would surface into key positions; there was no hierarchy, no way of knowing whom to butter up, whom to ignore. Some of the old Kennedy crowd left town with dignity. Others, grown dependent on power, were loath to disappear quietly on the off chance they might ingratiate themselves with the new President and hang on for another four years. Others, in typical Washington fashion, crouched down inconspicuously, in the hope they would be ignored and perhaps survive under presidential indifference. The more aggressive feathered their nests with the available Texans or Democrats who seemed likely to become influential when the turmoil subsided.

Lyndon Johnson had not been popular with the Kennedy

crowd, due in part to the circumstances in which he was put on the Democratic ticket in 1960, but largely because of Johnson's personality which, under the best of circumstances, was never congenial with the Kennedy style. Johnson and his spunky Lady Bird never fitted into the Kennedy social scene, and ridiculing the Johnsons' efforts to do so had become something of a parlor game for most Kennedy pacesetters during the three years Lyndon Johnson was Vice President. Their treatment of Johnson was obvious and cruel. Frequently he got more abuse than was called for.

The new President was proud, and he had a long memory and a reputation for revenge that caused the remaining Kennedy entourage as much discomfort in its anticipation as in its actual execution. Like the crafty cat he was, LBJ toyed with the mice before he swallowed them up or spat them out. He would soften up Kennedy egos by asking advice of them, hinting of his need for their loyalty. When he had them bleating for power, he fell upon them, bouncing them out of the White House or putting them back in their places filled with proper respect for Johnson largesse and muscle.

Those who had made sport of his Texas twang and dress began to seek out his staff with unusual enthusiasm. Johnson's employees, anxious to be pandered to by the people who had disparaged them for three long years, were not hard to cultivate. Such psychological reversals were compounded when the new President decided to keep some of Kennedy's top men in office, a decision that made other government underlings anxious to follow suit. Washington seethed with rationalizations: if, among others, the Secretaries of Defense, Commerce, Agriculture, Labor, State, and Interior could bridge the gap to serve two very opposite men, in two very different White Houses, then was it not all right for lesser luminaries to try to do likewise?

There was a rush of Kennedyites to place children in private schools, now that the White House playroom had changed overnight from Caroline's school to a recreation area for the two teenaged Johnson daughters. This was as tricky as the maneuvers to stay on Johnson's bandwagon, for crowded Washington private schools have never been noted for selecting students from among yesterday's political leftovers. The residual Kennedy people often turned on one another; women were not above dropping snide remarks about an associate's child who might also be a candidate for a vacancy in the same private school.

Few were above mentioning privately to a new Johnson insider a few choice words about how so-and-so who, while large in the Kennedy years, had been very anti-Johnson. As most important business is conducted over the Washington dinner table, social gatherings were the best barometers of who ranked where and above whom. During this period, it appeared that everyone and no one ended up seated on the wrong side of the salt. It was not uncommon for a member of the old guard to spend an entire dinner party persuading someone from the new administration that "I was, of course, always a Johnson supporter even back in the days when. . . ."

Not all efforts to cultivate Johnson favor were so obvious. Many were restrained by their wish not to alienate Robert Kennedy, who was watching the entire pageant. During the Johnson years, had the energy expended in serving two camps been funneled into constructive channels, Lyndon Johnson and Robert Kennedy, as well as the rest of the country, would have fared better. I believe President Johnson's worst mistake was to keep so many of Jack Kennedy's men in office. Not because they were dishonorable or incapable—often they were the best available help—but because there was every indication of bad blood between Johnson and Robert Kennedy, every indication that Kennedy would regroup to unseat Lyndon Johnson. Loyalty to both was impossible. To give Lyndon his due by day and mingle socially in the Kennedy world at night required Olympian stamina. Something had to suffer. My guess is that it was the country itself.

If Washington was slow to adjust to the new pace, not so Lyndon Johnson. He was in his element, secure in the office he thought best suited his talent and temperament: the Boss. His success with Congress during that first year in office, his popularity as President, however short-lived, remains part of Johnson's legend.

There was no better vantage point than the social circuit for viewing his administration. In fact at no time in Washington had I seen political socializing that afforded a better view of government and those who shaped policy than was available during the Johnson days. Johnson's people were always present at social functions, anxious to make the silhouette of LBJ more vivid.

The press learns more about power, who has it and how it is used, by sitting around dinner tables than it derives from the closed corridors of government. Whether that speaks well or ill of the system is beside the point; the cocktail party remains a vital Washington institution, the official intelligence system. According to these social jungle drums, it was apparent that the new President was in for hard times.

The respectful awe given Kennedy was not to be accorded Lyndon Johnson. He seemed unable to catch the country's imagination; there was little affection for his homespun personality. More than most presidents, he was the source of constant conjecture, appraisal, and gossip. Except as a political master, LBJ was a hard man to idolize. Perhaps Johnson appeared too much the average person. Americans like in presidents the glamour that they do not have in themselves. We expect exceptional morality in our leaders, desire that they be above reproach, be more genteel and refined than we are ourselves. Johnson was not Caesar's wife, and it became clear he would be afforded few gaffes before reporters and observers took him to task.

From the beginning, the prevailing Washington attitude judged Johnson to be on trial. He stirred early resentment by succeeding Kennedy too well in the presidency, following a sacred performance with a bit too much skill. The press began to consider LBJ the snorting bull that replaced the Holy Cow.

It was a comfortable time for me. I had not been sufficiently immersed in Kennedy life to be considered the Johnson enemy, and the Johnsons were low on untapped talent. Their quest for new faces, combined with my growing ambition, made us a natural combination: they had needs and I could be had.

Socially, the Dale Millers, Abe Fortases, Clark Cliffords, Homer Thornberrys, and John Connallys began replacing the more chic names in society columns. Where Jack Kennedy had separated his pals and his advisors to keep the office help out of the drawing room, Johnson extended his Texas hospitality to hired hands and brought them into his personal and social world. Had you "gone to the well" with Johnson in the old days, you were welcome to dinner in the White House during better times. The President's secretaries came for private and official parties, and several of them were bridesmaids in his daughters' weddings. At night, Johnson's employees did not cover their typewriters and fade into obscurity: they *were* The Great Society.

Old Johnson faithful were fast rising in the new administration: Walter Jenkins, Elizabeth Carpenter, Bess Abel, Warren Woodward, Douglass Cater, Horace Busby, George Reedy, later aided by Billy Moyers, Joe Califano, Harry McPherson, and the controversial Marvin Watson. Jack Valenti had come into the "family" by marrying Lyndon's good and dear friend and secretary, Mary Margaret Wiley.

But LBJ was smart enough to understand that his group, utterly loyal and adequate to his needs as Vice President, was not sufficient in number for his interim year as President or to secure reelection. Word went out for new talent, ideas, and people. The closer it came to the convention, the larger grew the list of "insiders"—much to the chagrin of the original nucleus of Johnson people. But power-selfish or not, they were faced with too much work and too little manpower; there was no choice but to be transfused with new blood. Besides, Lyndon Johnson had decreed it.

The 1964 Democratic National Convention was held in Atlantic City. I had been asked to work at Convention Hall as a Lady for Lyndon, a select group whose husbands or fathers were Johnson associates or supporters. We were united only in blind loyalty to LBJ. He was the anointed savior who would rid the country of Barry Goldwater, an amusing remembrance later when I would come to like the straightforward Arizona Senator. We "Ladies" numbered about twenty, all in our late twenties, all constructed to look sufficiently alluring in red crepe dresses from Nieman-Marcus. We spoke in varying southern accents and were largely political neophytes who did not know a delegate from a contributor until we became aware of the subtle differences in their demeanor: money-givers were aggressive and demanding, delegates were only boisterous and self-important.

We "Ladies" thought ourselves very special and did as we were told by Mrs. Johnson's companion, Scooter Miller, who at long last was having a moment of glory. If one wanted a similar moment for oneself, it was unwise to cross her. Outrageous flattery made one indispensable to her, but then in politics such practice was hardly a Miller original.

Ladies were assigned staggered hours throughout the convention, some of us meeting trains and planes, others registering delegates, guiding dignitaries around, jollying them up, and generally adding confusion to the teeming mass of small minds and large egos. In the evenings we were a bright red blur of enthusiasm for the TV cameras to pan during off moments on the convention floor.

As I would find throughout my political days, we with no blood or matrimonial ties to the President or his associates had to work harder to take up the slack left by those whose names carried more weight and fewer obligations. I was assigned each night to be a hostess in the President's Club Lounge, a private room where delegates and guests who had contributed more than a thousand dollars to the President's campaign fund were treated more graciously than those who had neglected to do so. Wearing a red, white, and blue name tag that said "Hi there! I'm BARBARA HOWAR," the first of many I collected over the years in the unchanged role of women in politics, I passed drinks, canapés, and endless hours of small talk with tedious delegates and their suspicious wives from forgettable delegations. I catered to their arcane rural whims as if my courtesy alone could nominate Lyndon B.

Johnson. If there exists a grand matron of the Eastern Star who takes herself and her title more seriously than I did in Atlantic City, I would like to be spared the acquaintance.

The convention keynote speaker was Rhode Island Senator John Pastore, a roosterish little man with a concealed sense of humor and an air of importance about being the evening's main speechmaker. His rhetoric was no more memorable than any before him, but I recall being impressed with his calm in the face of addressing such a vast audience, a unique cool for politicians who generally sweat profusely at large rallies. Pastore returned to the lounge without one drop of perspiration, no damp palm or beaded upper lip, and after according him the expected praise, I asked, "Senator, how come you're not wringing wet?"—a query he enthusiastically addressed himself to for fifteen minutes. He had, he told me, applied to his face an all-body antiperspirant used by chorus girls and majorettes. He offered to send me some of the solution but I declined on the grounds that speaking and strutting was more his line than mine, a questionable statement given my later proclivities for both. The exchange remained my single memorable conversation and was probably the only "new business" brought up at the 1964 convention.

The second night address was delivered with Bible belt sincerity by Indiana's Birch Bayh, the young Senator whose honest boyishness, his pretty, politically astute wife, and a visit to his home state by John F. Kennedy had combined to defeat Homer Capehart. The visit, a bit of political back scratching, earned Bayh his reputation as one of the new breed of men JFK swept into office. Birch and Marvella Bayh had been in a plane crash with Ted Kennedy while campaigning earlier in the summer and had pulled Kennedy to safety.

This increased the supposition that Bayh was a Kennedy man, not an altogether comfortable label given Bayh's ambitions with the new administration. The need for delicate balance in his speech caused the Senator great concern.

The Bayhs, the E. William Henrys, and Florida Congressman Paul Rogers and his wife Becky, were our houseguests in a drafty, overpriced place we had rented in Ventnor, a Monopoly-board move down the line from Atlantic City proper. All of us had definite ideas as to how Birch should address the assembled Democrats, advice he unfortunately accepted. We wrote that speech "in committee," but it was Birch who had to mount the rostrum, deliver it to the television cameras, and take the credit or blame for it, the ensuing criticism indicating the latter. The evening was not the highlight of Bayh's career, but it came close to being that for the rest of us, sitting in the audience nudging one another like enraptured king-makers while Senator Bayh waded through page after page of a most unhistoric address.

The rest of the convention afforded nothing more exciting than the gigantic, building-sized billboard that dominated the entire Atlantic City boardwalk. It showed Barry Goldwater's face and his personal slogan: "In Your Heart You Know He's Right"; which was altered one dark night to read: "*Far* Right." Until the prank claimed national attention as a clever trick, there were no confessed culprits. Afterward, every Democrat in Atlantic City wanted credit for it.

Our house during the convention was around the corner from the one lent to Perle Mesta, who was making an expensive comeback after three years of social oblivion during the Kennedy administration. Her gatherings, more than others, personified the old-type convention brawls and were probably the last of their kind. Perle entertained constantly and lavishly—more, I think, for the pleasure of the press than for her guests. People were crammed into rooms made claustrophobic by the lights, camera, and action of every reporter in the country, who thought nothing of flattening guests in a stampede to buttonhole the numerous political princes rumored as nominees for Vice President. Johnson had built the suspense about his vice-presidential choice in the manner of Bert Parks leading up to the selection of Miss America. With few exceptions, the army of candidates were present at Mrs. Mesta's parties, and they offered the only real drama at the convention; their presence made a Mesta invitation a much-sought status symbol.

Hundreds of tourists filled the Mesta yard every lunch and dinner hour watching for arriving celebrities, who tarried outside only long enough to say a few words into the microphone and to sign autographs. The crowd cheered actress Carol Channing while greeting Hubert Humphrey with puzzled silence.

There were parties for breakfast, lunch, and dinner. Cocktail groups met in every bar. There were dances at night and the usual convention brawling in the hotel halls until early morning. Each gathering surfaced new gossip as to whom Johnson would name as his running mate, new rumors that "Bobby Kennedy was in town" and "Could Jackie be far behind?" For me it was fascinating, and it would be a long time before I was cured of the notion that political conventions should be no more than good, unchallenged fun.

As I swept past the crowds in front of Madame Mesta's house one early evening, my own two sandy children were in the front ranks of the crowd, dripping chocolate popsicles and waving "Hi, Mommy . . . that's my Mommy." Our

243-pound nurse, Darnella, boosted both babies on her shoulders, whistled between her teeth and shouted, "Look at your mama strut her stuff!" With such an auspicious beginning, it was small wonder I proved to be such a political disaster.

6

Several weeks after Johnson received the Democratic nomination, I turned thirty. I never dreamed it would happen to me, and I took the birthday with much surprise and little grace. It continues to annoy me that my feminine conditioning is such that I have to struggle hard to convince myself of continuing value when I add a new year to my life. I handled the trauma of being thirty by going to Harry Winston Jewelers and buying a diamond necklace. When that did not prove sufficiently rejuvenating, I had an affair. Both the necklace and the romance were my first, and like my instinct to purchase jewels from the most exclusive source, I went to the highest quarters for a lover, the United States Senate.

The clergy and Elizabeth Arden be damned; nothing is better for the spirit or body than a love affair. It elevates thoughts and flattens stomachs, and while I doubt adultery will replace Billy Graham or the Canadian Air Force exercises, romance made me feel and look a good deal younger. Falling in love with a United States Senator is a splendid ordeal. One is nestled snugly into the bosom of power but also placed squarely in the hazardous path of exposure.

Washington will ever be a city for extracurricular romance

and undercover trysts, partly because of the high moral standards demanded of the politician by his constituency, and also because it is a town where women are more easily tolerated if they dabble with politicians rather than politics. There will be strange bedfellows in government as long as the double standard exists, as long as divorce is unacceptable in the high levels of politics, as long as the bed is the natural forum for women with political lusts.

Sometimes a man like Nelson Rockefeller gets away with divorce, but then the wealthy never live by the rules forced on the rest of us. Occasionally, men like Justice William Douglas manage to make divorce a way of life, but by and large, wife-changing and high office are not compatible. This inequity accounts for the many dull women in Washington and is the cause of much smug complacency on the distaff side of political marriages.

Some elected officials find it more convenient to take up with their employees, to indulge in intra-office liaisons that are safer than emotional involvements, and where the risk of embarrassing exposure is less. But not all politicians have egos that can settle for secretaries or airline hostesses, and this produces a unique kind of snobbery. They seek the company of lady journalists, New York poets and actresses, and quite often a colleague's more polished wife. In some cases, these lengthy affairs between prominent men and women last so long, the union acquires a respectability akin to marriage. More often, however, they lead to rumors of scandal.

Political power, like wealth, gives an otherwise ordinary man the sexual attractiveness generally reserved for movie stars, athletes, and playboys. The younger the man with power, the more exposed he is to temptations and the more vulnerable is his career if he is discovered. A Ted Kennedy had more to lose at Chappaquiddick than did Louisiana Senator Russell Long who divorced to marry his longtime companion. But the fear of destroying a carefully built reputation by getting caught at human behavior only seems to heighten the excitement and make trafficking in romance the supremely tempting challenge. Like most men with the drive and energy to excel, highly energetic politicians generally are possessed of equal lust for women, and rarely does the acquisition of real power dull their need for sexual conquest.

Except for the President, no man in elected office has to be as careful in his romantic activities as do those in the exclusive fraternity of the U. S. Senate. Given the average age and appearance of most Senators, I suspect few of them spend much time fending off women, but for those with pleasanter faces and more recent birth dates, the temptations are legion. So are the dangers.

For one thing, privacy is much less available than it is for the insurance salesman who takes up with a bored Des Moines housewife. Men with publicized names and faces do not have many hiding places and, unlike the average man who becomes something of a gay dog when his nefarious doings are found out, an elected politician can be ruined for his transgressions by a more chaste opponent. Washington love affairs are carefully conducted in the daytime, hours inconvenient for the male member if he has to answer roll call votes, for the cabinet member who must meet with the President, or the ambassador whose duty it is to be seen at the Queen's birthday party in the British Embassy garden. The lesser luminaries and members of the House of Representatives are more free than most to do as they please for they are less known, have less to lose, and nobody really cares.

My own affair was compounded by a middle-class sense of morality that prompted me to elevate it from the tawdry to the lofty by rationalizing the romance as true love. Both the Senator and I were novices, filled with guilt and handicapped by having no spare time to develop the relationship, to let it run a natural course and terminate gracefully. We both had families and active political interests. While he was dashing around the country righting wrongs, I was pressed into further service helping Lyndon Johnson get reelected.

I described this friendship not from an egocentric need for anonymous name-dropping but because the affair played a bizarre part in future events. It was a pleasurably dizzying interlude made more bittersweet by the shared understanding that his seat in the Senate was the most important thing in his life. Neither of us, as political animals, ever considered exchanging his life of power for a life together. However happy we were, we understood all along that there was no future to our liaison. We eventually fell prey to his ambitions and drifted apart.

Even if political mores had permitted the Senator and me a permanent and legal love, I knew I was temperamentally incapable of the obsequiousness necessary to court the favor of voters. Nevertheless, I felt a deep void when our relationship terminated. I was dazzled by men who held power or operated close to its source. I never dreamed to counsel the mighty myself, but I wanted desperately to belong with a man who could. My own life seemed vacant, and although I had a deep and nagging feeling that somewhere inside me lay another person who might possibly be capable of personal heights, I had no idea where my talents might lie and I lacked the confidence to test my desires. I only knew I wanted to be part of great and glorious moments and that I was bored and unfulfilled. The more I went to meetings with similar women who were sorting out Washington's charitable causes, the more I feared that my years would continue to be filled with trivia, and that I was good for nothing else. I would sit through a luncheon or tea while matrons in Zuckerman suits and diamond circle pins outlined which underprivileged or diseased area we would benefit, and I would be overcome with distaste for the life they and I represented. While we made lists of details for some philanthropic endeavor between sessions of gossiping and bragging, I became terrified that I would be inescapably mired in the life allotted the idle rich woman whom society considered responsible for all the stylish charity expected of their class. In moments I felt I would do anything to escape this destiny. I became so irritable with my daily routine, so trapped with planning meals and training servants, that I blamed my pallid existence on the husband whose enormous income permitted me such plush indolence. I had no appetite for comfortable domesticity. I felt a woman had to conquer the world on her own merits or be the partner of a man who could do it for her. Neither Ed Howar nor I seemed able to fill this need.

At about that same time, the corpulent embodiment of socio-political bossism, Scooter Miller, asked me if I would again serve the Johnson cause, this time as a hostess aboard the Lady Bird Special Train that was to tour the southern states getting votes for LBJ. I was dedicated to playing politics, and will not bore you by describing the alacrity with which I accepted her offer.

The train group was smaller in number and younger in age than we had been in Atlantic City, owing, I suppose, to the smallness of the train and the rigors of whistlestop campaigning. We were still a decidedly southern-speaking contingent. Our first strategy meeting was held at the home of Mary V. Busby, the Texas-talking wife of Johnson aide Horace Busby. From the cacophony of Confederate drawls came the decision that we would be outfitted in "Johnson Blue" shirtwaist dresses with voluminous skirts and wear equal excesses of white felt in ridiculously broad-brimmed skimmer hats. We would win the South for LBJ in sensible ground-gripper shoes, "Hi, there!" name tags, and wholesome Democratic smiles. Mrs. Miller relied on me to add sophistication to the project because of my background as charity ball organizer. At one time or other, I had been on the committee of every Disease Dance in Washington.

For reasons that eluded me then as now, I was selected to travel as Mrs. Johnson's hairdresser for the four-day trip. Peggy Goldwater had been criticized for taking a beautician on her husband's campaign train, and the Johnsons would not risk the censure of Lady Bird for doing the same. The week prior to departure, I followed the First Lady to the beauty parlor to observe her coifing ritual and then equipped myself with a straw basket decorated by a felt map of the Lone Star State, stuffed with rollers, combs, brushes, curling iron, and hairspray. It was hardly a diplomatic pouch but I thought myself as important as the man with the black bag who follows the President with the code to set off nuclear war.

We left Union Station on a rainy October morning in 1964, surrounded by television cameras, reporters, and well-wishers who crowded around the renovated train painted and buntinged with red, white, and "Johnson Blue." Everything was hung with LBJ Banners, Lady Bird Banners, Luci Baines Banners, Lynda Bird Banners, and a few personal ones that were made by friends and flown discreetly from the handles of my luggage: KEEP AMERICA CURLY! GROOM THE WAY FOR LBJ!

The Lady Bird Special had about a dozen cars: those for eating, sleeping, and storing campaign material; those that housed the press; the Johnsons; and finally, the "cattle car" which was reserved for the migratory dignitaries who were shuffled on at each stop. They were greeted by train commander Hale Boggs, who pumped their hands, clapped their backs, ran them past Mrs. Johnson for a quick audience and an autographed copy of *The President's Country*, then back to hostesses who plied them with liquor before the next stop where they were traded in for a whole new group. The official passengers were flaunted before the waiting crowds, allowed to speak a few kind words for Lyndon Johnson and kiss Lady Bird for the photographers, while the local high school band struggled through "Hello Dolly," to which we hostesses sang "Hello Lyndon."

Mrs. Johnson would be presented Texas-yellow roses by the curtseying daughters of county officials and would graciously accept the jellies, jams, preserves, and over-ripe carcasses of local livestock, while she extolled her husband's virtues and smiled bravely through endless choruses of "I've Been Working on the Railroad." The engineer would blow the whistle as a signal for the hostesses to disengage ourselves from the pawing crowd where we passed out banners, buttons, and LBJ candy kisses. The Secret Service would swing us aboard and amidst great cheering, waving, and bandstanding, the Lady Bird Train would chug on down the line where the same folksy politicking would begin again.

It would be a toss-up as to whether Johnson's book or Kentucky's bourbon got the wider distribution. Hale Boggs got the most exposure. At each stop, the late Louisiana Congressman would step to the open end of the train, take the microphone, and make the same declaration: "When Lyndon Johnson is reelected we're gonna have ham in every pot. We're gonna have ham and grits on every plate. We're gonna have ham with plenty of good ole red-eye gravy." When we reached New Orleans several days later, I had lost my taste for Hale Boggs or ham in any form.

When not actually stopped in a town, we had what was called "slow downs" where Mrs. Johnson, Luci, or Lynda Bird would stand at the back of the train to wave at the hundreds of people, mostly Negroes, who lined the tracks. The South is hot in October, and Mrs. Johnson would retire to her compartment to cool off and consult her staff while I combed her hair.

All of us were sticky and dirty, exhausted from constant contact with the daytime crowds and night rallies in auditoriums packed with thousands of people—not all of whom were friendly to the Johnson cause. We had encountered a particularly hostile crowd in Charleston, South Carolina, where hecklers stopped Mrs. Johnson's speech. From a platform on a football field, Mrs. Olin Johnston, the sick and elderly wife of the South Carolina Senator, became so infuriated with her people that she jumped out of her folding chair to take the microphone from a bewildered Lady Bird. With dignity and spirit the South Carolina lady silenced the crowd with shaming invectives. She called them "white trash," then said, "Shut your mouths and listen to a First Lady." They did, but at other times the temper of the crowds was such that the Secret Service would spirit us out of the mob and shove us back on the train, and we would move along to friendlier natives.

In Raleigh, our most triumphant stop until New Orleans, President Johnson joined us for a night rally in the Coliseum, addressing a crowd of nearly thirty thousand people. Carried away by the tribute, Johnson spoke too long and stopped only when Mrs. Johnson passed a note telling him to quit while he was ahead.

We did not see the President again until the end of the trip, but Mama came aboard in Raleigh and rode with us to Greensboro. When the train aligned itself with the decorated platform where the Greensboro hierarchy had gathered to greet us, it was my mother—not Luci's and Lynda's—who was the first to step through the open doors and onto the stage. Thinking her the First Lady, the band struck up and everyone cheered wildly, giving a prolonged ovation that Mama took as her due, bowing right and left as she descended the stairs, shaking hands with the parting crowd and disappearing into a waiting taxi.

I became expert at combing Mrs. Johnson's hair and was frequently asked by others on the train to see if I could do something with theirs. I combed my way through seven southern states, causing one little old lady with a flowered hat and an accent that put us somewhere in Alabama, to lean over and pat my hand, saying: "My, but you're a clever girl to have chosen a profession that allows you to travel."

In the Tallahassee bus station I ate my only meal with a knife and fork. Mrs. Johnson offered me the use of her train shower, but there never was time. When I was not campaigning in the crowds, I was attending Mrs. Johnson's needs, fixing her hair as she conferred with the President's advisors who had joined us in Florida. They brought the warning of a bomb threat, explaining to Mrs. Johnson that explosives were supposedly placed under an upcoming bridge. Their discussion in Mrs. Johnson's compartment that day was on the advisability of stopping the train, admitting defeat for Johnson in the South. I was as dedicated to Lyndon Johnson as anyone but my idea of political sacrifice did not include racing headlong into the certain death of a dynamited railroad bridge. So terrified I could scarcely hold a steady comb, I stood behind the First Lady, staring incredulously from one somber face to the next. With no thought to protocol, I interrupted Mrs. Johnson, tapping her shoulder with a hairbrush and pointing it at the Secret Service agent who was in favor of evacuating the train. "I think he's absolutely right, Mrs. Johnson. Yes ma'am, I'm with him." There was shocked silence as they noticed me for the first time, then stared past me again and continued discussing the risky business of my safety. To my horror Mrs. Johnson elected to continue, a decision that brought me as close to running water as I had come during the entire journey. I was threatened with the wrath of Lyndon Johnson and God Almighty, in that order, not to breathe a word of what I had heard, an easily executed command considering I was scared speechless.

White-faced, I went back to my compartment and stuffed my hairdresser's bag with all the worldly goods it would hold. Clutching it to me, I rushed through six railroad cars like the heroine in the last reel of an Alfred Hitchcock thriller. When I reached the open observation car where it was the despised duty of the hostesses to stand and wave, I volunteered to take the full vigil. Hanging on to the sides of the train railing with one hand, I desperately waved the other at hovering Air Force helicopter pilots as though they were the last living creatures I would see. I was ready to bail out but, to this day, the other hostesses think my long turn on the back of that train was motivated by generosity.

We managed to lose the South anyhow.

7

Something peculiar to the business of choosing a president, be it the primary, convention, or campaign, makes the candidates and workers stick together, prefer their own company, and form cliques like actors, athletes, and writers. Such political camaraderie generates friendships between men and women that perhaps would not flourish under ordinary circumstances. This is certainly true with Democrats and one can only hope it is the same among Republicans. Sometimes electing a man to public office splits the party, even the country, but campaigning has a way of coupling up the campaigners. It is the system's most redeeming feature.

At a rally, speech, or convention, certain people inevitably pair off for a sandwich, a drink, or whatever satisfies the hungers their politics engender. Gluttonous for the full cup, most people who play politics choose a running mate. I chose mine. A family man and seasoned campaigner, he taught me the tricks of campaigning. We drifted together quite naturally on the Lady Bird Train, and later on the Flying Whistlestop north to industrial cities. Just good friends at first, both dedicated to the same ideals and goals, loyal to the same candidate, we maintained a continuous but platonic acquaintance throughout Johnson's drive for the presidency. When not on the same junket, we were in frequent communication on the White House phone system, a direct and costless means of staying in touch. We became a minor political item.

He called from Texas the night LBJ won American history's largest mandate to be President. I was at a party watching the returns, a Washington tradition much in the same spirit as Hollywood people who group together on Academy Award night. With each call, I would cover the receiver to pass on the news from Austin to friends, "The Man is in fine form. Everybody he loves is here at the Driscoll. Connally just came in. Nellie looks great. Mrs. J. is worried that the Man's not eating. It looks good. It's official now, we've won. They're going to televise the President now. Can you hear me over the noise? My God, Barbara, Johnson has never been happier. What did you think of his acceptance speech? Well, we're in, we made it. I always knew it. Even back when he first ran for Congress. Stay put, he's calling me, I'll get back to you in a minute. . . ."

Since the day I turned thirty and began wondering if that was all there was to life, I had been looking for something special. The excitement of that night, all that led up to it, all it portended for the future, the staggering joy of success at the pinnacle of power, was in that moment everything I wanted. I wanted to spend every day campaigning, every night celebrating victory. That such pursuits meant spending those days and nights with the man on the other end of the telephone was no small part of it.

I was also coming to know the Johnson family, spending many evenings with them, and was fascinated as much by the complexities of their various personalities as I was by the immense power their position afforded them.

Lyndon Johnson will always be among my favorite men in history, by no means the vindicated statesman he fancied himself, but certainly one of the most original and funny men in contemporary politics. Rarely did he inspire idealism as did the Kennedy brothers, nor was his orneriness as endearing as Harry Truman's, but the man *was* different and quite special in his own way. One has only to listen to the hard and seasoned press corps swap stories about Johnson to know that he is strangely missed today.

Johnson should have been a more personally popular President. He was cut of native cloth; his homilies were in the best early tradition of America. But while Johnson was the last frontiersman in the White House, the country was no longer a frontier. Middle-class intellectuals and suburban sophisticates had closed in around Jack Kennedy, leaving Johnson no natural constituency. This change in American attitude, coupled with Johnson's unfortunate knack of publicly appearing as the villain, caused people to turn away from him. We did not feel secure with his policies, therefore we had little appreciation for his personality. Johnson also lacked the Truman-Kennedy ability to poke fun in his own direction: he thought himself many things but never the object of humor. The new President was also obsessed by the press. While Kennedy had charmed and used reporters, Johnson was wary of them and heavy-handed in his attempts to manipulate them. The press and the President came to distrust and dislike each other, and Johnson, the colloquial humorist, was translated into Johnson, the dogmatic egocentric. Later, when he left office, Washington would hear scores of LBJ anecdotes recounted by these same members of the press in precise Texas dialect and often with warm regard—

stories of Lyndon Johnson's terrifying hell-bent-for-leather drives in his Lincoln Continental over his Texas ranch as a back seat full of white-knuckled foreign dignitaries sat frozen while LBJ tossed out beer cans and shouted his observations about the great American way of life. Or of Johnson telling a visiting official from India, "Hell, man, we don't worship cows in this country, we eat 'em." But this appreciation of an earthy, down-home Lyndon Johnson was largely retrospective.

His unfortunate references to his own marital practices often left his listeners more repelled than charmed. His need to divulge family peculiarities to the press, as in his recounting of Lynda Bird's announcing of her engagement by crawling into her parents' darkened bedroom on her hands and knees, fell on embarrassed ears. While Johnson was almost fanatical in his need for personal openness, he was paranoid in his efforts to keep secret an official decision until it suited him to make a grand announcement. The nation's press quite rightly resented such access to the President's personal secrets while they were excluded from his official transactions.

Lady Bird Johnson and Johnson's staff, aware of this disparity, sought to protect the President from the members of the press who might not view LBJ in the same affectionate light in which they saw him. He was cut off from anyone who might find him lacking in the standard niceties which, in turn, cut him off from any constructive criticism or exposure that might have broadened his outlook and expanded him into the social lion he had the capacity and desire to be. In sheltering him, they did not enhance the man, but rather, they encouraged Johnson to become his own worst enemy.

In all fairness, they did not remove him kicking and screaming. Johnson was a cantankerous but willing prisoner.

[113]

His drive for power and the eventual exercising of it had left him drained. He was devoid of cultural or literary curiosity, too consumed by politics and too comforted by the underlings who surrounded him in his high but isolated office. He remained aloof from outsiders who, threatened by their exclusion, licked their wounds and awaited public opportunities to restore their pride by calling Johnson crude, corny, and impossible to deal with. While these charges were often true, Johnson's enemies neglected to add that LBJ was also capable of being a very warm, incisive, and humorous man. The real flavor of Lyndon Johnson was lost in a mountain of vanity, his own and that of those who could not get close enough to the President to appreciate him as a human being.

Lady Bird Johnson pulled herself together esthetically and intellectually, smoothed her edges, and made herself equal to her role. She learned to face crowds, later addressing them forcefully; she became expert at charming the people Lyndon felt insecure around, especially the Washington press that tended to glamorize the First Lady with the same lavish energy they expended in admonishing the President. Mrs. Johnson was an organizer and despite the thinness of her causes, she cultivated the rich and influential, pressed them into her service, and in general, took up the social slack within her husband's administration. She showed an early determination to be cultured, kind, and tolerant while underneath she remained a shrewd, hard-boiled, and clever woman. Already able to deal with orphans and welfare mothers, she became increasingly at ease in museums, concert halls, and the expensive drawing rooms of moneyed New Yorkers. Lady Bird Johnson blossomed in her role while LBJ shriveled in his. But, for me, Lyndon Johnson will ever be the more likeable and remarkable, the better parent, the more interesting human being.

I also came to know many of those people surrounding Johnson on the non-domestic levels of the White House. They came to consider themselves more important and valued than they were, or conversely, more impotent or bungling than was often the case. It was an acute form of power-schizophrenia engendered by Johnson's ambivalent feelings toward his workers, his habit of alternately chucking his employees under their trembling chins or bludgeoning them spiritless with their shortcomings. Assistants like Jack Valenti or Horace Busby could at one moment be paragons of wisdom and efficiency, and at Johnson's whim, he would cut them down as incompetent lackeys. Purposeful groveling was the price one paid for sitting close to Johnson's throne. His self-indulgent tantrums once caused Dean Acheson, present during a Johnson tirade, to comment to the President that he did not pay his people enough to talk to them like that. However, his staff took the abuse without once suggesting that the President of the United States might take the job and store it somewhere inside his personal anatomy.

But for every humiliation, I began to notice that LBJ had a way of tossing a wisp of praise to his subordinates that kept them coming back for more. By and large they remained loyal to him while he was in office. An exception later was myself, but I was never financially dependent on serving the Johnson cause, was never subjected to his mercurial disposition, nor granted a genuine power I feared to lose. I have not the slightest notion what I would have done had I been faced with the choice of sucking up or getting out. My guess is that I would have been no different from anyone else who becomes dependent on reflected power.

Given Mrs. Johnson's overzealous guard of her husband and his staff's constant vying for his favor, Lyndon Johnson was most attractive on the occasions he was without them. When relieved of playing the role they expected of him, Johnson was natural and likeable; even the press warmed to him in those unguarded moments. On White House evenings when Mrs. Johnson was off planting trees and braving the Snake River rapids in rubber rafts, LBJ was at his best. On the open deck of the yacht *Sequoia* in his leather swivel chair, dressed more like a White House maintenance man than the Chief Executive, Johnson was all charm, joking with the guests as he cruised up and down the Potomac River, and chatting calmly over several plates of his favored but forbidden creamed foods, easily chewed, and laced with rice or noodles. He would have more than the allotted one Scotch in his double-insulated plastic glass, and he allowed himself to be entertained and flattered, sometimes demanding the boat be turned around when it reached the dock and returned upstream for a prolonged cruise. He would watch the late television news with a pretty girl sitting on either side, holding a hand of each and calling out to a crony some bit of gossip or lewd reference to whoever had incurred his displeasure during the course of his strenuous day.

With style and cunning and the innate timing of a showman, Johnson monopolized all conversation. If a reference to dangling parts of the body "getting caught in a washing machine wringer" or his description of a lady's anatomy that reminded him "of a cow that kept stepping on its udders" made his audience wince, they did so inwardly. Outwardly they laughed, either because it was expected or because it was genuinely funny. If LBJ caught the difference between sycophantic giggling and spontaneous mirth, he never let on; he took both in his stride, both as his due.

He was never the kind of man with whom one made small talk—a president rarely is—but he would sometimes be of a mood to encourage timid jousting and could accept mild barbs with mild humor. Often he would tease me for concerning myself more with his daughters' attire than his own and would needle me into discussing his baggy trousers. I would reply, "Mr. President, we could upholster every chair in the White House with the extra fabric in those pants," a rejoinder he would take in good spirit. We had a running joke: he would lift my wrist full of jangling bracelets made of old U.S. gold currency and ask me why I wore coins instead of jewels. And I would answer: "This is my way of stopping the gold flow, Mr. President."

His attention to me on those relaxed evenings was such that many believed there was more to our relationship than met the eye. In truth there were moments when I also thought the President's interest was more than I had bargained for. In the White House theater, Johnson would sit in his ever-present leather swivel chair watching favorite spy-smasher movies while holding and stroking my hand. This would seem an innocent and silly recollection to anyone who has not cozied up with the President of the United States in a darkened theater and felt the conflicting stabs of pain and pleasure that the most powerful man in the world is making a pass at you, the bewildering realization that any move could be read as an affirmative or negative response, and not be certain which is worse.

Before any choice was offered, LBJ would fall asleep in his chair while still holding my hand. I will never forget the discomfort of my paralyzed left arm tingling from lack of circulation, afraid to move for fear of awakening the man and his interests.

After a brief nap, Johnson would wake up and demand to see the spliced reel of home movies from his younger days. The film was narrated by Lady Bird Johnson with background music by John Philip Sousa. There was footage of vanished Christmases and Halloweens, of Johnson at Lynda Bird's sixth birthday at their old house in suburban Washington, Johnson casually saluting the camera as Mrs. Johnson's voice pointed out: "Now here is a younger, slimmer Lyndon. . . ." The President would fall asleep again, only to wake up and order the film rerolled to the parts showing his ranch on the Pedernales in the days before he had turned it into an opulent showplace.

It did not take me long to see that Johnson was devoted to the telephone; he kept one handy in unlikely places. There was one beneath the dining table in the family quarters, and it was not uncommon for him to bring someone's name into conversation, reach under the table and either growl or purr for the White House telephone operators to get that person on the line. At dinner one evening, he turned and asked what my husband thought of my being away from home so much: "He's either mighty nice or mighty henpecked." Not certain which answer he would believe, I just smiled and nodded. Johnson picked up the phone and asked to be connected with Ed Howar who was waiting at home in something less than a cordial mood about my not being there too. I was horrified Ed might think the call a practical joke and cut the conversation short with an expletive, but Johnson and Lady Bird chatted amiably with my absent partner until the President abruptly ended the exchange by thanking Ed for "giving me your wife," confirming, I fear, Ed Howar's worst suspicions of my White House visits.

LBJ was unpredictable, and it was foolish to anticipate his responses to anything. I once took Don Carnevale of Harry Winston Jewelers into the President's oval office to show Johnson an assortment of diamond rings that Luci insisted he inspect for Mrs. Johnson's Christmas present. The President was recovering from his famous gall bladder operation and was still smarting over the ridicule resulting from the uninhibited display of his stomach scar that appeared on the cover of *Life*. I walked into the room and approached the President who was seated behind his massive desk, his back to the windows and flagstaffs. When he looked up, I extended my hand and came toward him without taking my eyes off his face. It was graceful carriage, but it kept me from noticing a three-foot square of clear plexiglass beneath his swiveling chair. My toe caught the edge of it and sent me sprawling headlong into the President's lap. When I tried to get up, the chair-rollers slid and sent us crashing back into the wall, bouncing us off it only long enough for me to fall clumsily a third time, a ricocheting process that was repeated once again before I staggered to my feet. To my relief and the President's credit, Johnson grimaced threateningly, rubbed his surgical scar, and announced simply: "You sure do know how to greet a fellow, Barbara."

His jocularity was shortlived as he looked over the diamonds spread on his desk. He buzzed for the handy Valenti who came so fast I suspected him of lurking outside the door. Both men expressed outrage at the price tags on the rings, and Valenti asked if he and the President might be in the wrong business, a query I would later make myself.

Regardless of his moods, I came to enjoy Johnson's electric personality, and if his amorous gestures toward me were disconcerting, they were also flattering. Mine became the dilemma of befriending a First Lady and her daughters while simultaneously fending off the advances of the man most important in their lives. The Johnson women were possessive of LBJ, and as he did with his staff and advisors, he played them off against themselves and others. He could get Lynda's attention by dangling Luci's virtues, and as was more often the case, he used Lynda to shape up his younger, more unconventional daughter. The girls never got enough of their father's time to be generous in sharing him with other women. Johnson never got enough time for other women.

My White House act involved some adroit footwork to keep the President gently at bay without incurring his rage or damaging his pride. At the same time I had to maintain equal rapport with both his demanding daughters while offsetting my influence with them against Mrs. Johnson's need to be all things to all three. A more complicated involvement with the President would have ruined my relationship with his women and wrecked my blossoming love affair with his trusted friend and longtime advisor.

The situation was straight out of a French boudoir comedy and according to my childish, self-centered way of thinking at the time, I fancied that everyone in the world craved my warm young body. I agonized over what I would say when the President made his interest in me a yes-or-no proposition, and on occasion went so far as to fantasize a dramatic moment when I would be forced to abdicate my position with the Johnsons because, as I envisioned I would say, "I cannot serve my country without the man I love at my side." I was never so far gone in my narcissism that the slapstick humor of the situation did not invariably reduce me to laughter, and I would be less than honest not to admit I enjoyed the whole thing enormously. Had Lyndon Johnson been the "younger, slimmer Lyndon" of Mrs. Johnson's home movies, I might be recalling different memories.

It was actually Mrs. Johnson who averted any confrontation between me and her husband. She was a woman of keen insight coupled with years of experience with Johnson's roving eye. She knew precisely when and how to interfere in his flirtations, a practice for her that bordered upon a second calling. She had already been forced to deal politely with several female employees whom Johnson fancied, and she was alert to keep me off the White House statistics list. When the President detained me too long in another room, Mrs. Johnson would call out: "Lyndon, don't be a hog, we all want to talk to you and Barbara"; or on the dance floor where the President would become most ardent, she would approach him firmly as she did the night of Johnson's Inaugural Ball. He and I had been dancing for fifteen minutes, he draped around my neck like a fox fur and I, not realizing protocol prohibited another partner from breaking in, was loving it but petrified that the President of the United States was "stuck" with me. "Now, Lyndon," she said, "I know a young girl who is very tired and a President who has a mighty big day tomorrow." With a steely grip, Lady Bird would lead Lyndon Johnson home, a tactic that may not always have been successful given Johnson's passion for women and having his own way. I only know it worked for me, and while I am not suggesting that the thirty-sixth President of the United States was a dirty old man, I would not bet the rent money that he was not.

8

My experiences with the Johnsons had only heightened my determination to remain entrenched with them. They, I rationalized, were my surest avenue to fame and happiness. Being close to the family in the White House gave me the unique and glamorous identity that closeness to power always permits in Washington. It was also the least complicated way in which I could continue my romance with Johnson's advisor. Together he and I went to work on the Inaugural. It had to be bigger and better than Kennedy's, for that was all that mattered, and every stop was pulled to make it so.

Several old temporary buildings on Constitution Avenue were turned over to Dale Miller, Inaugural Chairman, Texan, Johnson crony, and lobbyist. Those who had worked in the campaign were given prestigious jobs. Phones were installed on borrowed desks, secretaries and chauffeured cars were plucked from various government agencies, stationery printed, money allocated, and the vast machine that spends two months organizing a spontaneous welcome to a new administration was put into motion. Within five days there was a cafeteria, the absolute nerve center for any Washington bureaucracy. Thus the 1964 Inauguration of Lyndon Baines Johnson and Hubert Horatio Humphrey began.

I was appointed Coordinator of the Inaugural Ball sites, working directly under Co-Chairmen Warren Woodward and Mrs. Hale Boggs and responsible only to them for the five campaign advance men who were selected to organize the five ball sites: the District of Columbia Armory, and the ballrooms of the Mayflower, Shoreham, Statler-Hilton, and Sheraton-Park Hotels. The first site would be the largest, the last the most glamorous because it would house the Texans and be Johnson's final and longest stop. The other hotels were sloughing grounds for the thousands of people who come from all over the country to attend these circuslike calamities that are held every four years. It was my job to see that no one felt sloughed. Each site was decorated from the fund of one hundred thousand dollars allocated for that purpose; each presidential box was equipped with a public address system; each had equal provisions for booze, coat checking, seating, and dancing to the music of a big-name band. Like Dale Miller, my site chairmen were lobbyists for national business interests, each a crack organizer with his eye on the reward for serving a president-elect: influence. I had my friend Sherrye Henry named over-all Decorations Chairman. We shared an office, six phones, and a secretary and spent every weekday and most weekends putting together some semblance of a successful gathering for a crowd of fifty thousand people.

What had begun as a campaign flirtation turned into a full-fledged love affair at Inaugural Headquarters. We worked together every day. Our evenings were spent in constant company. I was never at home during those pre-Inaugural months, and rarely saw either husband or children. People talked but I was bothered by none of it; beyond concern, elevated at last from the role of housewife I had come to feel smothered by, happy, free, and very, very reckless. I had a title, power and identity, and that all-time Washington status symbol, a car and driver. I made two erroneous assumptions: I thought myself indispensable, and I also thought myself in love.

In the middle of those hectic months, Mrs. Johnson asked me to the White House to discuss taking charge of her daughters for the Inauguration, to organize their wardrobes while the girls were busy with school. I gladly took on the added opportunity to become more solidly affixed to life in Johnson's White House. Together the First Lady and I went through her daughters' closets, making lists of what was wearable and what had to be added. It was the beginning of the most complicated shopping expedition of my life—nothing that could vaguely be called a spree, given the size and taste of both girls and Mrs. Johnson's abiding caution with money.

Mornings were spent in my Inaugural office arranging for caterers, meeting with hotel managers, arguing about liquor licenses and special seating arrangements for Lyndon's Cousin Oriole or Hubert's Minneapolis Mayor. Afternoons were spent in department stores selecting dozens of ball gowns, suits, dresses, hats, shoes, gloves, and purses for the Johnson girls. I would charge and credit the items to my own account; the actual purchases would be billed to the Johnsons—a bookkeeping procedure that brought chaos to the Washington retail community. Eventually I put all purchases directly on Mrs. Johnson's personal account, an exercise in power I came to love: "I'll take those nine dresses and these six coats and charge them, please . . . Johnson, L. B., 1600 Pennsylvania Avenue, Northwest. Yes, the White House. No, madame, I am not a practical joker. . . . Yes, feel free to call the manager. . . ." It was some weeks before the White House chauffeur and I were not suspected of being the two slickest hustlers in Washington, but eventually we were given full run of every store. Like Mrs. Onassis, I would sweep through any department, selecting items at random without exchange of money or credit card, and sweep out, the package-laden driver in his White House uniform following behind me at a respectful distance.

Then there were evenings at the White House pulling garments out of tissue paper, trying them on an enthusiastic Luci and a reluctant Lynda, handing the rejected clothes to a maid for repacking, and setting aside the rest for the final selection to be made after dinner by the President and Mrs. Johnson. The elder Johnsons would settle into their private quarters at the opposite end of the enormous second floor hall that links the White House family rooms with Lincoln's bedroom and the Queen's official suite. The girls would model the clothes while the President looked them over and his wife scrutinized the price tags. The final decision was ostensibly the President's, but like anything else that affected the family, Mrs. Johnson had a way of making up his mind for him, subtly and diplomatically managing to have the last word.

The First Lady was, in fact, the only person who could handle the family obstinacy. She would listen quietly to all discussions, making invisible notes on her lap with an invisible pencil, thinking, always thinking. Some time later, plans would be formed to her satisfaction. She made these decisions appear as though they had been reached by her husband or daughters but it did not take long to see that she was in charge. Lady Bird Johnson, for all her obvious contributions, was best behind the scenes.

Because of an embarrassing evening Johnson suffered as Kennedy's Vice President, when he was the only man in white tie and tails at the French Embassy because he had not been informed that Jack Kennedy had decided at the last minute to wear a tuxedo, the President despised the full, formal attire and refused to wear it to his own Inaugural Ball. Luci was determined to dress the vamp and Lynda the schoolmarm, but one phone call to the First Lady and all three Johnsons showed up in costumes suited to the protocol of the occasion.

Mrs. Johnson could even persuade the President to eat the calorieless food prescribed after he had had a heart attack, a constant source of concern and struggle on her part. Johnson would say, "Bird is handling me," but except for one evening when he shoved aside a bowl of low-cholesterol bouillon with the suggestion to "leave this hot water in the sink where it belongs," he ate what she thought best—rarely at the proper hour, but usually in the proper manner. The First Lady became so good at managing the President that it was hard to avoid conjecture as to what mountains Lady Bird Johnson could have moved had she used her influence in matters more crucial than beautifying a troubled nation.

Regardless of all these complications, we managed to muddle through the 1964 Inauguration with the Johnson-Humphrey image as intact as, so it seemed, my sanity, marriage, romance, and reputation: all shaky but functioning. The night prior to the Inaugural Ball, a large Gala was held with a number of currently popular Hollywood and Broadway stars appearing on the Armory stage to salute the continuing Democratic regime. The evening was a great success, according to the newspaper accounts I read the next day in Georgetown Hospital.

Ed Howar and I had been in a limousine with Warren Woodward, the Ball Chairman, his wife Mary Ellen, and the Earl Deaths from Austin. Earl, a Texas version of Sir Toby Belch, ran Station KTBC, part of the empire Johnson amassed during his years of public service. Tearing down Constitution Avenue as part of the official motorcade, our limousine slowed slightly, lagged behind, and was struck broadside by a police car.

Mr. Death's several hundred pounds of jolliness were on the jump seat, with my legs stretched underneath. The impact of the collision threw Earl forward and the slamming of the brakes crushed man and seat back on to my legs. I recall little until I awoke around midnight in a hospital ward with an elderly lady whose broken hip caused her to moan from inside her oxygen tent. A radio broadcast from the nurse's station was interrupted for a news bulletin: "The first Inaugural accident . . . tonight . . . collision . . . several casualties . . . Barbara Howar . . . thirty-year-old Inaugural official. . . ." *Thirty years old.* I would never be able to lie about my age—the whole world would remember Barbara Howar was thirty years old at the time Lyndon Johnson took office. I went back to sleep.

Next morning I was in a filthy ward with ice packs on my legs, the old lady moaning, me weeping, envisioning life in a wheel chair, missing the Inaugural I had labored over for two months, and thirty years old. I slept some more.

When I awoke, my roommate and her tent were gone. In her place was a gigantic basket of flowers from the White House. An orderly was feverishly sweeping the room while three nurses changed my bed linens and fluttered over me with sponge and comb. A hazily familiar face behind dark glasses walked into the room, checked inside the closet, looked under the bed, and silently exited. This was the Secret Service's way of announcing a visit from a member of the First Family.

Lynda Bird breezed in with her current beau, twirled to show her costume for the Capitol swearing-in ceremony, plugged in a Sony TV, gave me cheery messages from her family, and promised to return with a complete account of what I would miss. She departed happily, saying, "Don't worry, Daddy will do this all over again in four years."

By mid-afternoon, I was wild. I had not seen a doctor. I rang for the nurses, whose interest in me appeared to have departed with the President's daughter. I called politely, then shouted, and was midway into a screaming fit when the orthopedic surgeon came in. Silently he and the cheerful nurse unwrapped my legs. He was an enormous man with red hair growing down a thick neck. He completely ignored everything but my legs which he bent back and forth with huge, red-haired hands.

"What is it, doctor?" I sobbed while he nonchalantly tapped and pulled. I was probably crippled for life, and this red-hairy doctor could not bring himself to tell me.

"Now, Doctor will tell *us* what *we* should know when he thinks *we* need to know it," was all I got from the simpering nurse who lost none of her cheerfulness at my suggestion that she was a stupid cow. Next came two interns who went through the same procedure as I repeated my hysterical questions. "No hablo inglés, señora. Buenos días!"

I was as concerned with improving international medical relations as the next terrified patient, but my interest did not include being practiced on by a couple of student doctors who spoke no English, and I let the entire floor of the hospital know it.

To stop my tirade, the orthopedic doctor returned and after a series of menacing nods, he said, "You're a very lucky girl. That long quilted evening gown saved you."

Dizzy with relief, I babbled, "I guess it was worth six hundred dollars after all," then remembered it was universally thought unwise to acquaint doctors with one's affluence. "Doctor, when can I get out of here?"

He deliberated. "Any normal, sane person would stay here a few days, but then a normal, sane person wouldn't have anything to do with Lyndon Johnson in the first place, would she?"

At the mercy of a Republican!

"If you stay quiet today and keep those ice packs on your legs, I guess you can leave late this afternoon. You're a fool but you can go. If something worse doesn't happen to you fooling around with Democrats, come in next week and let me take a look at you."

I grabbed his hand thankfully and recall him gratefully. For a redheaded Republican, he was a first-rate doctor and fortuneteller.

I went through the Inaugural Ball like a prizefighter whose physical discomfort is lost in the cheer of the crowd. In another hazardous motorcade, but one without casualties, we followed the President's limousine to the five ball sites, leaping out of cars and over snow banks, pushing and pulling each other through the mobs. The Hale Boggses, the Warren Woodwards, and I were too taken with our handiwork to notice how dangerously we had overpacked the ballrooms, too taken with Johnson's pleasure at his reception to worry about fractured time schedules or loudspeakers that went dead as the President, like the Pope on his balcony, rose to address his following.

Johnson set the evening's pace at his first stop, the Mayflower Hotel. He crossed the dance floor in his wide Texan stride and swooped Margaret Truman Daniel over the railing of her official box to begin both the dancing and the popular association between Johnson's presidency and Harry Truman's, a link with that previous Democratic order that LBJ continued to enjoy.

The doctor was right in his prediction that I would not feel like dancing and also strangely accurate in his suggestion that something worse might befall me for cavorting with Democrats. Prior to the Inauguration I had made the worst mistake a woman can make in marriage: I had been honest. I had told Ed Howar I was desperately unhappy, that my restless, chaotic need for there to be something special in my life beyond being a wife and mother was destroying me and everything I loved. I wanted a divorce. I told him I was in love with another man who might possibly be able to give me the sense of being real that I so desperately needed. I asked for nothing other than my freedom and the children. I told him the name of the man involved. While he was deeply hurt, I thought Ed Howar understood the depth of my fears and discontent and the irreconcilability of my decision.

I had begun quietly, prior to the Inaugural, to look for a job to support myself; it would be a small price to pay for autonomy. But even as I begged Ed Howar for my independence, I was suffused with guilt at hurting him and inflicting on my children all the horrors of divorce. Still, I felt a definite lessening of emotional pressures. I began to feel there might perhaps be better days ahead.

Three weeks before the Inaugural, Ed went to Florida for two weeks to, as he said, "think things over." I drove him to the airport. We were friendly, resigned, I thought, to the confusion of our marriage, and determined to do the quiet, honest thing that would be best for us and for our children. He called every night from Palm Beach and returned with lavish presents for us all: I could have a divorce and the children. I felt a strange sense of disappointment that worsened my guilt. I had an increasingly foreboding feeling that it had all been too easy, but I tried not to think of my situation as the Inaugural approached.

Two days after the Johnson-Humphrey triumphant sweep into office, I flew to Jamaica for a rest and some clandestine time alone with the man I was planning ultimately to marry. Our relationship had taken place amidst crowds, an atmosphere of fast political action that lent an aura of romance but was hardly a normal situation for making level-headed decisions affecting the lives of other people. Physically and emotionally exhausted, and strangely let down after the high-powered campaign and Inaugural proceedings, I became unsure that remarriage would put an end to my discontent. Locked into a situation of my own creation that I neither understood nor felt certain I wanted for the rest of my life, I also found that without those mutual interests in electing and installing a new President, this man and I had little in common and even less to talk about. I had the uneasy feeling I might be going from one empty life into another.

In the sultry, alien surroundings of the Caribbean, harsh reality became larger than my fantasy of finding peace by changing marriages. I became morbidly depressed for the first time in my life. I missed the children, my home, everything familiar and comfortable. I was melancholy and homesick, maudlin in my confusion, I wanted something to make me happy, something to give me reason not to care that half my life was over and that I had no real zest for finishing out the rest. Guilty and restless as before, I saw the future now as even more menacing. I wanted it all and I wanted out. It was the woman's primal feeling of being trapped, unable to live without marriage because it was all I knew, but incapable of projecting myself happily into more of the same. My anxieties grew. I had doubts about who I was and what I wanted to be. Why was I even in Jamaica?

I quickly found out *why*, as well as *what* I was. I was, according to five private detectives who dropped in on me, an adulterous woman committing the female's most unpardonable crime against society in a sixty-dollar-a-day tropical paradise.

Perhaps it was the sleeping pill I had taken to calm my nerves, or maybe just the uneasy feeling one has being in the same room with another person one is unaccustomed to, but I was in a misty stupor when the first sounds brought me out of that odd state of being neither asleep nor awake. I knew immediately that, like all those love-nest stories in *Confidential* magazine, I was being raided.

I recall shock and fear, then anger and outrage, that this could be happening to me. Criminals and anarchists live with this kind of terror, but I was nothing more than a foolish and reckless romantic—one, moreover, who was dangerously close to a nervous collapse. Without the fury, I would very likely have disintegrated.

Private detectives, for the uninitiated, bear no resemblance to Sam Spade or James Bond. My team of sleuths was headed by a wild-eyed fanatic, a man who was to haunt me for years both in nightmares and in reality. The other four detectives looked like bit players in a Mafia movie. With lewd suggestions and smirks, they busied themselves roughing up my companion and ransacking the room for my jewelry, which they found and confiscated. I was jerked around for a full-face photograph after they first tore off the strap on my nightgown. I was told such added spice would be very persuasive in court.

The chief detective waved a revolver and shouted that I was every kind of a whore. "All women are whores and sluts. You're all slime and dirt." I was left the suspicion that this thirty-thousand-dollars-a-case investigator was less disturbed by my particular infidelity than by that of someone in his own past. Screaming like an animal, he dared my companion to call the authorities on the phone which was, of course, dead. Over and over, the detective shouted that it was of no use to us to be "high and mighty." He laughed hysterically when no hotel employees investigated the noise, they, I suppose, having been bribed into the silence that surrounds Banana Republic assassinations.

I walked to the terrace after the detectives stormed out and picked up a forgotten camera, the film still intact. As they emerged below, I threw the camera over the balcony, striking the chief sleuth on the side of his head. Even in bad films, the gumshoe takes the evidence.

Photographs were incidental at this point. I was in trouble. My accomplice was crying as he clicked the receiver up and down trying to rouse the hotel operator to call his New York attorneys. We exchanged no words but I knew, quite calmly, that I was in this mess alone. The laws of society would find me guilty. There was no question of squaring things with Ed

Howar, even had I wanted to. He had been present in the hotel room throughout the entire episode, silently watching.

And so I left the sunny Caribbean. It was not an easy task at the height of the tourist season. We chartered a small craft to Miami where I got the last seat on a plane leaving for Baltimore within ten minutes. I placed a long distance phone call to the only person I knew I could count on: "Mama, I'm in trouble and I need you. Get to Washington as fast as you can. I can't explain anything to you now. Just hurry."

She asked me one question: "Have you killed anybody?"

"No, Mama."

"Good. We can handle anything else." She hung up the phone, took her purse, and walked out the front door in Raleigh. Without a word to anyone she drove straight to Washington.

I left the phone booth in Miami and shook hands with my companion, who was concerned with getting to New York to deal with his own problems this turn of events had created. I boarded a plane for the longest trip I had ever taken. Those three hours in the air were spent sorting things out. Ed Howar had never intended to give me the children. I later found that he had not gone to Palm Beach to think things over, but had spent those two weeks in Washington, in the basement of his sister's house next door to our own, where he and the detective had electronically monitored my every move, call, sound, and word. Nights he had slept on a cot in the basement of the detective's house in Arlington. Two thoughts tormented me: that the man I was married to knew me so little that he believed he could catch me at adultery in my own home with the children present, and that I was responsible for driving another human being to peeping and prying from basement holes.

My Catholic upbringing left me little doubt that I was beyond redemption; my southern culture had taught me that I had committed the truly unpardonable sin. I could have understood being shot for my crime, for that is a common occurrence in the South. What I could not handle was the idea and memory of all the things that had just transpired in Ed Howar's full vision. I could understand his desperation but never the manner in which he dealt with it. The impact of recalling the morning's events—my carrying a suitcase past the drunken detectives who lounged around the hotel's courtyard swimming pool while my own husband watched and listened to them make vulgar catcalls—hit me in midflight. It is the only time I ever threw up on an airplane.

From Baltimore, I took a taxi to Washington, to the house of my friend and obstetrician, Jim Walsh. He and his wife were having a dinner party, but he calmed me down and drove me to the home of Thomas Wadden, the partner of famed trial lawyer Edward Bennett Williams. Both men were sensitive to my situation, but I knew their attitude was one I would encounter in equally decent men: I was guilty. Tom Wadden listened somberly to my story, made a phone call privately, and came back into his library to tell me he was sorry, but Wadden and Williams did not handle divorce suits and could not take my case. He would find someone else. I was to go home and wait.

I was dropped in front of my empty house. My car was gone, and the locks had been changed on the doors. I sat alone on the front steps in the cold dark, hugging my knees, too scared to feel sorry for myself. By the time Mama arrived I was hardly capable of talking.

"I want my children, Mama. I want Bader and Edmond."

Without a word, she threw a brick through the kitchen

window, climbed inside to turn on the lights, then came to let me in after first closing the doors to the children's rooms where the signs of hasty departure were apparent. We talked and cried all night, my third without eating or sleeping but by no means my last. Aside from feeling I had done wrong, my sense of inadequacy and self-loathing were pushing me to the breaking point. Whatever anyone else was to think of me, it could be no worse than I thought of myself. Not once did anyone try to relieve me of that notion throughout the entire ordeal.

Next morning there was nothing. No contact with Ed or my children. I did not know where they were or what would happen to them or to me. Mama telephoned Ed's parents but was turned away by a servant. She went to the Howar house and was received coldly by Mrs. Howar, who demanded that Mama remove her wanton child from Washington: "She is finished in this town."

Tom Wadden called to say that all the reputable lawyers in the city were busy. The shrewdest Washington divorce attorney was already in the employ of Mr. Howar and, I was told, the rest have "heavy schedules"; they were all "very sorry." I was at the worst crisis of my life right in the middle of the legal rush hour. No one would take my case. Mama talked to several lawyers herself, telling them that my family would pay any fee, anything. "Sorry, Mrs. Dearing, but at this time of the year. . . ." Ed Howar's lawyer would speak to no one but "Mrs. Howar's attorney," and Mrs. Howar could not scare up a third-rate quack at any price.

Finally Tom Wadden came up with an attorney who would at least give me an appointment after hearing the details of my predicament. He had no partners, no receptionist, no secretary, but he took my case. Ed Howar's lawyer talked with my attorney and gave him the verdict: "Mrs. Howar is to relinquish everything. She must give up the children and leave town with nothing more than the clothes on her back. Mr. Howar is prepared to be generous. He will permit her to see the children three weeks each year, for three consecutive weeks and in a place only he may designate. During the remainder of the year, Mrs. Howar may write or call the children only by communicating through Mr. Howar. He will also pay the divorce costs provided Mrs. Howar assumes her maiden name and leaves for Reno by noon on Friday."

It was further stipulated that if I did not sign the necessary papers within thirty-six hours, Ed Howar would file for divorce in a District Court, suing for adultery and naming as co-respondents a United States Senator and an advisor to President Lyndon Johnson. My lawyer was advised that in his efforts to prove me an unfit parent, the private detective had monitored phone calls from the Senator, and while they did not have actual proof of a liaison, no judge would take lightly the double breach of morals. Ed Howar's lawyer alluded gravely to the public outrage over the conduct of such highly placed people and suggested outright that the ensuing publicity would damage any chance I had of proving I was fit to keep my children.

So, there it was. Either I was hopelessly paranoid or all those upstanding lawyers were not as busy as they would have me think. No law firm in its right mind wanted to become involved on the wrong side of a custody fight that would have repercussions reaching into the White House, touching off a scandal that would be embarrassing to the most influential man in the world. It was an open-and-shut case of *get out of town by sundown or else*. I had never heard of Gloria Steinem or the American Civil Liberties Union.

I told my attorney that I was not a "street-walking, dope-taking whore" and that "I would see them all in hell and the front page of the *Daily News* before I would give up my children."

"Surely," I asked him, "no judge on earth would take my children from me on the basis of two indiscretions on an otherwise clean record?" My lawyer advised me to sign the papers and make the best of it. I refused.

The night before the deadline, a meeting was arranged between me and the man involved in the affair, our first and only contact since Miami. Sherrye Henry drove me to town, crying, saying nothing but "I'm right here, pal, you know that." It was a lot from a friend whose identical social conditioning made her think me as guilty as I thought myself. She and I, along with Mama, took for granted the fact that I had broken the big rule. We did not look for or expect social sanction, we just wanted to get my tail out of a crack and hush up the scandal.

I met with the gentleman in question alone. I told him I was going to see the thing through to the finish, that I was going to fight. He begged me to change my mind. He had been, he told me, with Abe Fortas all afternoon and the White House was very upset. He pleaded with me to consider what the scandal would do to his career, his children, his wife. Finally, "Think, Barbara, how good the Johnsons have been to you, how they have trusted you as a decent woman around their children. Think of the embarrassment it would cause them if you go through with this." He also mentioned the disgrace to the United States Senate. I shook my head in disbelief and disagreement.

"Look, Barbara, the country doesn't need this right on top of the Walter Jenkins and Bobby Baker affairs." The *coun-*

[138]

try! I burst into hysterical laughter—he had kindly spared me a reference to Billie Sol Estes. I was about to lose my sanity and children, and I was being classified with graft and perversion and asked to throw away my children for the sake of my country.

He never paused in his appeal. "We'll see you are taken care of. I promise. I have the highest authority to offer you a job with the Protocol Department on the West Coast. You're young and resilient, Barbara, you'll have other children."

I could not win, and I could not abandon my children to grow up with people who thought they had the right to separate them from me. I signed. I insisted my husband be present as I did, and afterward, I asked Ed Howar if he would take me out for something to eat. Two days later we reconciled. My children returned but my tolerance for the traditional role of women never did.

9

I began a two-year sentence in a personal hell. I grew accustomed to entering rooms filled with people whom I imagined to be both curious and hostile. Despite my efforts at secrecy, everyone appeared to know the details of my amorous escapades and fabricated some additional versions of their own. I learned to fill awkward silences with flippancy, taking thinly veiled innuendoes from the Johnson people as something I had coming.

A slip from grace in the Washington of those days and you were fair game, an easy mark for those who had resented your moments of power. Fall beneath the hypocritical standards of morality that Washington pretended to live by, and you were beyond the social pale, the target of righteous female indignation and the object of suggestive advances from every man in town. In her lifetime as a Madame, Polly Adler never received as many propositions as I got in the six months before my red-hot reputation cooled down. The Senator never knew how close he came to moral notoriety. The influential "other man" bought his wife a mink coat and went on a prolonged cruise until the conversation subsided and was replaced by other juicy gossip. This man I had thought my salvation acquired a new interest and became something of a swaggering ladies' man, thoroughly enjoying, I think, his unaccustomed reputation as a gay blade.

Ed and I spent many an evening at home in the silent resignation of couples who are bound together by social mores and little else. But gradually, like all Washington gossip, we became yesterday's news. It was Mrs. Johnson who brought me back from oblivion. Luci called one day to ask me to go shopping with her, an invitation I appreciated but declined on the grounds that I did not think her mother would approve. Luci assured me her mother had said it was all right and later told me: "Mother was very upset about the whole thing. She was very sad that two nice people had such personal misery. She was proud of you for doing the right thing."

With all her ambitions, Lady Bird Johnson was tolerant and sympathetic of human failings, an undisputed lady when it came to giving the benefit of the doubt—impressive generosity, considering her own exemplary conduct. It was she who spoke out publicly for Walter Jenkins, and although I never felt our behavior was on a par, I was happy to be included with Mr. Jenkins under that part of Mrs. Johnson's wing reserved for the blacker of the sheep.

Slowly, I resettled into the old White House pattern, and for nearly two years I enjoyed a solid relationship with the Johnsons. On the outside little was changed, but on the inside, I was no longer the little do-gooder lusting after political glory. I felt I had paid in full for every ounce of glamour my association with Lyndon Johnson brought me. He and his associates had been willing to sacrifice me, and I was quickly learning to use them right back. I felt the President owed me the chance to restore my reputation, and I took my second opportunity coldly and calculatedly. No matter how questionable my behavior may have been, the fact that I was in with the Johnsons again would be sufficient to make my detractors accept me. If I were close to the source of power, Johnson's Washington would sugar me up and swallow the bitter pill.

I never strayed from the path of proper moral behavior, and I became almost pristine in avoiding encounters with the opposite sex. However frigid I appeared, I never intended to lose my children again on the grounds of being warm-blooded. Instead, I would play the gay, frivolous socialite and keep myself too busy to see the mess I had made of my life.

And so I became the complete Johnson satellite. My prestige returned, and I did what I chose, whenever and however I felt like it. While morally strait-laced, my social attitude was one of abandon. If LBJ did not like my outspoken irreverence and iconoclastic attitude, it was just too damned bad. I had committed myself to an empty life in order to keep my children and to protect the Johnson image. I felt the White House owed me at least simple freedom of speech. I proceeded to break the rules of Washington political and social etiquette, rubbing any available nose in my publicity, and flaunting my regained power in every handy face. It was my way of getting even, of showing Washington it had make a mistake to count me out.

At Mrs. Johnson's request, I began to purchase clothes for Luci and Lynda directly from the merchant princes of Seventh Avenue, which is how it should have been handled all along. The Johnsons were in their second year in the White House, and the First Lady was becoming wise in the ways of couture. She stopped dressing as though she were merely one of the great American public, and as she took on worldly sophistication, so did the White House.

The Seventh Avenue designers were delighted to have the Johnsons as clients, and the Johnson women were happy to be wearing the best of American couture. They set an example to other "moderately priced" dressers around the nation who had been flocking to buy the European imports that glutted the ready-to-wear market in 1964. My task took me often to New York. It was my only escape from Washington and the increasing demands on my time to serve as a companion and chaperone for the President's daughters.

Now that the White House found me desirable, the Howars were again acceptable in polite society. People who had struck us from their list six months earlier began to cultivate us again. But Washington social life had not changed in my absence. Johnson people still did not enjoy the friendship of journalists, nor did they mingle with those other Washingtonians with continuing power who deliberately avoided the Texas-dominated social arenas that the newspapers referred to as the Great Society.

The word "great" was largely used to mean "sizable." There were indeed an enormous number of Johnson parasites, lobbyists, old Capitol Hill cronies, and members of the Texas State Society. Together with the smaller group of genuine insiders, they swelled to bursting that raucous crowd in which we traveled.

The Great Society was a peculiar lot, a robust breed that dominated by sheer numbers. I never cared to know them well, but they were vivid props for my personal drama. I was not unaware that no matter how flamboyant my behavior, it was still tasteful when compared to that of the Texans.

The people who came to the front under Lyndon Johnson were insecure as social lions. It was a time when Washington belonged to Perle Mesta and mobs of Westerners. Parties were vast gatherings where Walter Jetton dished out spareribs and bean casseroles, conjured from deep inside Mexican borders as though it were a national revenge against the United States.

Following the Lone Star party circuit demanded a sturdy constitution in every way. There were always the raised voices of hundreds of Texans, who appeared to exist on the premise that if there is nothing to say, say it loudly and in unison. The lack of true style troubled no one, least of all me. I was there to beat them at their own game; I thought it was the only one in town.

Only those presidential advisors and cabinet officers who were Kennedy holdovers could get away with fraternizing with Bobby or Ted Kennedy. On more than one occasion, I was warned about treading the dangerous line that separated the Johnson and Kennedy strongholds. It was not infrequent that Luci or Lynda would remark on a newspaper account of a Kennedy gathering that listed my name or showed my picture emerging from a party. The implication in those remarks was that I and the other stray from the Great Society, Bill Moyers, were consorting with their father's natural enemies. At a French Embassy dance in the waning days of the Alphands' glory, while I was down on all fours in the huge tent in the Embassy garden helping Lynda search for her perpetually lost contact lens, she snapped, "Don't get your dress dirty. Your Kennedy friends won't dance with you."

On another occasion, I was hobbling around on crutches as the result of an accident at Hickory Hill. I had been driving a wicker pony cart filled with children attending one of

Ethel's afternoon charity benefits. Her horse trainer irritably smacked the back end of the pony, Geronimo. The animal took off at a bucking gallop while I held on to the reins trying to stop the pony before he pitched me and my passengers to the ground. We tore over the crowded grounds of the Kennedy estate while the pony kicked through the front of the antique cart and I careened away from the children in our path. When we were finally halted, I had sprained both my wrists and my legs were critically damaged by the kicking horse. I was rushed to the hospital where, again, I was ministered to by my old red-headed Republican orthopedic surgeon, who asked me, "Why are you so determined to give your legs for the Democratic Party?"

When I told the Johnson girls how I had mangled myself, neither Luci nor Lynda showed the sympathy they had expressed when I had injured my legs in the service of their father. But my pain was well worth the memory of that afternoon at Hickory Hill: Bobby Kennedy hovering over me before I went off to the hospital and, in turn, being hovered over by dancer Rudolph Nureyev. Bobby introduced me to the famous Russian and even in my agony, I was vain enough to note that Mr. Nureyev was not as interested in my anatomy as he was in Bobby's. Happily, the reverse was not true.

To the Johnson's way of thinking, Washington belonged to them; the Kennedys had had their turn. The city was also claimed by the lobbyists who, like the Texans, had been kept in the background during Jack Kennedy's presidency. Now they openly joined administration office-holders at massive soirées where their every move was chronicled by the society reporters, who had also just emerged from a Kennedy-imposed oblivion. There was rarely any justification for the glowing copy they filed. Often a new government recruit would ask where he might find all the excitement he had read about in Betty Beale's columns in out-of-town newspapers. There was little, and what there was, was over-tabascoed fare that ran straight through the system like a Tijuana plate lunch. The important thing socially was to see and be seen, and many evenings were passed trading gossip in lieu of significant conversation. Texans like their tall tales and Lyndon Johnson rarely made them privy to anything more substantial.

The diplomats were, as usual, coordinated with the administration whose favor they were sent to curry. The French and British Embassies that had swelled with importance under Kennedy shrank to obscurity under Johnson. When Johnson dealt with world powers, he dealt directly and had little concern for the ego of the ambassadorial middleman.

The Johnson crowd took up with the Arab countries, the richer in oil, the better. The new-moneyed Arabs and new-powered Texans were exceedingly comfortable in one another's society; Johnson's people appreciated lavishness and this was what the desert diplomats had to offer. Both factions had been outsiders so long that it seemed natural they should come into season simultaneously. Together, the Arabs and Texans flowered, and while not exactly subtle in their smells, they made for a colorful and dazzling arrangement.

If one had an inclination to hear Arabs speak English with a Texas accent, one had only to be a vaguely influential member of the Great Society in 1965. There were grandiose evenings at some Arabic-speaking embassy at least once a week for the greater part of Lyndon Johnson's presidency. These were costly social productions, boisterous and crowded, the

Easterners and the Westerners exchanging customs and mannerisms, one group as comfortable eating a pigeon pie as the other was with a platter of barbecued beef.

The tiny country of Kuwait was put on the map by an enterprising, squat little Palestinian refugee who was the Emir's ambassador to LBJ; his zaftig wife became the most photographed woman of the Johnson years. They had unlimited energy for entertaining Texans and the resources to finance it all; their English was good, their embassy immense, their labor cheap. It appeared their time and money were well-spent, for the Kuwaitis became the insider's outsiders, which is to say they were the pet foreigners of the Texas crowd. The Ambassador was never without Cuban cigars, and his wife, when not being photographed from every conceivable angle, was painting her face in anticipation of it. Her make-up and hairstyles were the most elaborate in Washington, and her eyes were so incredibly landscaped that I once asked her how long it took to decorate them. "Hours," she told me, "but what else have I to do? It is my job."

I was never certain what the Kuwaitis received in return for their perpetual hospitality, but there was no question that, for the Texans, the Kuwait Embassy was something of a small-town country club, a place where there was always something going on.

Arab ambassadors were inveterate bridge players, and there were generally all-night card games in rooms off the main drawing room, where the rest of the guests would dance all night to the most expensive rock bands on the East Coast. Society columnists favored by the Johnsons gushed over those evenings where East met West. One of them was known to take free trips to the Middle East, where nothing was spared to insure the fantastic visit that inspired columns encouraging American tourists to see the charm of the old country.

The program was similar at the Moroccan Embassy, although their constantly changing ambassadors were usually better educated, their wives more stylish. Moroccan food was richer than the Syrian fare of stuffed lamb and grape leaves. Buckets of fresh caviar, pigeon pie, and a sweet version of North African cous-cous were served on low tables for the guests to eat with their fingers. These parties were served by liveried waiters elegantly trained in the European fashion, and a Moroccan party generally ended with at least one belly dancer. Dinner was sometimes taken on floor cushions in the Moroccan Room, sometimes in French chairs placed around skirted tables in heated tents. Dancing partners were abundant from among a special platoon of French-speaking, heel-clicking embassy underlings whose qualifications for foreign service included bachelorhood and native rhythm.

The Moroccans entertained for anyone, as did the Kuwaitis, whose ambassador once phoned to ask if I knew of any senator or White House staff member who was having a birthday or anniversary because he felt like giving a party and needed a guest of honor. Society reporters themselves were honored at massive gatherings and the Arabs ran through the list of Washington dignitaries so quickly it would have surprised no one if they had given a seated dinner for the White House kennel keeper.

Moroccan parties were especially lush when the King or his kin came to town. No expense was too great for a proper welcome, and I often wondered if the foreign aid the King came to seek was not actually spent in the United States cultivating the Administration. With the exception of Kuwait, the Middle Eastern countries who reigned in social Washington in these times had the world's lowest per capita incomes and the highest rates of illiteracy. But poverty among their citizens was overlooked in the glittering diplomatic scramble. Washington men of power would sit crosslegged on the floor ogling dancing girls while their wives paraded about wearing billowing Moroccan kaftans—difficult attire for the slimmest of women, a grave error for most Texas ladies.

Standing alone among the perpetrators of Washington's Arabian Nights was Chérif Guellal, the handsome and brilliant young Algerian freedom fighter. He represented his country in American diplomatic circles. Unmarried, he often carried the Arab standard into rooms less public than the grand salon. Along with his constant companion Yolande Betbeze Fox, a former Miss America from Alabama who had used her title to cultivate her brain as well as a number of the country's living legends, he entertained less often and less lavishly but in a certain swashbuckling style that drew together the keener political minds, celebrated academicians, international radicals, and show-biz luminaries who were the residuals of Mrs. Fox's years of salon-keeping in New York and Los Angeles.

Guellal was Algeria's roving intellectual, a serious diplomat who used his Embassy, the former estate of Perle Mesta and the residence of Vice President Lyndon Johnson, to his country's best advantage. It was there that I met Russian Ambassador Anatoly Dobrynin, a bearlike man whose social grace contradicted the American image of the gauche and war-hungry Communist. He was charming and far more outspoken than his counterparts from the Free World. He and I had a delightful argument one evening on the drinking habits of American women in contrast to Russian women. The

Communist ladies, he claimed, could hold their liquor better than Westerners. I was not one to be challenged by a foreigner, especially a Red one. I embarked with Dobrynin on a drinking contest; we clapped our hands for the waiter to bring us three tumblers of Russian vodka, pronounced "wod-ka" by the Ambassador. One glass was for him, one for me, and the other was thrust into the hands of Emily Scheuer, the tiny wife of the Democratic Congressman from New York City, who happened to join us at just that moment. I explained to Emily why she must drink the six ounces of "wod-ka" which, to the credit of American womanhood and the quality of her stomach lining, she did. I gulped mine without taking my eyes off the Ambassador. When finished, I wiped my mouth with the back of my hand and smashed the goblet in the fireplace. Ambassador Dobrynin and Mrs. Scheuer did likewise.

The room fell silent and the formally dressed crowd turned to the sound of roaring laughter. Dobrynin and I fell into each other's arms, laughing and clapping one another on the back. When he asked if I had learned that Russki-Winter-Palace trick from reading Tolstoy, I told him I had seen it in an old Yul Brynner movie. We were fast pals at the moment, but the relationship was never quite the same on later evenings. The Ambassador's portly wife would inevitably steer him clear of both me and the vodka, leaving me to think that capitalists' and Communists' wives have more in common than we are led to believe. Some time later, Jim and Emily Scheuer were expelled from the Soviet Union during a visit there, but their untimely exit was precipitated by the Congressman's views on the oppression of Russian Jewry rather than his wife's drinking habits—which, like my own, never equalled our display that evening.

In the grip of a colossal hangover the next day, I felt compelled to replace the three expensive glasses we had smashed, and later became more circumspect about upholding the image of American Womanhood. I once whimsically suggested to Dean Rusk that the State Department should reimburse me for the cost of the goblets. He quite seriously replied, "We have no funds for things like that. . . ." So much for the Voice of America.

10

1965 was also the height of the charity ball business; a time when official Washington believed the federal government needed all its treasury to wage war and that if it were anybody's concern to stamp out cancer, polio, deafness, blindness, multiple sclerosis, or the sundry diseases of the heart, liver, lungs, or brain, it fell to those with a suit of formal clothing, and the price of a dinner-dance ticket. Charity had been a prime interest of the wealthier in the Kennedy administration. They had made cocktail philanthropy a way of life, and as in everything social, the Johnson crowd followed their example. One by one the ladies of the Great Society took turns organizing opulent fund-raisers. Nieman-Marcus sent up fabulous prizes and politically oriented business firms donated cases of liquor. Free champagne paved the way for the guests to make their much publicized cash donations to charity.

Usually an astronaut was present at these invitational soirées, astronauts at that time being a big draw for officials and socialites alike. During Johnson's years they were featured attractions everywhere. Work stopped in government agencies for any excuse, but never so much as for the opportunity to fawn over the men from Cape Kennedy. Huge turn-outs of federal employees banked Washington's streets when the moon travelers rode triumphantly into town amidst flags, confetti, bands, and the cheering, littering crowds. The astronauts and their families came in motorcades to the White House, where they were warmly received by the Marine Band and the First Family.

Today, astronauts are nameless, faceless men, but at that time they were genuine celebrities and certified household words. Men like Buzz Aldrin, whose celestial adventures gave him the credibility to promote foreign car sales later on television commercials, drew admiring crowds in hotels taken over for Heart Balls, Mental Health Balls, and Eye Balls. The opportunity to dance and dine with them sold many hundred-dollar-a-plate tickets. Frequently, the astronauts were aided in soliciting cultural and charitable contributions from Washington socialites by a star from the favored Johnson television series, "Bonanza," and sometimes, by a whole-some Hollywood movie star like Pat Boone.

The social coup of such an evening would be for the likes of a Scooter Miller, dressed as a prima donna from some Wagnerian opera, and hanging onto the arm of a uniformed, beribboned Scott Carpenter, to lean over a numbered, gaily decorated table and screech: "I was with Bird all day, and Bird told me that Lyndon said. . . ." Assembled Washington would strain to hear the White House gossip, then pass the word along that so-and-so at Table 63 was on good terms with both Johnson insiders and astronauts, hence in a position to petition highly placed connections for official audiences and perhaps even a political favor or two.

It was never important that the name-droppers actually be close to power, only that they appear close. No one questioned the authenticity of the purported friendships; it simply made things easier for lobbyists and social climbers if they looked close to the White House. It was also handy when the time came to square income tax deductions and pad expense accounts. The Johnson people were masterly insinuators of connections, and I must confess, they were credible pretenders. It never seemed to bother the Johnson family if their names were taken in vain socially, just so long as they were not used in print in any way that took away from the First Family as the fount of all authority. The Johnsons were so new at being droppable names that they enjoyed the headiness of it all, which was, I think, one of LBJ's greatest problems in his desire for good public relations. He never seemed to realize that his image ultimately suffered from the behavior of those he allowed to free-wheel in his behalf.

He was surprised to be blamed for the New Hampshire slur against Democratic presidential candidate Eugene McCarthy in the 1968 primaries when broadcasts, instigated by Johnson staffers, backfired in their suggestion that McCarthy's antiwar stand made a vote for him, "a vote for Hanoi." It was also reported later that Johnson was taken aback by the outcry from some of the public against his high-handed maneuvering of the bloody 1968 Chicago convention. The President would have been still more shocked to learn of the bad blood his staff generated on the less political but equally significant cocktail circuit. A crowing Jack Valenti was a decided displeasure to journalists. They resented having to get their news second-hand from Johnson's aides, who were often less than polished in their manner of speaking for the White House. His people were considered an extension of Johnson himself, and every phrase and action was filed away in the mental ledgers of the Washington press corps as a plus or minus beside the President's name. With every asinine statement, every loud and boastful soliloquy, the Johnson image suffered like a political portrait of Dorian Gray.

Evidence of discontent with LBJ was mounting daily in Washington, creeping into conversations everywhere. I would like to insinuate that I was waking up with the best of them during this period, but that was not the case. So wrapped up in my personal misery, so desperate to regain my social footing and hide my frustrations in crowded parties, I was blind to anything that did not pertain directly to me. While others began to disassociate themselves from the Johnson administration, I was busy gathering publicity that proved I was more than ever a substantial part of it. There were no important events in the world other than those involving me.

But no matter how fast I raced away from my own problems or blindly ignored the troubles of the world, I was still given to long fits of depression, which I dealt with by running harder and laughing louder. For short periods this worked. I could wake up each morning with a man I did not like and forget him while I read a newspaper account of how adorably I had performed the night before. If my two phones were ringing with requests for interviews, I could pretend I liked myself and the life I was enduring. Like Satchel Paige, I knew better than to look back, because something was indeed gaining on me.

I loved my children, became almost hysterical at the thought of being separated from them, but they were too small to be more than reminders of marital bondage. The time I spent with them did not obliterate the futility of my predicament. I had a second chance at my particular American Dream, and still I was a miserable malcontent. Engulfed in self-pity, the more I got my way, the worse I became. Nothing was enough. I was plagued by terrible nightmares in which private detectives were chasing me and I could not run, agonies in slow motion where my legs would not move. Increasingly I would look at Ed Howar and his face would fade into the chief detective's face. I would squint my eyes and shake the vision away. Then the man reared his ugly head into reality. He turned up around town with my Caribbean photographs, flashing them about, trying to sell them and alluding to a proposed plan for blackmail. We tried through several lawyers to silence him, but it seemed that most Washington law firms used his services and were in no position to do more than request politely that he keep my business to himself. After much haggling and chasing about, Ed reported that he had acquired the wire-tap tapes and photographs which he had paid such an inordinate amount of money to commission in the first place. He said they had been burned. I believed him.

My feeling of being trapped worsened to the point where I could no longer take the children to the zoo, for the sight of caged animals would depress me. Emotional claustrophobia depleted my energy, and I was reduced to long periods of what I came to call "the lying-down disease." I could not get out of the bed, sometimes for days.

I applied the Puritan ethic: a little hard work would leave no time to indulge the malady. It did not work. I took to my couch, leaving it only to drag out to buy clothes, have my hair done, and shine at some party. After a bout of lethargy, I would try harder, then fall back harder. There was no one I could talk to, because more than anything else, I feared reproach, the fleeting looks which suggested that I had brought this on myself and that my life was not so bad. Mama was happy that things had been worked out quietly, although not completely deceived by my gay public image. She was beginning her long and violent bout with physical pain, and I did not have the heart to drag her through more. The fight was mine.

And so I went to a psychiatrist, the American panacea for all ills. He was recommended by Ed Howar's psychiatrist, and although I had little faith in therapy, I hoped that time on somebody else's couch might help. I thought I was going crazy. Certainly I was the world's worst malcontent, a spoiled misfit torn apart by alternating moods. I thought I could lie down in a quiet office and tell some wise Freudian that I was schizophrenic, that I had recurring dreams of being in a bird cage chirping loudly to get out but surrounded by admirers who thought I was singing for them. I would tell him of my visions of addressing a vast audience, and when I opened my mouth, no sound would come. Of horrors both day and night that people were stealing my children. I would explain how more and more frequently I could not catch my breath, how I needed to press my forehead against something clean and cool, a tiled bathroom wall, a glass of ice, a window pane. I thought I could talk it all out and he would make me normal and happy.

After the doctor established that I could afford to visit him an hour every day, we discussed my case. I launched immediately into my problems, never pausing, too familiar with the material, too desperate for a miracle, to be hesitant.

He was a heavy-set man in tinted spectacles who sucked an empty pipe and wore black silk anklets that showed most of his hairless calves. He kept four Weimaraner dogs penned outside his suburban office window. They had hostile blue eyes and would run back and forth, leaping on the wire walls of their cage, howling, scratching, and pawing. Beside his leather chair, there was a gurgling tank of tropical fish that the doctor poked with his pipe stem to keep the fish moving. After weeks of soul-baring, the only "transference" I made was with those trapped creatures in the aquarium; my rapport was with the doctor's dogs. Finally he talked to me: "Do you think your depression is the result of guilt from your improper behavior?"

"Yes, yes, sir, I do." This he accepted with a sage nod.

"Why do you think you want to break rules, make others suffer?"

"I guess I'm just spoiled and selfish, doctor. I'm trying to be better, only I can't seem to get the hang of it." More nods.

"Why do you hate men?"

"I don't think I do. My problem is that I like them too much."

There was a long leer over the rim of his glasses. "You say you can't talk to your father or your husband?"

"It's not that I *can't* talk to them, it's just that I *don't like* talking to them. They don't ever say anything."

"Do you know why you are so close to your mother?"

"I like her, she's a strong woman."

He made a long entry into a notebook. "Why do you like to read about yourself in the newspaper?"

"Well, I don't know. It's what I do best. People notice me and . . . oh, hell, doctor, reading about myself beats a sharp stick in the eye." I was dismissed eighteen minutes before the hour was up.

We progressed to the Role of Women, our duties and obligations, what happens to the female psyche when women assume the aggressive role nature intended for the male of the species. I honestly tried to do and think everything he made me suggest. Nothing worked. At the end of six weeks I was just as confused as on the day I had walked into his office. By the time he got around to: "Life is not always something we can control. We must accept certain things as inevitable . . . make the best of them. Play ball. Happiness can't be found reaching beyond your station . . . Good wife, good mother, good, good, good. . . !" I dismissed *myself* eighteen minutes early and took my business down the street to Lord and Taylor, where my time and money were spent to better satisfaction.

I am sure there are psychiatrists in this world whose ideas on women are more contemporary, doctors who do glorious things for troubled people, but I had had lectures like his in Catholic school and they had not done me any good. I was cured of nothing but a mild belief in psychiatry. The lying-down disease took over again, and I thought it would be better to disintegrate on my own. I decided to beg another divorce. Before I could get myself together, my son was stricken with spinal meningitis.

11

Edmond had been ill for nearly a week and was visited several times by a pediatrician who did not recognize the deadly affliction because he had never before encountered it. The case was undiagnosed, untreated. The baby cried constantly. One night I went into his room, where he was lying almost lifeless in his crib, staring at the ceiling, emitting low, deep, and constant moans. The smell of death was staggering. We rushed him to the hospital where, to placate me, his spine was tapped.

I waited in the room he had been assigned, paralyzed with fear that my son was dying or that he was only in the grips of an ordinary childhood sickness and I was indeed losing my sanity. I was staring vacantly into space when hospital attendants rushed past the room, a black orderly carrying Edmond in his arms, followed by a resident physician and a nurse who held the bottle of fluid being fed into the child's arm. It all happened fast. I darted into the hall and reached toward Edmond's mass of sweaty curls, trying to stop them, telling them they had passed his room. "Lady, keep back, this child is dying." I would have settled for being crazy.

For days Edmond was in isolation with nurses around the

clock, medication pumped into his little wrists until his veins broke down, then his legs, then his neck. There was little hope he would make it. Ed and I were told to make funeral arrangements; the law requires immediate burial for victims of contagious, killing diseases.

We spent those days and nights in the waiting room, surrounded by people whose faces did not register. Of all the things Ed Howar and I had been through, this was the worst. We clung to each other as to every drop of encouragement. Scrubbed and gowned, we were allowed into Edmond's isolated glass box, but the baby showed no signs of recognition. I will always be amazed at stronger people who find spiritual strength during a medical crisis; I had none. I could fight anybody who tried to touch my child, but I had no way of striking back at this. My Catholic God had finally caught up with me, the wrath and vengeance I had been threatened with by the nuns and priests of my childhood were being visited on me. I was to be punished through my baby. Ed's view of a vengeful Allah did little to alter my fears. In my frayed mind, I was an adulteress and now, a murderess.

It was Mama who first caught on to my silent determination to take the blame for Edmond's impending death. Instinctively, she kept pushing and pulling at me verbally until I broke down and cried "Yes, yes, *yes* . . . it's my fault. I did this to him. If he dies, I killed him." I sobbed until she struck me across the face.

"You listen to me, Lady Jane. You are not the beginning and the end. You are not so important that everything that happens in this world is the direct result of you, you, *you*. That baby out there needs somebody pulling for him, not a self-centered zombie resigning him to death because *you* think *you* deserve it. You get in there and make peace with whatever God it is up there that you respect. If Edmond dies it has not one damned thing to do with you and your theatrics. Stop thinking about Barbara Howar and think of that baby."

Edmond was in the hospital for a long time. When he was released, he was cured of meningitis but seemed little more than a vegetable. It was weeks before he could lift his head, sit up, or move about with the motor skills of even a six-month-old infant. It was months before he could make sounds or stand again, months and months and months before the extent of the damage would be known. I did not think about a divorce any more.

Life settled into a new pattern: appointments with specialists, therapists, doctors; tests and evaluations; time, for waiting, hoping, praying. There was less time for the lying-down disease. Ed and I worked with the baby trying to help him regain lost ground. We spent more time with his sister who, at four, understood something was wrong with her brother that made him the center of all attention. She needed reassurance to know she was loved in spite of being healthy. It was the first time I had thought of my children as having individual needs, that they were more than two creatures I had spawned, extensions of myself that I need only love and provide for. They became real. Bader and Edmond replaced Barbara Howar as the center of the world. It was altogether a better place for my affections.

Back on the Texas party circuit at night, my afternoons were filled with children: mine and the Johnsons'. While the President's daughters offered a healthy alternative to becoming neurotically possessed by my own two children, they were growing more and more demanding of my time; they were always with me. As the presidency of Lyndon Johnson stepped up, so did Mrs. Johnson's outside activities. Her girls became mine. They needed a companion to steer them through public places, someone to shop with them, to chaperone their parties, go to movies, restaurants, discothèques. It became understood that I would accompany them anywhere at any time at any expense.

I was more available than special, and the girls were accustomed to me; I was comfortable, familiar, and convenient. Lynda was coming out of her schoolmarm period and her transformation took a good deal of my time, but she did not need me once she came into her own. She occasionally wanted someone with whom she could talk about the things that were happening to her, where she was going, how she looked, what she did and with whom she did it. Lynda became enamored of herself, calling me on the White House phone system from Hollywood, telling me about her transformation at the hands of makeup artist George Masters, her social evolution on the arm of make-out artist George Hamilton, what fun she was having, how much attention she was getting. She was full of herself, a pastime I certainly understood, and much of her smugness was deserved. Lynda had worked hard to change skins, a difficult metamorphosis at any time, but especially so under public scrutiny.

While this was fine for Lynda, and it pleased her doting parents, it did not sit easily with Luci, accustomed as she was to bearing the Johnson beauty standard. She was glad for Lynda to add style and grace to her conventional and somewhat humorless academic manner, but the competition of a new Lynda Bird was too much. Luci was a threatened, jealous little girl. She missed the parental approval all children seek. Mrs. Johnson preferred Lynda's company, even as an ugly duckling; her attention tripled as Lynda came out of her shell. Progressively, the elder Johnsons were irritated by Luci's impetuous nature, and although I doubt they had anything but love for both girls, Luci Baines thought herself the odd-man-out around the White House.

She was embarked on a nursing career at Georgetown University, but Luci was not a student. Her scholastic ineptitude added to her sense of inadequacy; she knew she was not the perfect presidential daughter. Her parents did not have the time to give her the vast quantities of attention her insecurity demanded. She came to avoid her mother and would do anything to please her father. Once, late to greet a group of ever-arriving astronauts on the southwest lawn of the White House, Luci ran ahead of me and her Secret Service agent to catch up with the President in the Rose Garden. The Marine Band was playing "Hail to the Chief" as the President crossed behind the thick foliage that separated him from the waiting crowd. Luci darted into the group of men trotting alongside Johnson and thrust her arm about his waist, a fast-moving blur of kelly green lunging at the President of the United States. One of Johnson's agents leveled a gun at what he took to be the President's assailant. A second agent shoved the gun toward the sky saving Luci from being shot. Rufus Youngblood, the agent who had thrown himself over Johnson during the assassination of John Kennedy and whom LBJ had elevated to head the Secret Service when he took office, lectured Luci in a manner only a man charged with the safety of the First Family could get away with. Luci accepted it with the equanimity of a circus-child of politics. "Rufus," she countered, "I'd just as lief be shot as have Daddy mad at me for being late."

She contrived to spend more time away from her family and with mine, passing endless hours with me talking, giggling, and becoming something of an older child–younger sister member of the Howar household. I loved Luci but came to resent her limousine outside my house, came to loathe the pulling and tugging at my affections, the constant vying for my time between Luci and Lynda, who demanded my services like two housewives who share a mutual day worker.

There were rewards for pandering to the Johnson assumption that all the world was anxious to dance attendance on their every whim. When the White House entertained for England's Princess Margaret and Lord Snowden, Washingtonians from all levels were commanded to a dinner dance—all but the Howars, a source of great embarrassment. Lynda inquired about my costume for the occasion and shrugged at my admission that we were not invited. Luci, however, was one to take care of her own. She managed to be plugged in to White House gossip. She was current on in-house jealousies and feuds, and just as Lynda did not share her mother's devotion to her chief of staff, Liz Carpenter, Luci was not enamored with her mother's social secretary, Bess Abel.

"Your being left out of Princess Margaret's party is Bess's doing, Barbara. I bet Mama doesn't know you're not invited." I protested mildly. That afternoon, Mrs. Abel phoned to say there had been some confusion with the invitations, and would Ed and I please come to the party? We just happened to be free.

That party was my exposure to Lyndon Johnson at his best. Entertaining royalty in the flower-filled East Room of the White House was much to his liking, with the Marine Band playing "hail to him" in the hall while Peter Duchin made dance music in the ballroom. Everyone the Johnsons thought special was there, slicked up and paying court to

LBJ while he gave each an audience. He extended his largesse to include Joan Kennedy and a few Kennedy holdovers who, along with a number of Beautiful People of the day, had been summoned to the President's mansion for the occasion. Like a prom king in a high school gym, Johnson nodded to the subjects trotting back and forth before his throne.

Henry Ford had brought his new Italian bride to the party, and it was only with her that LBJ shared the spotlight. Mrs. Ford wore a clinging, strapless gown, a turquoise and diamond necklace, and very little else. She danced to the rock music with Hubert Humphrey, whose demeanor in Johnson's presence was, as usual, a bit clownish. Together they threw their arms in the air, wiggling and twitching, as Mrs. Ford's dress slipped down and exposed her generous Mediterranean chest. She went through the same routine with Secretary of Defense Robert McNamara. Usually a sedate and taciturn gentleman, he appeared as helpless to stop that spectacle as he was to end the Vietnam war.

Peter Duchin's wife Cheray approached several of Johnson's aides, wailing like Chicken Little, "Her dress is falling down, her dress is falling down!" She found Jack Valenti and told him that he must immediately inform Mrs. Ford that "her breasts are exposed." Without once taking his eyes off Mrs. Ford, Valenti, with equal Italian bravado, answered, "You want *me* to tell Mrs. Ford her dress is sliding down? Not on your life, Cheray." He stood with the rest of us as the totally unabashed Christina danced exuberantly with a long line of highly placed partners. Pausing only when she felt a draft, Mrs. Ford would look down, tug her bodice into place with a whispered Roman *"scusi"* and go right on with the business of being the belle of the ball.

It was still Lyndon Johnson's night. The Princess, I recall, sat rather petulantly on the sidelines. I am sure Her Royal Highness Margaret Rose had had better moments than her U.S. visit, but she was not this country's most gracious guest. Mrs. Johnson introduced me to Lord Snowden and we danced. I felt it was I who took *him* into my arms; he was the shortest man I was ever paired off with until I stood next to Eddie Arcaro at Santa Anita. Like an over-vitamined American lummox, I swept the Little Prince around the dance floor, towering over him. We could think of nothing to say as we pumped away in deathly silence, my high heels digging into his tiny Savile Row slippers. The Earl of Snowden dyes his hair and wears a thin layer of pancake makeup, and while this was at least something we had in common, I did not think it a proper topic of conversation. I merely smiled down, clutched him to my meager bosom, and danced on. I later saw him in the same embrace with Mrs. Ford, and I could only hope he enjoyed the contact a good deal more.

There we all were, having nothing valid to say, but going through all the imperious motions of very important people anyhow. This was fine for me; I would not have recognized a deep thought or a piece of vital information had it been dispensed to me in a portfolio stamped TOP SECRET. I understood only that there was little worth understanding.

This is not to say that there were no intelligent people moving in and around the Johnson White House, but they were more quiet than thoughtful. By no stretch of the imagination were they rebelling against LBJ's policy. After Johnson's abdication, scores appeared from nowhere saying, "I told you so," vowing they had seen the folly of Vietnam all along. But at the time they were strangely mute. I respected Joe Califano, a Johnson man who never went to the mat for the President's war tactics. I liked Bill Moyers enormously and came to have a high tolerance for Harry McPherson, one of Johnson's better speechwriters. My ambivalent feelings for Lloyd Hand, Johnson's Chief of Protocol, leaned to the positive side, and I still get a giggle from an old *Life* photograph showing a group of the female faithful that Lloyd assembled to act as official greeters of visiting foreign dignitaries. There were eight of us, dressed and hatted, standing in single file under the canopied entrance to the White House diplomatic receiving room. We would extend our white-gloved hands to the President of Italy or the Premier of Korea, give them short curtsey-like bows, and murmur hellos in the visitor's native tongue.

Actually, it was Lyndon Johnson who was most taken with this assembled pulchritude of the Great Society. He would pause before each of us, squeeze a hand or pinch a cheek, and stare warmly into our worshipful eyes. Lloyd would nudge the President along, often making himself the object of LBJ's worst rages; but then, that is about the most useful purpose a protocol chief is put to anyway. Of all the protocol chiefs I had watched bow and scrape through official Washington, Lloyd Hand took his job most seriously, always managing to be at front and center when the pictures were taken. Once he was photographed next to the Pope, and the picture became a sly joke circulated around Washington with a message written below: "I don't know about the old gentleman in the long, flowing robes, but the man on his left is Lloyd Hand."

The Great Society often met for dinner parties, the ladies later withdrawing to join one another for coffee and endless chatter about children, servants, and absent members. The men, as was the somewhat southern habit of Washington in those days, would closet themselves in libraries, drink brandy, chew cigars, and jealously swap scraps of political information in somewhat ponderous discussions of their government. For me these were tedious evenings, only slightly more redeeming than those spent alone at home with the partner of an unhappy marriage.

Given this monotony, I was filled with an uncontrollable desire to shock—to say or do anything that would raise voices and eyebrows or boredom's threshold. I had a natural ability to alienate people I found dull. I would rudely cut short any matron lady who dwelled too long on her wonderful children, her indispensable housekeeper, or her husband's unheralded political abilities. I once interrupted a woman deep into her monologue about the great Lone Star State with, "If I hear one more exaggeration about Texas, I'm going to throw up on the Alamo." I became incautious in my descriptions of Texas habits, asking one gentleman sporting a hammered silver belt studded with ersatz stones: "Did you make it at summer camp?" And to a Dallas lady in reference to the Tex-Mex delicacy she had proudly served for dinner: "Did you get this recipe off the back of a Frito bag?" I also got a bit too good at imitating Texas accents and could, quite frankly, speak more like Lady Bird than the good woman herself.

With those women who worked for the First Lady, I shared nothing beyond a mutual dislike. They did not care for me, and I dealt coolly with them when I bothered to deal with them at all. Mrs. Johnson had opened a direct line of communication from herself to me that heightened the existing rivalry between her hired help and me, her most unhumble of servants. When Lady Bird Johnson finally turned her thumb down at me, her staff was ready to close in. Luci had often warned me that I was incurring female wrath in her mother's side of the White House. "Bess and Liz are out to get you, Barbara." They did.

Luci had decided to get married. Her father would not bless the proposed union of his youngest daughter and Patrick Nugent. However, no Johnson of my acquaintance ever took no for an answer, even from another Johnson. Luci persisted, and the banns of matrimony were published everywhere but in *Hairdresser's Manual*. Wedding plans began immediately, and Luci would agree to none of them unless I did. Pat Nugent went away to do his National Guard duty while we arranged the details for the event, which was scheduled for August of 1966. The President and Mrs. Johnson were in Texas during much of this time, and the White House, always a lonely place but unbearable when empty, ceased to be Luci's home; she operated out of our house. We arranged for the purchase of her wedding rings, selected bridesmaids, talked flowers, food, and clothes until all hours when Luci would finally go home to sleep and then only at the urging of her exhausted security agents. Over bridal magazines and endless lists, we talked of The Wedding, Bader's role as flower girl, and my own elaborate plans to give Luci a dinner dance scheduled for early June. Luci Johnson's impending marriage took on the air of a family affair, with me in the uncomfortable and risky position of surrogate mother of the bride.

Some time in May, shortly after Bill Moyers had suggested I play a more demure role in Luci's wedding, Ed's secretary received an anonymous phone call urging her to inform the Howars that "a movie magazine is about to hit the stands with the whole story of Mrs. Howar's past conduct, complete with pictures of all the Johnsons and Howars." The informer added that Lyndon Johnson was furious. Stunned that this could happen nearly two years after the fact, I called Ashton Gonella, Mrs. Johnson's private secretary and resident lamb among wolves. "Ashton, what is going on down there?" I explained the strange telephone message and she promised to investigate. Meanwhile we raced to every magazine stand in Washington, bought dozens of Hollywood trash publications, thumbed them dog-eared, and found nothing.

Ashton called to say the Johnsons knew nothing about a magazine story. The next day Liz Carpenter called and said bluntly: "If the invitations to your party for Luci have been mailed, please recall them. Mrs. Johnson is canceling all Luci's large parties."

"Liz, for God's sake, what is going on? You know our dance is Luci's only big party."

"Mrs. Johnson wants Luci to be a rested bride. No parties!"

Eventually the resting bride called. It was my final personal contact with her. Luci whispered into the phone that the party was being called off because of the war. I was struck dumb by the second excuse. It was 1966, and this was Luci Johnson's first reference to Vietnam in all the years I had known her.

The crank call was successful. My reputation for doing the direct and impetuous thing had preceded me. There was, of course, no movie magazine exposé. Someone had counted on me to overreact by calling and alarming the White House, and I did not let them down. Added to my irreverent style and tight influence over Luci Johnson, the fear of a prewedding scandal was too much for the Johnsons. I had become more trouble than I was worth. For the second time in two years, I was Washington's social outcast, the target of open insults, the subject of newspaper gossip columnists. I was hurt and bewildered. I had understood my ostracism two years back. That time it made sense; this time it did not.

The White House ladies had no intention of letting me fade silently into oblivion. First, the Howars were publicly dropped from the Washington Social Register, along with, I might add, Justice Douglas, who by marrying his fourth wife Cathy, had taken one too many for Washington's sense of decency. Douglas responded in *Time* that he never even knew he was in the thing, and I was reported in the same issue to say, "Being kicked out of Washington's social book is rather like being asked to leave Nedick's." I could not have cared less.

What I did care about was the growing clamor that I resign my "Lady Bountiful" posts around Washington. I was pressured to quit as Vice Chairman of the International Horse Show. The Show's public relations man explained to me that a local society editor had told him, "You can expect no publicity from us as long as Mrs. Howar is connected with the event." I was also Chairman of Washington's oldest charity celebration, the International Ball. What publicity we could get for it was all bad. Sponsors and donors dropped off and tickets were impossible to sell. When the committee worked up the nerve to suggest I ease out of the chairmanship, I had hardened into a "screw you" attitude. If I was to be unloaded, these do-gooders would have to force me out. I would not go quietly. I had done the "right thing" before.

The International Ball benefited the children's hospital that had done so much to bring Edmond through his bout with meningitis. They desperately needed the revenue from the ball. I wrote Mrs. Johnson a letter asking her to call off her dogs in the name of charity. There was no response. I remained with both benefits to the end and have never since authorized my name to appear on any invitation for a Washington charity. On my second and last exit from polite society, I paused long enough to integrate the International Ball by including some Negro friends. The evening was a financial success, but it was touch and go as to whether half the guests would stalk away in indignation. I will always admire Cliff and Adele Alexander, the first friendly black faces to block-bust this Washington bastion; they were splendid. My chairmanship marked the end of the annual International Ball, which was probably my only meaningful contribution to Washington society.

I spent the six months following my last encounter with the Johnsons trying to appear as if I did not care, but we both know better. The more I lived with this second disgrace, the more I wondered why I had cared at all. However late in the game, I was growing up. I might no longer be the darling of anybody's society, but I no longer thought I was cracking up. Reevaluation was slow, but I began to feel more secure than I had in years. With the return of that same need that had brought me to Washington only a dozen years earlier, I had to be moving on and smartening up. For the third time in as many years, I decided to get a divorce.

12

Smartening up was difficult; moving on was impossible. There was no question of following Moslem law, facing East and shouting thrice: "*I divorce thee.*" I had to adhere to Western culture and dissolve my marriage in the courts. My newest attorney informed me that I had no legal grounds for leaving a husband: not bigamy nor adultery, brutality, or desertion. As long as Ed Howar was not beating me up between periods of abandoning me for a harem, no court would honor my need for freedom. Without grounds, I still had to have his permission to break up the marriage.

My husband's attorneys advised my own that I could not remove the children from their legal residence, and were I to do so, Mr. Howar fully intended to "collect the children in an unguarded moment and return them to his domicile." It was strongly hinted that my old Caribbean caper, while not actually admissible evidence in a divorce trial, would certainly prejudice any judge against the "checkered Mrs. Howar." My old photographs and wire-tap recordings had been filed away by Ed Howar two years earlier in anticipation of another bolt for freedom.

Furthermore, Mr. Howar would not "leave his home for

the civilized calm of bachelor quarters during the negotiations." After six months of living under the same roof in alternating moods of violence and silence, I was finally offered my freedom if I would (1) agree to joint custody of the children, whom I would (2) never remove from the District of Columbia, but would (3) support on a monthly allowance per child only slightly higher than the standard welfare subsidy in (4) a house other than the one I had lived in with Mr. Howar.

With sly insinuations from my lawyers that I had a rich man lurking in the bushes to take me away from all this anyhow, I was encouraged again to do "the nice quiet thing": sign. When Carl Sandburg wrote: "Why is there a secret signal when a lawyer cashes in? Why does a hearse horse snicker, hauling a lawyer away?" he anticipated my legal transactions and response to them. I signed. Little did anyone know, however, that I would gladly have settled for less.

I lost custody of everything but Bader and Edmond; Ed retained the money, most of our old friends and their good will. The children and I had one year to live in the house—which gave me precisely the same amount of time to carve out a new life for us. We eyed one another suspiciously. I was never sure whether they—or I—were comforted or nervous that we were dependent on one another. At that time our lives were dominated by a sinister nurse of Chinese extraction. She was not the "godless communist" variety, but a more fearsome breed of oriental who, in addition to being a vegetarian, was a fanatical follower of some obscure religious cult. She had severe missionary ideas which she pressed on us when she was not zealously forcing the children into character building coolie labor and me into nocturnal courting patterns compatible with her godly beliefs. Hard work, she held, was good for the souls of small children, while their mother could do nothing but profit from complete social abstinence.

She announced one day that it was not "Christlike" for her to live in a fatherless home, that it was alien to her religion. I replied that her Christian intolerance was alien to my heathen household, and we parted company, the Dragon Lady and I. Unloading her, a domestic relief, began the difficult task of finding that Holy Grail of all divorced women, a good mother-substitute. We went through so many candidates from employment agencies that our assortment of white unite uniforms rivaled Sears Roebuck's. The salary offered did not entice a Mary Poppins: there was an Irish lady, wonderful and jolly until she emptied the liquor closet; a Welsh woman whom Bader terrified with stories of the Georgetown hippies "who will eat you all up in their tummy"; an elderly British type who left huffily because the children insisted on calling her "nanny-goat"; and finally, a Scottish lady of high temper who packed her bags when Edmond bit her hindquarters as she was bending over the bathtub to wash his howling sister's head of tangled hair.

There were several other suffering souls of indiscernable nationality who could not cope with Edmond, whose illness had temporarily left him able to communicate only in gestures and a strange childish language that no one but his sister could understand. Bader had the unhappy faculty of translating his conversations into dialogue not always flattering to the mother's helper of the moment. And so we were alone at last.

Faced with the major support of a three-year-old son and six-year-old daughter, I started getting myself together to supplement the small child support. I did not know where to begin. My old guilt was replaced by a newer burden that subjected me to a deep concern over the rearing of "small, fatherless children" who the textbooks warned "would resent the mother for depriving them of an average, normal home life." I also could not do anything that society remunerates with a paycheck and still holds the laborer in high moral esteem. There were no ads in the classified sections of the paper seeking ex-debutantes experienced at dishing up tea. Freedom was one thing; survival would be another.

I concluded that I was skilled, however poorly, at only one thing: marriage. And so I set about the business of selling myself and two children to some unsuspecting man who might think me a desirable second-hand mate, a man of good means and disposition willing to support another man's children in some semblance of the style to which they were accustomed. My heart was not in the chase, but I was tired and there was no alternative. I could not afford freedom.

Finding a husband is not easy when one is young and unencumbered. It is worse when the stalker is disinterested in the hunt and is followed everywhere, partridgelike, by two small people. However, I mapped out a strategy. We needed a rich man, and I methodically began to search. That is how I came to subscribe to *Vogue, Harper's Bazaar, Town and Country,* and *Women's Wear Daily*. These publications specialize in the idle rich, where they hang out, what they wear and say while at play. *Vogue* advised me to: ". . . look at super Sue Baloo . . . the model everyone loves . . . isn't she adorable . . . her dazzling white blond prettiness perfection . . . in Biba's new duds? Everything is made in a shade of white because Biba believes white is right. . . ." Eugenia Sheppard told me where to get my face lifted; syndicated "Suzie" columns touted all the right playboys, and Mrs. Alfred G. Vanderbilt allowed in print what happiness it all was "to spend long hours with paints and brushes, books and records, son and daughter, husband and friends, Corgi and Dachshund. . . ."

I did not need a facelift, only a rich man who wouldn't put wrinkles in the old one. While the beautiful life appeared to suit Mrs. Vanderbilt, I was exhausted from "long hours with my son and daughter." I had no husband and few friends and did not even know what a Corgi was. Undaunted, we packed up and followed the rich into their lairs, taking a house in Southampton for the month of August, 1967, a month that took most of my funds and all my patience.

I do not know about the Sue Baloos of the world, but the watering grounds of Southampton bored me witless. I found, of course, the available mates as advertised, but they were already attached to wives, rich wives. My single conquest that summer was the aging White Russian colonel, Serge Obolensky who, while charming, was quite hard of hearing, and given to forgetting my name and sometimes his own. Even the sun did not shine for me around the Beautiful People. We spent thirty drizzly days in Southampton before returning to Washington, manless and penniless. I eventually managed to unearth a respectable number of eligible men, but the ones I liked were looking for rich mates themselves. Those who could afford me were generally exacting, moneyed conservatives. I had tried that once before.

As the year ran out, I began selling my jewelry, the revenue from which lasted about as long as my belief in the commercial myth that diamonds are forever. Mama sent us a little money when she had access to any, and it was not unusual for the children and me to have a couple of free meals a week at a small café owned by a distant relative of the children's grandfather, old Joe Howar. The immigrant proprietress, Mama Ayesha, never forgot my earlier kindness to her when I would invite her, unbeknownst to my disapproving mother-in-law, to come and visit Bader and Edmond. After leaving her restaurant, I often would find a roll of grubby five-dollar bills she had stuffed into my coat pocket. I was thirty-two years old, not exactly a charity case, but broke and with little more to show for the first half of my life than two children with growing feet and growling stomachs. When we had nothing left to sell, I contracted with the *Ladies' Home Journal* to write a "tell-all" story about Lyndon Johnson and how he ate his peas mashed up in a bowl, Chinese-rice style.

Since I had first laid hands on a *Big Little Book,* I had wanted to be a writer, going so far as to invest in a correspondence course from the Famous Writers' School. While spilling her guts to a ladies' magazine was not Flannery O'Connor's route to literary success, it was my single journalistic option. The *Ladies' Home Journal* article caused endless inquiries as to "Why have you done such a thing?" and began what would become for me a standard response over the next several years: "I need the money."

I did not know at the time that writing the article would be a healthy and final break with my social past. I spent two agonizing months closed off in the dining room writing about LBJ, dredging up Johnson memories for the *Journal*'s readers that would be juicy enough to justify a fee I would not be paid until the article was completed and accepted. To save money, I turned the heat off in most of the house, an unnecessary thrift when attacking a President. I was in a state of clammy warmth during the entire ordeal. The magic trick of "telling all" without disclosing painful personal events took away my appetite, but the children, accustomed to sizable Arab coffers, still thought themselves the Nile Queen and Heir to the Peacock Throne. Their preference for the better cuts of meat was quickly replaced by the notion that all steak came straight from the cow either chopped or ground. We took to being nouveau poor with as much grace as possible.

Crossing the reigning First Family at the typewriter is more fearsome than angering them socially. The word went forth around Washington that I was more untouchable than ever. A local television station that had queried me about hostessing a talk show terminated the discussion on the advice, I later learned, of the White House. Mrs. Johnson's Elizabeth Carpenter phoned the *Journal*'s editor, John Mack Carter, raging that he would stoop to printing my story, promising him presidential mayhem, and threatening a future moratorium on White House coverage. Mrs. Carpenter demanded equal time to tell about Barbara Howar, but Carter stood fast and I continued at the typewriter. I was not your celebrated fledgling writer nor sought-after controversial journalist, and I came to know a ringing phone meant nothing more promising than abortive exchanges with creditors. When lame vows to pay up no longer mollified my debtors, I unplugged the phone and withdrew completely.

I did not have the stuff of a true recluse and will be ever grateful to Ethel Kennedy for summoning me to reality. She asked me to work on a fund-raising telethon she and Bobby were staging to benefit the orphans of Washington's Junior Village. Grateful to be included, I would have canvassed door-to-door to save the Boston Strangler. Instead I worked with the telethon's executive producer and found television fascinating. During the actual five hours of the show, I was often on camera with imported athletes and celebrities answering phones and registering pledges for donations. My enthusiasm was surpassed only by that of Jack Paar, who mastered the ceremonies. It was also my task to take charge of one of the movie stars in town to promote the telethon. My choice was between Angie Dickinson and Bobby Darin.

Bobby Darin and I became the best of friends. For all his show-biz flamboyance at the time, he was a self-styled intellectual, a young man with a political conscience and the Elmer Gantry ability to convert those who did not share his convictions. I know it would make better reading to report that I began thinking of the world's problems through an exposure to John Kenneth Galbraith or, at least, Paul Newman, but it was Mr. Darin, the teen-rage of the fifties, who led me through the maze of bigotry in which I lived, backed me down on every narrow-minded point, and made me care.

When I was not working on my *Journal* article, I traipsed gypsylike over the nightclub circuit where Bobby was performing. We ate greasy hamburgers and talked race with Flip Wilson in Philadelphia; discussed censorship with Tony Franciosa in Puerto Rico, before we started a brawl with a bar full of San Juan hookers; and talked life and times with Sugar Ray Robinson, Gore Vidal, and Liza Minnelli in a Copacabana dressing room. I met Gloria Steinem, who planted in my mind the seed of discontent with the second-class lot of women. From Bobby Darin I learned that there really was a Mafia and that there were such things as loyal friends, that the former was to be avoided, the latter cherished. Many times a day he would shout, "Open your eyes and look around." I did.

What I saw ranged from barroom mob murder to the free-spirited qualities of a new breed of people, people who ultimately became good friends. Whatever my Washington reputation suffered, Bobby Darin did fine things for my soul. At the very least, he showed me I might have one. When the New York *Daily News* confirmed everyone's worst suspicions that I had become something of a nightclub moll by running a full, front-page picture of Bobby and me, I had come far enough not to care about that kind of publicity, and was only amused to see myself retouched by the paper's photographic artist into an unaccustomed state of mammary voluptuousness.

My story on Lyndon Johnson reached the stands precisely one week before his announcement not to seek reelection. I did little to discourage an association between my silly story and his historic withdrawal. Unfortunately, Johnson had a full year left in his term, and his political decision to step aside temporarily elevated him from the role of warmonger to that of elder statesman. I had written about the President of the United States in the hope that it would lead to bigger things for me and my typewriter, but the crafty gentleman in the White House had foiled me again. Journalistically, I was a very tacky flash in the pan. Public appearances to promote the article were abruptly canceled, and those honored were travesties. I had secretly hoped to appear on network television and be discovered by CBS; or that Otto Preminger, lounging before his television set, would see me and shout, "Get me that girl for my next film." What I got was a lot of hate mail. I was on an obscene-name basis with most of the country's lunatic fringe and not a few members of the John Birch Society.

I went on the "Johnny Carson Show" looking like an exaggerated kewpie doll interviewed between Nipsy Russell and S. I. Hayakawa. Orientals and Negroes have little need of television makeup men, who, to pass the time and earn their keep, spent hours painting me for the camera. Waiting my turn to go on stage, I sat petrified in an NBC Green Room with an unknown singing cowboy named Glen Campbell, who took as news the five-day-old revelation that Lyndon Johnson had decided not to run for a second term. Mr. Campbell asked, "What kind of act do you have?" and I was damned if I could answer him—or Mr. Carson, who wondered the same thing later on camera. Carson did not like me, had not read my article, and used both as an excuse to make me the brunt of some pretty silly bathroom humor and slapstick mugging to the audience. It was not fashionable in 1968 to go on television to criticize either the war or its promoter; nor was I intellectually capable of defending my new liberalism against Johnny Carson, which, as you may have surmised, placed me in the most ignorant period of my adult life. But for Nipsy Russell and an antiwar audience, Mr. Carson would have ground me up for the tawdry upstart he thought me. I certainly looked the part.

The press tore into me, too. Even an idol, Harriet Van Horne, whose aversion to LBJ was legendary, took me to task on the opinion-editorial page of the New York *Post*, ending her dissection of my Johnson story with, "I think there's a vicuña coat under the woodpile someplace." Would to God there had been. I saw another long, cold winter ahead.

If character is actually improved by struggle, life afforded me a rare stint of moral rearmament. Washington passed me by and busied itself inventing virtues for Lyndon Johnson. I had nothing left to sell and nothing to do. The time had come, according to my divorce agreement, to sell the house and shift for myself. My lawyers informed me I was legally obliged to do so, but, if I had learned nothing else, I knew I could screw up my own business without having to pay attorneys to do it for me. I simply refused to move; if necessary, I would chain the children and myself to the banister when the sheriff came to evict us.

Slowly, things started to look up. Washington never really had its heart in lionizing Lyndon Johnson. Soon the press began to view the last days of LBJ as the lame duck period it was, and as Washington's awe of Johnson's historic abdication diminished, tolerance for me increased. Bob Bennett, then general manager of Metromedia's Channel 5, offered me a spot on the "Ten O'Clock News" doing three-minute commentaries on Washington, three times a week. I could, he told me, choose any subject I could handle, which considerably limited the field. I did it anyway.

During the 1968 Poor People's Campaign when the Rev. Ralph Abernathy's followers camped out on the grounds near the Washington Monument, I did my first televised comment, called "Viewpoint." With Minnie Mouse eyelashes and a Fannie Flagg voice, I stood before the camera and pontificated on the plight of the nation's poor. If anyone watched, Barbara Howar on poverty created the largest credibility gap outside the White House. It was not long before I saw the necessity of cleaning up my image or taking up a new line of work.

I began to read everything from *The New York Times* to chewing-gum wrappers, sought out newsmen and politicians and learned to listen. Hours went into each commentary. I wrote and rewrote; scores of tape recordings screeched back my twangy voice until, six months later, I could almost stand the sight and sound of myself on camera. I was never certain anyone else reached that level of tolerance. Doggedly, I went on camera three times a week, airing my opinions on anything from abortion to renegade priests to Abe Fortas.

I was sent to the 1968 Republican National Convention in Florida and did little to distinguish myself, so politically ill-informed, was I that Spiro Agnew had to be identified for me. Since the early 1950s I had lived and breathed Washington politics, but had only managed to absorb the social ramifications of power. Gradually, however, I came to see the motives behind the political maneuvering around me, began to understand why there was such gloom in Miami the night John Lindsay abandoned the Republican liberals and seconded Agnew's nomination for Vice President, and why a male friend with whom I happened to fly to the convention could conveniently switch from working for the moderate Nelson Rockefeller to campaigning for Spiro Agnew. Lindsay would lose in his gamble to throw in with the Nixon crowd, but my Rockefeller turncoat would sign on permanently as a tub-thumping employee of Vice President Agnew. Power, or rather a new form of it, began to rear its head. A different variety from what I had seen in Congress, it was more subtle than the wheeling and dealing of Lyndon Johnson. This personal powermongering was often devoid of any motivating sense of right or wrong. I came to see it as sheer political greed.

Flaws in the governing system had started to become apparent to me in the course of my awakening even before I had gone to work on television. In the spring of 1968 I had done some volunteer work at Robert Kennedy's headquarters. Bobby had taken up the cause begun by Eugene McCarthy, and regardless of the ruthless measures he used to usurp McCarthy's liberal, antiwar stance, I believed in him—perhaps because Kennedy started to articulate publicly the thoughts I was forming privately: there was not equality and freedom for all; the Vietnam war was wrong whether we won or lost. I found myself in step with the new Robert Kennedy. I thought he had the answers.

What he did not have was a smooth campaign headquarters. There was as much greed and petty rivalry among Kennedy followers as Lyndon Johnson's people could display on their worst days. It was more disappointing because I had expected better of the younger men packaging Robert Kennedy for the White House. They worked grudgingly alongside the older men Bobby had inherited from Jack Kennedy's administration. The two factions suffered one another poorly, victims as they were of differences in age, style, and, sometimes, ideology. Each group was determined to be in charge and bent on being Bobby-powers. They were like matron ladies squabbling at a bargain basement White Sale. The really powerful figures in the Kennedy entourage scarcely kept themselves above open in-fighting, and if the rumors were true that the Ted Sorensens, Fred Duttons, and Pierre Salingers disagreed with the fellows known because of their youth as Bobby's kiddie car brain trust, they did so behind closed doors. But the scent of internal disorder seeped down to the underlings and took hold. If the person in charge of Indiana fund-raising were absent, the coordinator of Oregon volunteers did not dare interfere; even if things went undone, no one was permitted into another's territory. The legendary Kennedy humor and sense of fun were not apparent at headquarters. The outs were organizing to get back in, and it was a deadly serious business.

None of the campaign workers ever satisfactorily explained the Kennedy mystique, that overwhelming phenomenon that could reduce grown men and women to servitude. Perhaps, like the regime they sought to displace, the Kennedy revolutionaries were only looking for personal political spoils. Certainly this new breed of Democrats was every bit as jealous of anyone who caught the imagination of its leader. I recall an afternoon shortly after the publication of my LBJ article in the *Journal* when Bobby dropped in at headquarters. I had been quoted in the papers as replying to a reporter's query on what I would do if Johnson took retaliatory measures. I had answered, "Go aboard the *Pueblo*. Johnson seems unable to reach anyone there," a reference to the ship currently captured in North Korean waters. Bobby came over to ask if I had actually said that. We laughed and chatted and when he left, there was a new attitude toward me. Some thought I might be a power to be reckoned with in the campaign, to either ingratiate or badger. It was the same insecure curiosity that personal notice had caused in Johnson circles: the man in power may change, but those seeking it are all alike.

Some weeks after that, Bobby was gunned down in Los Angeles. As with the death of his brother five years before, not all his people behaved as the idealistic Kennedy follower would have wished. There was pushing and shoving to get on his funeral train, and—although not all the interlopers were as obvious as Los Angeles Mayor Sam Yorty, who deposited himself uninvited in St. Patrick's Cathedral for the services—there were many faces in the televised crowd that had remained outside Bobby's shadow during the Johnson years, faces that should have been red from embarrassment to pass among those genuinely loyal followers of Robert Kennedy. I was reminded of a time when Bobby Kennedy was alive and sitting in front of his Hickory Hill fireplace while children, dogs, athletes, mountain climbers, movie stars, and journalists roamed through the sprawling, noisy, colorful house. Bobby was wearing a string of love beads popular with the youth movement of the late sixties. They had been given to him by football hero Roosevelt Grier, as Bobby said, "so that I can keep count of how many children I have." It would have taken a much larger necklace to account for all those men present at his grave who had been strangely missing from the scene when Robert Kennedy was alive and struggling to replace Lyndon Johnson.

In our long history of shooting politicians, I have felt the repercussions, from the gunfire in the House of Representatives gallery that wounded Alabama Congressman Kenneth Roberts, to the disaster in a Maryland shopping center that crippled Alabama Governor George Wallace. I have come to feel that Washington politicians look upon these events as little more than temporary setbacks in the continuing process of government.

When Martin Luther King was murdered in Memphis, Washington's inner city went up in flames. While the black community erupted in rage and frustration, the press and the people they write about defied the curfew and gathered together under the flame-red sky to hash and rehash the death. Perhaps this was a healthy sign of resilience, but more likely it was the result of the callous attitude of a city that during the sixties had seen political shootings become almost as commonplace as massive political demonstrations.

The attitude that life goes on is strong in government circles, and once the initial shock and sorrow wears off, interest is centered upon the new leader. It is a contemporary version of "The King Is Dead: Long Live the King"—except that in Washington's higher levels, the line of succession is never that clear. The phrase is altered to: The King Is Dead: Who

Is the Next Best Bet? Only those whose immediate lives are changed by political assassination manage prolonged grief. The rest are looking over the coffin for the approach of a new bandwagon.

This type of opportunism was evident at the 1968 Democratic National Convention in Chicago, where a score card was as much a requisite of survival as a crash helmet. It was difficult to keep straight which Johnsonite had taken up with Hubert Humphrey, which follower of Gene McCarthy had switched to Robert Kennedy, and which of the same had re-aligned themselves with McCarthy after Kennedy's death, in contrast to those who had fallen in behind the latter-day candidacy of George McGovern. Most curious was the second-guessing about the ones who could be counted on if the groundswell for Ted Kennedy should begin as rumored on the convention floor and in the Hilton Hotel bar.

I had sat through boring hours of the Washington-based Democratic Platform Committee, watching the proponents of the peace plank deal with the party opposition to it. When the plank was voted down on the convention floor in Chicago, I lost what was left of my political virginity. Belief in any person or platform seemed impossible. Rumors abounded that Ted Kennedy's brother-in-law Steve Smith was hiding, Howard Hughes-like, in a Chicago hotel, pushing buttons for Teddy's candidacy while Kennedy colleagues canvassed the delegates for support. Humphrey people were secondary to Lyndon Johnson's man at the convention, and new McGovern people like Pierre Salinger and Arthur Schlesinger wore campaign buttons proclaiming GEORGE MCGOVERN IS THE REAL GENE MCCARTHY. No one knew what the old Gene McCarthy was up to.

Democratic ladies jammed the ballrooms and private dining rooms off the main lobby, amusing themselves with card parties, teas, luncheons, and style shows where models from the ranks of the Women's Democratic Club wore historic gowns from past Democratic administrations. The distaff side of the Democratic Party, in fact, was the only group with any vestige of solidarity: Abigail McCarthy, Muriel Humphrey, and Eleanor McGovern sat side by side at head tables during the women's events. The role of women at that bloody convention was summed up by Lady Bird Johnson in her *White House Diary*. She related a phone call from Elizabeth Carpenter, who was reporting on an afternoon fashion show with Mrs. Johnson's social secretary Bess Abel, "looking adorable as Dolley Madison." While kids and journalists were clubbed in the streets, while television correspondents were hauled off the convention floor by special police, while gestapo methods were employed to search delegates and journalists at the convention hall, while official press seats were filled with Daley's city employees holding counterfeit passes, while delegates snake-danced around the hall singing and the peace plank died a Democratic death, Democratic wives played lady.

Despite the fact that Lyndon Johnson had been forced aside and that his anointed heir, Hubert Humphrey, had taken up his war standard without so much as dropping a vowel, despite McCarthy and Kennedy primary victories on a far different platform, Humphrey won the nomination. The night of his acceptance speech, the spotlight was turned to the flag-draped box where George and Eleanor McGovern took gracious bows. All was over; all was forgiven. No one knew or cared where Gene McCarthy was. Ted Kennedy had the good sense to absent himself from the scene of Lyndon Johnson's final triumph. While everyone raced around mend-

ing political fences and ingratiating themselves with the
Humphrey camp, I shared fourteen bottles of cheap red
wine with four reporters and five yippies. I had come a long
way from my Ladies for Lyndon days in Atlantic City.

13

It was Mama who announced that I was a boring radical. I was, she said, like the pubescent child who discovers sex and is unable to leave herself alone. I had, indeed, made it my business to unearth and dissect every national inequity and then fling it in any available face. My prime conversations centered around atrocities committed in the name of democracy, and I was comfortable and satisfied only with like-minded people who fed my lust for fault-finding. While Mama was not one of them, critics were not scarce. I recall adhering to every rule of radicalism, stopping only this side of going unbathed. Mama suggested I grow a beard.

I learned all the rhetoric, the arguments, the nihilistic gestures of despair, that mark the converted radical. Politicians who yawned and backed off from my monologues were, I decided, fearful of the truth. I was avoided in the same way I assumed the enlightened had been shunned by the Philistines. I was too naïve to understand that most politicians concern themselves with society's evils only in an election year. Burning issues are tiresome harangues in Georgetown parlors.

Either because I was so good or so bad at political commentary—one is never certain in television—I was given the female spot on a live Washington talk show called "Panorama." For two hours each day I sat with two male hosts and belabored all the things that concerned me. If I was not exactly a card-carrying intellectual, neither were the members of my audience. While I muddled through issues and crises, they stormed along with me, either agreeing or taking exception, and judging by my mail, it was mostly the latter.

Not exactly the queen of daytime TV, I was nonetheless watched. The ratings climbed, and I was tolerated, however grudgingly. It was a long while before my public aggression leveled off, before I learned that if there was anything worse than a bigoted keeper of the status quo, it was a recycled socialite with a newly aroused public conscience.

Eventually, I also came to understand that I had rare access to large numbers of people, and that if I could come up with thoughts that merited attention, I had a unique opportunity to express them. In the meantime, I blithely went about breaking every rule in the staid world of television: my skirts were too short, my opinions too radical, my respect for the medium and those who ran it nonexistent. If the uneasy station manager lost advertising because of my attitude, the ratings continued to go up.

At first I was delegated all the frivolous interviews that producers consider women's work. It was I who stood outside in the windy parking lot to interview the trainer of six gargantuan Clydesdale horses newly purchased as the symbol for a nationally known firm of meat packers: "Sir, how does the public react to *horses* used to advertise *edible* meat?" The station lost the meat-packers account.

I attacked the national lobby of diamond miners and sellers for racist conditions in South African mines and the commercial exploitation of "sentimental women who trade their freedom for a wedding ring that does not accrue in value." I dismissed author Jim Bishop after he made what I considered to be derogatory remarks about the assassinated Robert Kennedy. I called Mr. Bishop "a very good second-rate writer." Bishop stormed off the set, and I was instructed next day to make an on-air apology to him. It came off so much worse than the original insult that I was ordered to deliver another mea culpa. My public apologies to Jim Bishop nearly became a regular part of the show. I tangled with gossipist Sheilah Graham, the Right to Life anti-abortionists, fundamentalist Carl McIntyre, the promoters of the Miss America pageants, and the better part of the entire United States Congress.

Only once did the management of Metromedia come down hard on me, and that was done prior to an interview with the ultraconservative millionaire sponsor of "Life Line," H. L. Hunt. I was warned not to argue, dispute, or challenge the old bigot in any way; I was to afford him the same courtesies I lavished on guests whose political beliefs resembled my own. Mr. Hunt, diagonally across from me on the set, was an elderly man, given to non sequiturs and lascivious leers. He sat holding a cup of hot coffee in his lap while he extolled Capitalism and the need to keep power out of the hands of common folk if they happened to be poor, uneducated, young, black, yellow, red, or female. While Hunt droned on, I sat before him in a suede skirt that stopped twelve inches above the knees, exposing my legs which, off camera, I crossed and uncrossed with the high precision of a Rockette. Between kicks, I scratched my chest area with jangling bracelets that jammed the network more subtly than Communist countries fuzz up Radio Free Europe. With every scratch and flying leg, Mr. Hunt became more and more disconcerted, finally spilling his coffee in his lap and becoming embarrassingly incoherent. He was led away by his shapely young secretary, and I fancied myself as having saved the day for the liberal cause without once opening my mouth.

After severe lectures about taste and protocol, Metromedia selected me to anchor their East Coast coverage of the Nixon Inaugural Ball. Four years had passed, and instead of running a Democratic Inaugural, I was about to broadcast a Republican one. We were given the exclusive of the Nixon-Agnew party arriving and reveling at the first official stop of the presidential party for the evening. Metromedia stations were on the air at ten o'clock with the networks following up at the other ball sites around midnight. I was very aware that the first glimpses of the triumphant Mr. Nixon would be narrated by me. I prepared for this with long hours at the hairdresser, surrounded by wives of Washington officials who watched the portable television sets either in a state of depression because they were no longer to be a part of the pomp of government, or with the manic gaiety that grips new official wives who would be tasting the public spotlight for the first time. I sat under the drier making notes for my grand performance that night and watching the televised departure of the Johnson family as they boarded Air Force One for the last time amidst sad well-wishers and the final musical salute of "Hail to the Chief." The Johnsons were going home to Texas, and either because of or in spite of all the good and bad blood that had flowed between me and that family, I cried. I was sorry to see them go. It was the same complex sadness I would feel nearly four years later when Lyndon Johnson died. However strained our relationship, I would grieve at his death with that certain knowledge that he had been a powerful figure in my life and that I cared deeply for him. I mourned him as a person mourns the loss of a formidable and difficult father. Part of my youth had dwelled with him.

Unfortunately my preparations to narrate the first social appearance of the Nixons were mostly cosmetic, consisting of an elaborate coiffure and an equally elaborate gown. My makeup was perfect as I sat on a specially constructed platform in the middle of the grand hall of the new Smithsonian Institution, the engineers checking the light and sound while hundreds of people I knew crushed onto the dance floor awaiting the presidential party. It had not occurred to me that Richard Nixon would not walk into that room at the precise stroke of ten; it had not crossed my mind that the intercom system connecting my left ear with the remote control truck in the parking lot might not function. The engineer on the platform with me began counting down the minutes to air time.

"I'm not hearing you through my earphone. I'm not hearing the director either. No signals are coming across."

"Four minutes to air time. Forget the earphone, Barbara. Watch my hands for your signals. When I hold up three fingers, switch to Meryl Comer on the floor; when I give you a fist, take a station break; four fingers will mean Jack Cole has a live interview in the crowd. When I give you a V sign, fill air . . . stall."

"Wait a minute, fellows, I can't follow all this."

"Two minutes to air time, Howar. Shape up."

"Jesus Christ, you all, I can't do this."

"God damn it, Barbara, watch your fucking language. Your mike is open."

"Oh, God, you guys."

"One minute to air time, Howar, and Nixon is nowhere in sight. Fill till he comes. God damn it, run your mouth till I signal you the President is in the Hall."

"How? What the hell can I do?"

"Too late for that, baby. Eighteen seconds to air time. Ten seconds . . . five . . . stand by"—and down came the engineer's index finger straight at me; I was ON THE AIR! My monitor was not working, the intercom was useless, my signals were confused, I could not turn toward the stage because I had no way of knowing whether the camera was on me or not.

"Good evening, ladies and gentlemen, welcome to the Inauguration of the thirty-seventh President of the United States . . ." For forty minutes before Richard Nixon arrived, I sat on that raised platform in a cold sweat, wallowing in the worst banalities of my life: "Why, did you know that Grover Cleveland at his Inaugural . . ." or, "Few of us will recall the fêting of Theodore Roosevelt but . . ." I was calm, polite, tasteful, and dull. The fear of God and unemployment had been placed in me not to equate this Inaugural with Lyndon Johnson's, not to discuss the ridiculous inner workings of an Inaugural with which I was well acquainted. I was not even allowed to comment on the silly press controversy over the inappropriate length of Judy Agnew's white kid gloves. If millions of people from Miami to New York were interested in the little-known trivia that accompanied the Inaugural of Herbert Hoover, they loved me that night.

Variety said I was overdressed, the hierarchy of Metromedia Television called me professional, and Mama thought me distinguished. I was a thumping bore.

When it was over I went home and propped my over-dressed self up in a kitchen chair with a full bottle of bourbon which, combined with the evidence of the equally chaotic coverage by the television networks, soothed me through the remainder of Richard Nixon's Inaugural. I had blown another Big Chance, and my final thoughts as I went to sleep were of my personal ill omens of four years of a Nixon Administration. I recall making plans to open a very distinguished and professional house of prostitution.

The reemergence of Richard Nixon on the Washington scene gave the city, if nothing more, a brief period to sort itself out. There had been no such respite during the previous eight years—the swift-moving Kennedy era, political murder, the rise and fall of Lyndon Johnson, and more political murder. The hectic pace slackened, journalistic carpings ebbed, and if the scramble to advance oneself politically and socially was not halted, it was at least conducted on a temporarily subdued level. It was a time of political wait-and-see. With Richard Nixon there would ultimately be more waiting than seeing.

I was pleased with myself and my job. Less the radical, I was beginning to understand that given the available information and the same exposure as other Washington journalists, I could form opinions of my own—opinions that appeared to be at least as valid as those I had spent the previous year parroting. I progressed from doing television's women's work to working right along with John Willis and Maury Povich, the male hosts of "Panorama." They may or may not have been ready to deal equally with a "new woman," but the "new woman" was determined to deal with them. Accustomed to more docile females, the gentlemen sometimes suffered me with little grace. However, I was allowed to argue, interrupt, and dispute them, all of which I did with jolly regularity. The surer I became of my politics, the more forceful my on-air personality became. And this worked for me socially, the two never being far removed in Washington.

Hubert Humphrey gave Maury and me his second televised interview after his presidential defeat. We had both been cautioned to exercise good taste while raking him over the coals, but we were young enough and disgusted enough to sting the old Vice President into making asinine assertions that surpassed even Humphrey's reputation for the ridiculous. I was thirty-three, Maury thirty; neither of us could remember Humphrey's bygone glories in the heyday of the Americans for Democratic Action. Maury and I demanded to know what HHH had done for us lately.

To me poor Humphrey was a dead politician, a corpse of the 1968 convention, only he could not seem to let go. He personified the most sorrowful in American politics. He was the tragic mask of Chicago, of Lyndon Johnson's highhanded assumption that he could tap Humphrey to continue his own presidency without any concession to the public pressures that caused Johnson not to seek a second term. Humphrey had ignored the primaries that had shown the Democratic voters wanted reform and change. Like every one of those kids working for Kennedy and McCarthy who believed the system would work fairly, I was furious that Humphrey had received the nomination. I held him personally responsible for my disillusionment in the convention process. Somehow it did not seem important that he almost beat Nixon; it only mattered that Humphrey caused me to despair of my country.

But blaming Humphrey was pointless. I should have shown him sympathy. I recalled him vividly from my Johnson years, often remembering the stories of Johnson's earlier acute discomfort as Kennedy's Vice President, and curious as to why Johnson was not more sensitive to Humphrey's role. Johnson, never a kind man, was cruel to Humphrey. He used him conveniently, generally as a buffoon, dressing him up in ten-gallon cowboy hats and boots for the press, making snide and vulgar remarks about Humphrey's vital organs "being in my hip pocket," suggesting breeding Humphrey to Calvin Coolidge. Johnson often said Hubert's mouth ran "worse'n a woman's."

Regardless of how much more potent a politician Johnson was, he resented the kindly, joy-loving Humphrey, and seemed somehow jealous of his gregariousness and popularity. LBJ never liked his daughters to pay much attention to his Vice President. Both girls felt comfortable with Humphrey; they enjoyed the Vice President's bantering and teasing. Luci called him "Uncle Hubie," an endearment that brought disgust to her father's face. Johnson seemed to think Humphrey far too weak for his daughters' admiration. The President was quick to remind listeners that for all Hubert's concern for civil rights, it was he, Johnson, who "got the job done," that for all Hubert's scrambling for high office, it was Johnson, who by the crooking of his powerful finger, had beckoned Humphrey into national prominence. Lyndon Johnson had a "the Lord giveth and taketh away" attitude about his Vice President, and for Humphrey, there were too many reminders of his bondage to Johnson's largesse. HHH had sold his soul to LBJ, and Johnson was always there to collect his debt.

It was no secret in the White House that Lyndon begrudged Hubert any private political ground. Humphrey could not oversee the country's education policies; these belonged to Lyndon and Lady Bird. He could not even have the dandy's role as the administration's official greeter, the goodwill traveler, the roving keeper of America's hospitality flame. Occasionally Humphrey was tossed a bone, but Johnson had picked it clean before relinguishing it. The few missions permitted Hubert were stripped of real authority or importance before Humphrey departed, often dispatched on Johnson's whim without adequate backgrounding or preparation. Humphrey was Johnson's pet whipping boy, a palace eunuch among eunuchs, politically emasculated by Lyndon Johnson.

During my White House days, Humphrey was persona non grata owing, I later learned, to a mild disagreement with Johnson on the Vietnam war. Obsessed by a need for total commitment to his policies, Johnson never forgave Humphrey for expressing a contrary opinion on Southeast Asia.

For all the complaints of the Johnson people about their ungracious treatment at the hands of Kennedy's staff and family when they served Vice President Johnson, they seemed indifferent to the same abuse directed at Humphrey. He was alternately ignored or patronized. Johnson people had no more tolerance for Humphrey than did the President: if LBJ held you in low esteem, his devoted assistants held you likewise. Lyndon Johnson demanded absolute loyalty from his underlings even in their personal friendships.

Like the unfavored child in a large family, Humphrey tried to endear himself to Big Daddy, talked him up to the press, and spread the Johnson word regardless of his own convictions. But if Humphrey hated his role, he never showed it. Rather, he went to great pains to appear solidly entrenched with Lyndon Johnson. Humphrey brought it all on himself; there were no chains to his ankle. He was a willing prisoner. This, of course, made him all the more unadmirable, which was perhaps what Johnson intended all along.

I recall a large White House reception where Humphrey was chattering away in a far corner. Luci suggested we go over and "fluff up Uncle Hubie . . . he's so lovable." While I never shared her affection for Humphrey, he was pleasant and likeable. His excess of exuberance only made him the more pitiable, and I grew to think of him as "poor Hubert," almost as though "poor" were part of his Christian name. The man selected to be a living memorial to Johnson policy was not worth rancor. He was only a sour reminder of Johnson's ego.

For me personally, the early Nixon years coincided with my new feeling of contentment. If I did not know precisely who and what I was, I had some indication and was not alarmed by what I suspected. I was being invited out by new people I liked and could respect, frequently seated high above the salt, close by those Washington personages in both press and government whose power has continuity from administration to administration. They had not been part of my Johnson-Texas world.

A frequent complaint of Washington women married to politicians and columnists was that they were invariably asked by dinner partners: "What does your husband think of the anti-ballistic missile system?" or, "Where does your 'better half' stand on busing?" For most Washington wives, this is as much intellectual stimulation as the traffic can bear, but for others it is insulting, boring, and ample reason for staying socially aloof. This did not happen to me because I had no husband, and because my opinions reached hundreds of thousands of homes five days a week. Very few Washington women are allowed public exposure on their own merit, and however small and insignificant my domain was, it was not easily dismissed. At last I had a small amount of influence that was my own, independent of another person. If at a dinner party I began a discussion with Senator Fulbright on some issue of the day, I would spend the entire salad course trying to persuade him to come on "Panorama" and discuss it. When the head of the Immigration Service had an interesting theory on narcotics traffic, I booked him during dessert. For those with an idea or a book to be peddled nationally, I convinced them to practice their dialogue on me before they appeared on the "Today Show" or the "Tonight Show." "Panorama," you might say, became a television version of the off-Broadway tryout.

I was granted a pass to the House and Senate Press galleries. My face and—oh God—my voice were quickly recognized. I could make appointments with and get phone calls through to almost any office in Congress, the government agencies, and in some instances, the White House. For a woman who three years earlier had had all the social and political clout of Mary Magdalene, I was not displeased with my sketchy eminence.

One of the first events during the Nixon administration was the annual black tie dinner of the Association of Radio and Television Correspondents, stag except for the handful of women from the media. CBS newscaster Roger Mudd, the

Association's president in 1968, asked me to assist Fishbait Miller in receiving distinguished guests in the Shoreham Hotel's VIP room before they were marched to music into the ballroom to take their seats on the stage. Fishbait is the oversalaried and legendary Doorkeep of the House of Representatives, whose sole function, as I see it, is to proclaim to the television audience: "Ladies and Gentlemen, the President of the United States," while whoever holds the office strides down the aisle to address a Joint Session of Congress. Fishbait and I, taking the role of greeter with equal seriousness, stood at the door and pinned carnations on Melvin Laird, Barry Goldwater, James Westmoreland, Daniel Moynihan, William Fulbright, the heads of all three networks, the leadership of the House and Senate, most of Nixon's new cabinet, and Spiro Agnew, who now did not have to be identified for me.

Unemancipated, I wore a dress too short and too low-cut to indicate I thought myself above the level of sex object. Still, I was delighted to be a part of all this official display, a professional part—not the employee, the socialite, or the controversial outcast, but a working part of the Washington press corps. There was not a man in a carnation more self-important than the skimpily clad girl who pinned on their boutonnières.

At dinner, the tables jammed with the important men in media and government, each partaking generously of the bottles of liquor in front of him, I decided that I had at last found my place. It never crossed my mind that there was any inequity in the fact that there were less than fifty women amid the hundreds and hundreds of the most important and powerful men in the country—the men who controlled the system and those who reported on it. I was perfectly content to be, as I thought, a rose among the mighty oaks.

During the intermission between the speeches, I dashed toward the Ladies' Room through a kitchen door to avoid the crowd and ran into Ted Kennedy and CBS's Myra McLaughlin, who had come off the dais with the same short-cut in mind. We chatted and walked down the empty kitchen corridor, Myra on Teddy's right, I on his left. Midway, it struck us simultaneously that this last living Kennedy brother was in a kitchen, alone, unguarded, in very much the same kind of surroundings in which Robert Kennedy had been killed in a Los Angeles hotel kitchen less than a year before. I felt panic and a strange sense of giddiness which, though we never spoke of it afterward, must have been close to what Myra and Teddy experienced. We fell suddenly silent. Teddy reached out and pulled Myra and me closer. We walked quickly down the rest of the long, dim hall. The remainder of the evening was not the same. My triumph was somehow diminished, replaced by a nagging feeling that there was never anything lasting or permanent about Washington or its politics.

In the aftercrush of private parties in the hotel suites, I chanced to be in a packed elevator with Gene McCarthy, who only months before had been the Don Quixote of all that was right and good. He looked tired and done with it all—another reminder of political impermanence.

Always the late reader of omens, I recall a vivid encounter with a handsome man in a tuxedo who followed me about during the evening, inviting me to go to the lobby bar and have a drink. "I would like to talk to you." After coolly brushing him aside several times, I turned on him, "Look, fellow, I didn't come with you, and I'm not leaving with you! Got that?" I transferred my attentions to Walter Cronkite, airily asking, "Who the hell is *that*?" Walter allowed that *that* was Elton Rule, President of ABC Television. Knowing there were still two networks left did little to lift my spirits.

14

While Washington tiptoed around the Nixon crowd, I reacquainted myself with the city: the monuments, parks, government buildings, restaurants, shops, the diplomatic salons as well as the plain old living rooms of old and new friends. *Life* columnist Hugh Sidey wrote of the new administration as a breath of different if not fresh air. He suggested the Republican administration would bring new life to the city as well as a change in entertainment styles and hostesses: legendary Washington party-givers "Perle Mesta and Gwen Cafritz are over the hill," he said, "and Barbara Howar never really made it. . . ." I was delighted to be included even unflatteringly in his roundup. I sent him a telegram saying, "I've made it now. Thanks, Barbara Howar," which the good Mr. Sidey modestly took as the compliment intended. By return mail, I received a letter from Hugh saying he had hoped I would be a good sport about his column and inviting me to lunch in the mysterious Sans Souci, the restaurant that is Washington's official clubhouse—the place where politicians and the press meet to eat and swap secret documents. It is done exclusively over lunch.

It became my opinion that more dallying than document-dropping was done at the Sans Souci. A credit card heaven, it continued to be the place where the powerful men in Washington gossip. If a cabinet appointment or a resignation was imminent, the person in question generally showed up at the height of the lunch hour with a "highly placed source," or a "close White House partisan." Rumors would fly around the plush, carpeted, brocaded room. "John Connally is three tables over with so-and-so from the White House," someone would observe. The next day, there would be an official announcement: "President Nixon today appointed former Democratic Texas Governor John Connally as Secretary-designate of the Treasury." If Nixon press secretary Ron Ziegler lunched with a syndicated columnist, the columnist invariably had a special slant in his next outpouring.

The Sans Souci was where Henry Kissinger lunched with Clare Boothe Luce or the starlet of the moment, where Edward Bennett Williams would be cheered if his Redskins won a football game or hissed if they lost. Nothing went unnoticed. If the place closed down, three-quarters of influential Washington would be rendered dumb and starve to death, literally and figuratively. Over cold artichokes or hot onion soup, it has always been possible to plug into state secrets or constant government gossip. On a good day, it could be a highly accurate barometer registering who had been sleeping with whom on all the interesting levels of government. For powerful regulars, there has always been an available table.

Regardless of the administration, the restaurant's flavor, like Washington, remains purely Democratic and liberal. Republicans leave the city when their term is over and go back to running General Motors. Democrats stay on. More than their counterparts, they contract what is called Potomac

Fever, that pernicious disease that keeps men close to power even when they no longer deal directly in it. Democrats retire to write books on their Washington experiences, go into law practice, or take up the less elegant but more remunerative pursuits of lobbying. Along with the usual Democratic majority in Congress, and the decidedly liberal character of the press, they comprise the backbone of Washington, a Democrat's city. Never would this be more apparent than in the lunch line at Sans Souci. For at least three administrations, influential Washington men have been judged by where they are seated and with what speed they are served. A bad day at the Sans Souci could herald hard times.

Above all, it has never been a restaurant for lunching ladies. An unwritten law has prohibited women from eating there from noon to three unless they have power or beauty—Washington rarities. Other acceptable women are members of the working press at a working lunch. But, unless she is seated with men whose credentials are known to the other lunchers, a savvy woman would hunger in the street before making the wrong kind of entrance into the Sans Souci.

Not all the new aspects of the town were as pleasant for me to discover as Mr. Sidey's famous restaurant. There is, sadly, an uncelebrated part of Washington, ignored in the guidebooks. The White, Rich, and Powerful live in what is geographically called Northwest, and in a small area of Southwest, a section near the Potomac waterfront where vast sums of government money were expended moving the poorer blacks further into the city to make way for garish high-rise apartments with equally lofty rents. Downtown, there is the maze of monuments and government buildings. Some sections of Southeast, near the Capitol, have been renovated

[209]

for white living, and there are large areas along Sixteenth Street in the Northwest section that house the affluent, middle-class black community of doctors, dentists, and businessmen. The rest of Washington is one vast ghetto. Low-income whites have moved to the suburbs to avoid the black people who migrate to the city in hope of finding the promised higher welfare or at least some of the equality or social communion that large cities tease the disenfranchised into thinking they will find there. The real nation's capital is the rat-filled area that packs in the majority of Washington's population. The standard of education is low; traffic in dope is high. Crime is perpetrated by blacks against blacks. Policing of the area is done mostly by white officers who commute from suburbia and know little of inner-city problems, hopes, or griefs. Even the firemen are unfamiliar with the neighborhoods they work. Rape, theft, and muggings, common happenings in Washington, are worse in the ghetto areas. Little is done for these Washingtonians. The premise is that "Little can be done for *those* people."

Washington has no self-government. It is America's last colony. The White House appoints the mayor and the city council. City funds are allocated by the Congress, which takes its attitude from the congressional committees established to rule the city—committees chaired by somewhat indifferent men, generally southerners. Rarely do they come from cities with populations of more than twenty-five thousand; they know nothing of the horrors of large cities crowded with uneducated Americans who, under the system, have come to expect as little from the federal government as they receive.

Serving on the House or Senate District of Columbia Committee is, in fairness, not a choice committee assignment.

Not only is the city an apparently insoluable mess, but there is nothing connected with such an assignment that is impressive to the voter back home. A high-ranking member of the House District Committee cannot use his influence to do anything for his constituency in the South or the Midwest. There simply is no political gain for the congressmen who babysit the national capital.

The fever to give Washington home rule rises and falls. Many official reasons are cited for the city's inability to govern itself, but these invariably come down to the harsh truth that Washington is predominantly Negro and Congress will never, or certainly not in the forseeable future, turn over the town that houses the United States Government to the blacks. The city remains the ultimate center of white racism in America.

The main street of Washington, F Street, stretching between the White House and Capitol vicinities, has been all but abandoned. Regardless of how much federal money is spent to light and landscape the old downtown area, it remains a larger version of the ghostly business sections in cities across the country. Better stores have moved to affluent white shopping centers, taking the few good restaurants with them, and leaving the center of Washington filled with pornographic book shops, X-rated movie houses, souvenir stands, and block after block of alternately vacant stores and those selling overpriced credit-plan merchandise. The Washington City of the Founding Fathers is gradually dying.

It was not until I made an embarrassing on-air blooper that I came to know this other Washington. "Panorama" cohost John Willis and I were discussing the annual arrival of the circus. My daughter Bader had noticed during the clown parade a half-dozen Negroes in astronaut suits. I mentioned on the air that she, at ten, had questioned the use of Negroes in this space act when she had never seen a black astronaut on television. A little to the right of Alley Oop, John argued that the space program was certainly open to Negroes but that those blacks who had participated in the earlier programs had been drop-outs, intellectually uninterested and unable to train for a moon shot. After a harangue about the entire space business and my rebuttal that black Americans could be educated at NASA as well as the present white astronauts, I blurted, "Don't be ignorant enough to go along with that flimsy Canaveral propaganda, John. If NASA can train a monkey to operate the controls of a rocket, they can train a black man."

Regardless of how well-intentioned my statement, it severely angered black Washington. The station switchboard lit up with indignant callers and my mail further suggested the impact of the innocent insult. My thoughtlessness, however, was not taken so seriously by a handful of black city leaders who thought I might still be redeemed. One by one they contacted me and acquainted me with facts I found unbelievable, facts underscored by frequent trips with these men and women into the inner city, eye-opening visits to which no white woman of my acquaintance had been exposed. By day I saw practices of national food chains, my own included, where inferior produce, meat, and household needs were sold at prices higher than the same merchandise was marked in the white, Northwest Washington stores. Management-customer relations were nonexistent, courtesy wholly absent, food stamp holders barely tolerated; the stores fell below required health standards. The black community, dependent on credit, was gouged by high interest rates for overpriced consumer goods. The repossession statistics were appalling.

The nighttime view was worse. Government-subsidized housing was full of hazards that ranged from faulty wiring to infestations of rats better nourished than the humans with whom they shared quarters. White-owned bar-and-grills were filthy, dope easily obtained. There was an astonishing number of white prostitutes. I saw little sign of the police except those officers seated in the nicer and more highly priced establishments. Block after block of burned-out buildings, unrepaired since the rioting that followed the King assassination, were boarded up and littered. Invariably they bore fading signs saying "Soul Brother" that had been hastily painted over old announcements of "Wings and Things: Lowest Prices Anywhere."

When I brought up these subjects on the air with Nixon-appointed city officials, I was met with lame and distant plans for change. Off the air these self-important appointees would acquaint me with the ignorance of the black population and tell me earnestly, "These people don't take care of what we give them." It appeared Washington would have to come up with a higher caliber of poor people before conditions could be improved.

Now that Washington has a Negro holding the newly created seat of Non-Voting Delegate to Congress, there is more publicity focused on the problems, but still there is little change. Knowledgeable black organizers learned to stave off the use of Washington for antiwar demonstrations; they knew a million college kids, however well-intentioned, destroyed scenic Washington and that the carefully hidden black areas would suffer as thousands of city dollars were spent policing and tidying up after parades or rallies.

White liberal hypocrisy about the black situation was made clear to me by George Wallace. Midway between Wallace's abortive runs for the presidency in 1968 and 1972, he was the main speaker at the American Independent Party's convention in Richmond. Since he was never able to attract much press notice unless he looked dangerously close to upsetting the complacency of the Democratic or Republican Parties, Wallace went virtually uncovered during the convention, which is probably how I happened to be sent to interview him both for television and for a national magazine.

Wallace drew from his frenzied throng twice the enthusiasm we liberals afford our demagogues. I had never been party to an ovation like the one George Wallace received. The spirit of his audience was so much more gut-serious than that of the followers of Johnson or even Robert Kennedy. These people had something to lose compared to their liberal counterparts who fancied they had something to gain. The force with which they stood behind Wallace was frightening—and strangely moving in its genuineness.

George Wallace is crude and sharp, a fox-like manipulator of crowds. He is also forceful; hence, a sexy and magnetic man. For me, it was impossible not to take him seriously and, quite frankly, it was difficult not to like him.

Wallace, another journalist, and I, along with an even dozen of Wallace's staff, all southern gentlemen with university degrees and Brooks Brothers suits, retired after the morning session of the convention to a Chinese-American restaurant, certainly not found in the *Greater Richmond Guide to Good Dining*. Wallace neither drinks, smokes, nor admires those who do. As the only female in the group, I found it necessary to do both, closed off as we were in an unairconditioned private dining room whose only remotely Oriental decorations consisted of long strips of flypaper hung from the ceiling.

It was the week of Chappaquiddick, a beastly hot July, and as the ceiling fan fluttered the flypaper, there was much earthy talk of Ted Kennedy's caper, his sexual motivations, and a handful of obscene stories about past transgressions of other political personalities. By comparison, Wallace's conversation made Lyndon Johnson sound prudish. But there was an honest quality about Wallace that, if it existed with Lyndon Johnson, eluded me. Johnson had a tendency to be all things to whoever was listening. Wallace was Wallace, a calculating racist, but an open and honest one. He did not lie; he did not promise, making him, for me, a unique breed of politician, hardly palatable, but unique.

There are no such things as good politicians and bad politicians. There are only politicians, which is to say, they all have personal axes to grind, and all too rarely are they honed for the public good. If we would stop expecting the good politician to suddenly appear for us and realize that, as Mencken said, ". . . a good politician, under democracy, is quite as unthinkable as an honest burglar," we would all be much the better for it. The politician could stop making asinine promises he could not hope to keep, and the public could stop expecting miracles and experiencing disillusionment every four years when one crowd replaces the other. This is the point about George Wallace; he is no savior, no walking panacea, no hypocrite. While I was disgusted by his attitudes, even frightened he might prevail, I could still afford grudging respect for his candor.

Wallace has bigger eyes for women than ears. But, since I was seated to his right, he had no choice but to deal with me. And deal he did. I started my wonton soup with questions about school integration and busing, asserting between spoonfuls that he was wrong, that his bigotry was opposed to the principle that all men are created equal, and progressed to the egg rolls on the theory that "society must afford everyone the same opportunities." We had reached the business of a totally integrated society and racially mixed neighborhoods by the time the sweet and sour pork arrived. Wallace had listened to my postulations through three courses, silently wiping his sweaty face on the steaming towels the Chinese proprietor kept handy. He blew his nose into his napkin, swatted a few flies, and retaliated:

"Why, Miss Barbara, how did a good southern girl like you get such a head full of trash? What business is it of yours what happens to nigrahs?"

"Governor, it's my business, and everybody's business, that all Americans get the same breaks regardless of color."

"But, Miss Barbara, what business is it of yours to tell people who don't live in fancy big houses in . . . Georgetown, isn't it? Yes, Georgetown. Now what concern is it of yours to tell people who don't live like you do *how* they are supposed to feel about nigrahs and *why* they are supposed to let them in their schools and in their neighborhoods?"

"Governor, it's the business of every American to . . ."

"But it don't affect you none, honey. You got it in your pretty little head that you can sit here and tell me I got no right to fight for folks that don't live in Georgetown, folks that ain't been handed a free ride. You been gone from home too long, been spendin' too much time with fancy liberals. You can't tell folks how to feel about nigrahs just because

[216]

you got some fancy notion that other folks should live and go to school with them—not when changing all these things ain't goin' to affect *you* none at all."

"Look, Governor, right is right and wrong is wrong, and . . ."

"Look here yourself, little lady, this is not your fight, you and your limousine liberals. You got nothing to put on the line. All you folks want to do is run your mouth. Make other folk live the way *you* think *they* ought to live. It just don't concern you none, and it's time you come to know that."

"Look now, Governor Wallace, I'm just as willing to do whatever is necessary to . . ."

"But that's the point, honey, ain't nothin' necessary for you. Where your children go to school?"

"Well, they're in private school in Washington and . . ."

"And how many nigrahs you got there that can pay money for special schooling?"

"Well, there are several in each child's class."

"And their daddies is more white than nigrah?"

"Yes, in the sense of education, but . . ."

"Well, honey, the nigrahs you want my children to go to school with is nigrah nigrah."

"But Governor, unless black children are afforded the same basic educational opportunities as the whites, then nothing will ever equalize."

"You mean *my* kids are supposed to suffer to help the nigrahs catch up, but not yours?"

"That's not what I mean at all, I mean . . ."

"Now, Miss Barbara, you tell me how many your neighbors is nigrahs? How many nigrahs you have to your fancy dinner parties? Who you have? Ralph Bunche, Thurgood Marshall, Roy Wilkins? Now, honey, you're too pretty and sweet to sit there and tell me and my people to integrate with nigrahs so you'll feel better about things when you don't do it your own self. I'd be pleased to have Roy Wilkins eatin' lunch with us today, but he ain't no real nigrah. You and your friends in Washington want to ease your guilt about your black brethren? Then you fill your schools up with nigrahs, you move 'em in next door to you, have 'em three meals a day. You want integration, then you go right out in the streets and ring yourself a bell, holler for all the nigrahs to come on to your house. Just don't go hollering for 'em to come to my house, you heah?"

All the frustration of that conversation returned to me two years later in May of 1972 when Roy Wilkins' nephew, Roger Wilkins, a brilliant *Washington Post* editorialist, came for dinner the night of the shooting of George Wallace. I tried to recount to Roger the confusion I had felt that day, my inability to sort out and to articulate what I thought was right, or even to overcome a sense of fair play that made me admit that, though I abhorred what Wallace said, he had a point about me and my "limousine liberals."

Roger did not understand my confusion, but his companion Patricia Matthews, a strong-minded black friend, did. She told me that, at fourteen, her mother gave her a choice: "Pat, you can be a day worker, or you can learn something in school. If you learn, I'll mop all the toilets it takes to send you to college." Pat chose the latter. She is adamant that a college education does not mean equality and feels deeply for all the girls whose mothers could not give them alternatives. She understood that most whites are invariably still racists, even though unwitting; she knows that, like herself, I do what I can with the racial prejudices I have been handed. There was an exchange of sympathies between Pat and myself that I cannot really explain, but I wish she had been in Richmond that afternoon. I think she would have gotten through to Wallace where I could not. She lives it; I only espouse it.

Unfortunately, like every other slick-tongued southern male bigot in my life, the Governor got the best of me and may again in the future. It was not that he backed me down or changed my mind; it was that I could not back *him* down or change *his* mind. When the happy day comes that I can convert the male symbol of my childhood, I will have arrived.

15

Actually, there were other things that were not working out as I had hoped. I had only wanted contentment; I was not prepared to face the problems that come to the open-minded. I wanted to be something other than a woman doing a man's job. I wanted acceptance as a human being.

My blood rose with every statement beginning: "For a *woman* you have one of the best jobs . . ." "Women, of course, can't relate to . . ." "As a woman, your best approach is to . . ." I began fighting with the show's producer, the arguments always ending: "God damn it, Barbara, try to be more feminine. You are so strident, you turn men off, and women can't identify with you." Instructions to "act like a lady" were my personal red flags. The suggested soft approach crossed my eyes in fury. None of my counterarguments that we women did not all have "smaller brains and skimpier emotional stability" fell on sympathetic ears.

While this kind of rhetoric was becoming commonplace in New York, it was still blasphemy in Washington. But, as in the early stages of my political radicalism, I glommed onto the idea that I was as good as the next fellow and ran with it ad nauseam. I became more outspoken with my colleagues and superiors at the station—all of whom were male to the core, often a rarity in the performing side of television. I was as demanding that they reevaluate their attitudes toward women as they were that I conform to my traditional role. Neither of us was subtle in our suggestions that the other was wrong: I thought them archaic and chauvinistic, which they were; they found me a foot-stomping and opinionated bitch, which I was. It never crossed anyone's mind that all of us were conditioned by society to believe firmly the woman was the lesser creature. It was supposed to be enough that I could be seen and heard on television so that Channel 5 could say, "Yes, we employ women," just as they later came to expand their tokenism to include, "We hire blacks."

Eventually most television stations around the country achieved their minority quota by hiring "twofers," which is a trade expression meaning a "black, female, on-air personality," two television unthinkables, at one salary—a salary, I might add, that generally falls short of the "equal pay for equal work" cliché.

If what I was seeking was hard for others to understand, it was pretty fuzzy to me, too. All that stuff of my background was not for nothing: I felt second-class. Unlike the role of wife and mother, the role of television woman is not clear. I knew neither what was expected of me nor what I expected of myself. I was finding, alas, that I did not fall into either acceptable television category. I was neither a crack controversial debater nor a genuine sex object. While I was unsure I wanted to be either, I certainly was not entertaining men on camera and most assuredly not pleasing those who run the industry off-camera. Though I thought myself better than any woman on the air, I never thought I was good enough, an evaluation which became, I fear, the only point of mutual

[221]

agreement between me and the corporate television structure.

If my male counterparts made strong critical statements, they were "blunt" or "forceful"; similar candor from television women is "cutting," "catty," and "bitchy." A television man of strong convictions is wooed and pampered; he is a paragon of "strength," and "tough-minded firmness." Women who exhibit similar traits are "aggressive." Television executives beat themselves senseless looking for controversial, authoritative males, preferably those sufficiently aged and haggard to look distinctive, but the female counterpart is anathema. There are a few young, pretty, and engagingly efficient female reporters or interviewers, but once they approach forty or dare express too many contrary views, they become risks.

Marya Mannes, whose television exposure in the sixties was terminated, according to her words and my instinct, because she was too old and too opinionated, says in *Out of My Time* that television "harbors a deep aversion to controversial or authoritative females over forty. The gray temples and deepening furrows that are the marks of distinction of Walter Cronkite and Eric Sevareid are . . . marks of disaster in women of equal years and value . . . as fatal as the white crosses on the windows of abandoned houses."

I was not close enough to forty to wear the fatal white cross, but I appeared to be approaching it faster than I was gaining on television stardom. I decided to cast an ambitious eye toward the networks: the big time. That, I deluded myself, was what it was all about. Local TV was what was wrong: once I became a network darling, the attitude would surely change. Ego aside, I needed big-time money, too. Very few women's time is money in any industry, but it means very little indeed in the smaller television markets.

What I still really wanted was for some man to ride in on his white horse, take me by the hand, and lead me off to a new world. So deeply fixed in my consciousness was this fantasy that I still believe it is possible, even hope for it. But Washington has fewer white horses roaming the streets than other cities do, and I was learning that the ultimate price a woman pays for independence is the loss of her promised savior; only to the complacent go the spoils. Most men, it would appear, pay nothing but lip service to the female who manages for herself. The emancipated male will nod, shake an encouraging head when he discusses the new breed of women who can cope, but it is to the clinging, game-playing cuties who have emotionally never come off daddy's knee that the tangible tribute is given. Most liberal men will verbally champion the female cause, but these men who want to free women for a place in the sun, want them in somebody else's sun. It is a sexual variation on the old theme: "I like visiting liberated women, but I wouldn't want to live there." Fine and good for celibates and lesbians, but lousy for the likes of me.

There is almost no man tolerant, on or off the air, of "uppity" women. If every man in Washington had given me a crisp dollar bill prior to the following lecture, I would be solent enough to retire: "Now Barbara, for your own good— and I'm telling you this because I genuinely *like* you—stop being so fast, so quick on the trigger. Learn to edit your conversation, sit back and show your lovely teeth once in a while. Don't always get the point so quickly. Stop besting and topping men. Learn to be feminine and soft. Don't work so hard." God Almighty, how many men take another man to lunch and tell him, "Don't be so clever. Edit your intelligence"? I liked men too much to become one of them, but I also liked me enough to become what I truly was.

There were many women in the television audience who began relating to my confused charges that too much was withheld from women, that we deserved something more. They wrote, called, stopped me in stores, street corners, even cocktail parties—nothing like a cult, but straggly voices that in varying ways said, "Me, too." These women helped me endure the hostess who, upon inviting me to dinner, would jocularly chide, "Now, no women's rights talk tonight, okay?" Not entirely, but I needed and wanted to stay in the political and social mainstream of Washington life. I also found dining out economical; a woman in television learns to partake of all free meals.

Partake I did, not exactly satisfactory fare either intellectually or dietetically, given the new Republican crowd quietly ensconced in the Nixon Washington of 1969. At first I believed my absence from Republican dinner tables was attributable to my anti-Nixon politics, and much of it was. But Nixon's people did not fatten the calf for their own, let alone the prodigal. They simply did not entertain each other or anybody else. I met only those members of the administration the permanent residents of Washington found tolerable, and them only in the homes of the most socially secure hostesses. Regardless of politics, the professional hostess needed power figures sprinkled about her drawing room in order to stay in the party business.

Only a few of Nixon's cabinet, it seemed, could be made palatable, and those luckless creatures were trotted out endlessly for social functions. The others were well-kept secrets. One did not see the Haldemans, the Erlichmans, or any of the lesser-known administration officials who, in addition to bearing German names, carried most of the White House authority. One met instead Dr. Henry A. Kissinger, Harvard Professor, Advisor to Presidents, secret swinger. I caught his act before he became the token conservative in liberal Washington, the gay blade of Republicanism, the phantom of Peking and Paris, the Hollywood press agent's dream—before he became the first man of any political party to move Jacqueline Kennedy Onassis off the covers of movie magazines and tabloids all over the world.

I met the legend we now call Dear Henry in June of 1969, several months after Nixon's Inauguration. It was shortly after the moratorium on criticizing the new President had expired, and immediately before the world acknowledged that Richard Nixon had no plans for stopping the war in Indochina right away—that quiet time in the new administration when, like puppies at a fire hydrant, famous men sniffed each other out.

It was an unseasonably hot, dull June; the political cease-fire had given everyone some spare time—time to lose weight, read books, travel, ski, or do whatever was the personal pleasure of political types whose prime hobby was bragging about their accomplishments or justifying their lack of them. I had used the hiatus to visit a California health spa to tighten up my midriff, which I thought to expose in the popular bare fashions before either the fad or my muscles slackened.

There was a black-tie dinner given with flair and taste in the Georgetown home of David Bruce, former Ambassador to both France and the Court of St. James's. His wife Evangeline, an intelligent diplomatic wife, managed to dispense more American charm than the combined efforts of the entire Department of State. On this night she had brought together some of the best minds in Washington, sprinkling among them the odd and even numbers necessary to make a capital party memorable. There were beautiful foreign women, sweet young things of both sexes, glittering New Yorkers, cabinet members past and present, senators, columnists, and diplomats.

Dinner was served at round, draped tables scattered throughout the house. Seated between a pompous columnist and a velvet-suited New York fashion designer, I talked skirt lengths to my right and "the approaching welfare state" to my left. The columnist's political leanings bored me past the point of argument, he being a pillar of reaction whose opinions were unfounded and equally uninteresting. The fashion mogul, a subdued homosexual, was a fount of ready-to-wear information, a likeable but dogmatic little man whose sexual predilections troubled me not at all. His interest in an artist at an adjoining table left little doubt that his interest in me, as mine in him, was purely conversational. I was restless, and looking for something more interesting than projected fall fashions.

After dinner, the guests reassembled into smaller groups through which I wandered, searching for someone suitable for the long haul of the evening. In the main salon I found myself near former New York Governor and Ambassador to the U.S.S.R. Averell Harriman, who was engaged in a heated discussion with Kentucky's Republican Senator John Sherman Cooper. Both these legendary men are decent and well-intentioned. Both are also quite hard of hearing. They were arguing loudly on two entirely different and completely unrelated subjects.

I moved along to columnist Joe Alsop, engaged in the business of carving up Palestine on a French settee with the wife of a syndicated columnist who, I felt certain, was the direct descendant of Isabelle Archer in *Portrait of a Lady*.

In another corner, resplendent and haughty, sitting queen-like was Washington's all time status-symbol guest, Alice Roosevelt Longworth, a lady of vast years, humor, and intellect. Mrs. Longworth is always a delicious and easy conversationalist, thin, antiquely chic, and sharp in the best and most contemporary way. I never chose to compete with her; rather, I would have preferred to vie for the attentions of a dinner partner with a nude Raquel Welch, for the competition would be less keen. One never beat Mrs. Longworth at any game. This had been so since she took over Washington long ago with her father, Teddy.

A grand old gossip, she can extract from her listeners as much information as she gives. Refreshing in political Washington, which is so often like a Victorian house—stuffy with things unsaid—Mrs. Longworth will take pokes at the deserving with wit and dignity, before grandly driving away in her aging Cadillac with her aging driver, both of which are pleasant parts of the Longworth legend. Some of the most memorable gibes recorded in Washington come from her. It was she who devastated Thomas E. Dewey's image by likening him to the "little man on the wedding cake." She, too, slapped Senator Joe McCarthy verbally when most of Washington was engaged in licking his boot. Responding to this question, "You don't mind if I call you Alice, do you?" she said, "Senator McCarthy, my gardener may call me Alice; the policeman on my corner may call me Alice; all New York taxi drivers may call me Alice, but *you* may call me Mrs. Longworth."

One night driving back from the Washington International Horse Show, she and I were seated in the rear of her limousine, a lap robe over our knees, while she told me a fiery story concerning her longtime Negro chauffeur and friend. It seemed they had been driving through the snarled streets of downtown Manhattan when they got in the way of a New York cab driver. The cabby leaned out yelling, "What do you think you're doing, you black bastard?" Mrs. Longworth zipped down her window and replied, "Driving me to my destination, you white son-of-a-bitch."

On this night a year later, the petite, Dresden-like lady was already surrounded by a half-dozen Washington women whose habit, like my own, was to pay court to her and, not incidentally, to collect some of the best dirt dished in the nation's capital. I was too impatient to wait in line.

In the large entry hall of the Bruce home was Katherine Graham, who, in addition to being one of my favorite Washington people, remains one of the most powerful women in the world. As owner of the *Washington Post, Newsweek,* Washington's Channel 9, and sundry other news outlets, Kay Graham carries obvious clout. Though painfully aware that her empire was inherited, she plays down the fact that she took each of these businesses and built them into the powerful network she continues to control.

She was, that humid night, in the middle of a dozen and a half of Washington's brightest men, surrounded like Miss Scarlett at the Twelve Oaks barbecue. I have never been certain that Kay Graham believes these men would seek her company so exclusively were she not *the* Mrs. Graham of Washington. She has the personal magnestism to warrant the attention, but given the aggressiveness of powerful politicians and columnists who need her endorsement, her newspaper, or magazine, it is understandable to wonder if these same men would be attentive to anyone, regardless of sex, unless they wanted something.

Kay Graham, more than most, has learned a great deal on her way to being a person. Humility for one thing, how to laugh at herself for another. She has always been kind to me, a kindness that goes beyond the advantage of a handful of years. She has that capacity to put herself in other people's places, a rare grace in women dealing in power. To me she had shown an amazing ability to help extricate my foot from my mouth. I was once misquoted making a reference to her in a magazine. Horrified when I saw the article, I mentioned it to Joseph Alsop. No one chooses to hurt a friend, and only a fool would deliberately insult Katherine Graham. Joe suggested everything from a retraction to a lawsuit, but it was too silly a misquote to belabor. I sat down and wrote a note explaining the circumstances of the blunder, but, before she had received the letter, Kay phoned one night to say she had heard I was upset and that I was certainly not to be. I was to forget it, she said, and then proceeded to tell me an amusing anecdote about a similar gaffe she had made many years before and how the person had called to smooth her feathers. It was my first and only Washington exposure to that kind of class. I liked her all the better for it.

Kay was standing that night among the penguins of politics, listening and nodding. On the fringes of her group was a short, portly, curly-haired man with a florid face, one of the few without a cigar. Henry Kissinger had a passionless, bland look of studied attentiveness. He was being cultivated from both sides and did not appear bored by it. I circled the group, caught his eye, and with a crooked index finger, motioned him to follow me into the drawing room. He began to settle into a gilt chair. "Dr. Kissinger, let's sit over there on the couch where we can touch knees." We did, he Germanic and correct; I, coyly certain I was shocking the stodgy Harvard academician by my boldness, giving, I thought, the old conservative the thrill of his careful life. We complimented ourselves that each of us already knew who the other was and exchanged polite flirtations. Shortly, he rose. "I must accompany the President to the summit meeting in Midway in the early morning so I must leave. May I call you when I return? Perhaps I could take you to dinner?" I suggested that if the good Doctor could persuade Saigon's President Ky and Richard Nixon to take American troops out of Vietnam, "you can take me anywhere." He smiled and bowed. "Dinner will do."

So much for shaking up the academician-turned-politician. If I had indeed given the stuffy professor the thrill of his life, it did not show. Observing all this from her corner was the gleeful Mrs. Longworth. Before Dr. Kissinger had set foot on Midway, his name was linked romantically with mine. Even in my days of radical politics, this did not displease me. What I did not know was that I was only to be the first in what would become an overpublicized series of romantic escapades involving the President's Advisor on Foreign Affairs who, as Henry later put it, was the first in that office to dabble in domestic ones as well.

16

I would like to be above a dissertation on Henry Kissinger, to think that he and I are better stuff, that our friendship deserves commitment to private memory, that we belong outside the relationship of exploiter and exploited. Ridiculous! To ignore Dr. Kissinger is unthinkable. His personality and the extent of his power are such a part of the real Washington of the late 1960s and the early 1970s that he cannot be passed over. Moveover, my exchanges with him point up vividly my own Nixon-era confusion as well as that of a large number of political people. To omit Henry from a contemporary Washington memoir would be like writing of the pop culture and skirting the sexual orgy.

From the time Richard Nixon took office, Henry Kissinger was the solitary accessible power figure in Washington. It was as though the hierarchy of Republicanism caucused with the world press and decided the conservative image as well as the gluttonous public needed a key figure on which to focus during the reign of Richard Nixon, one of the most boring periods in Washington history. Had it been necessary to invent Henry, they could not have done a better job. Between the power of the President and the power of the press,

Kissinger became an overnight legend. They got a lot of help from Henry.

I make no apologies for liking Henry Kissinger. I came to terms with that a long time ago. Though I disagreed with, even loathed his politics, I had and have a decidedly friendly attitude toward him. Quite simply, as the man overrode his Dr. Strangelove stereotype, I stopped making fumbling apologies to liberals for consorting with the enemy. The enemy was Henry, my friend, and if you do not have my ability to rationalize the friendship then you may mentally shave my head as a social collaborationist.

Henry Kissinger has managed to associate with radicals, anarchists, journalists, the elected political figures to the far left, and the social parasites of whatever political leanings are currently expedient. I do not know what Kissinger's own party thinks of him. Those men and women who have lived within the Nixon mold and found Kissinger distasteful have kept their own counsel, for even in Republican circles it is unwise to publicly disparage a man so anointed with presidential power.

Kissinger is the second most powerful man in Washington, which makes him one of the most powerful men in the world. Aside from his war policies, his tastes and social interests have been decidedly progressive. He has sought the company of liberal politicians in their offices and in their dining rooms. He has been given a fair press, and if the press has not always adhered to the cultism created by ambitious Kissinger hostesses, it has seldom been vitriolic in its discussions of him. That he became a pain in the collective conservative fanny is someone else's problem.

In four years I was with Henry on only two occasions where he was ostensibly with his own kind: Republicans. One evening we were in the President's box during a concert in the Kennedy Center, alongside Postmaster General and Mrs. Winton Blount, and a top Kissinger aide, Alexander Haig, and his wife. When the house lights went up and the audience looked to the presidential box, Kissinger was recognized immediately and given silent tribute. Unless one is prepared to exceed me in the belief that all music lovers are Republicans, it must be conceded that Henry was an object of admiration from both parties in celebrity blasé Washington.

On another occasion, we went to a small dinner party at the Blounts' home, shortly before Blount resigned as Postmaster to run for an Alabama Senate seat. The Blounts' Georgetown house was filled with administration figures gathered to eat Alabama quail and other southern delicacies not served on Republican plates until the recent schism in the political South. After dinner the men were separated from the women to watch Nixon's televised address to the nation concerning his Vietnam policy. More addicted to southern cooking than to customs, I whispered to Henry, "I have no intention of joing a bunch of women upstairs while you and half of Nixon's cabinet are in the library."

"Just try to behave yourself for once, Barbara. Go *upstairs!*" This from Henry in the heavy German accent he has until recently refused to allow to be recorded.

For about two minutes I considered playing lady, but the lure of watching history with Nixon's cabinet got the better of my manners, and certain I would never be invited back without Henry anyhow, I went into the library with the men, pulled up Herb Klein's empty chair between the Secretary of Defense and the President's Advisor on National Security and thoroughly enjoyed dissecting both the televised speech and the interaction between Kissinger and his growing enemy, Melvin Laird.

Red Blount graciously offered me brandy and a cigar before we fellows rejoined the ladies for some old-fashioned parlor games organized by Mrs. Nixon's social secretary, Lucy Winchester. We played "hot potato" and did a little shimmying under a broom held level by enchanted Nixonites. Henry and I were the last to leave. I was not, of course, invited back.

The rest of my social appearances with Kissinger were made on the political left, and if he spent many other evenings in the bosom of his White House colleagues, they went largely unreported by either the press or Henry. It is well to understand that little that Henry Kissinger has done and thought has gone unreported by either the press or Henry.

Although he is a fascinating companion, Henry is a bit hot to handle for anyone from the left with real political aspirations. I was invited one night to a party at the Ted Kennedys', and when I called Kennedy's press secretary to ask if I might bring Dr. Kissinger, I was assured that Dr. Kissinger would be most welcome.

We arrived by White House limousine at the Virginia estate and were greeted by a large contingent of press and photographers, the Kennedy aversion to publicity being somewhat equal to Kissinger's—nonexistent. Joan was in a pink and gold brocade hot pants outfit, which she told me she designed herself and which I believed. She greeted Henry warmly as they both mumbled how much they had heard about the other and how nice it was finally to meet. Teddy was gracious but stayed discreetly away from Kissinger in the presence of the photographers.

I have not been there since, either with or without Henry, which closed the circle on Kennedy invitations. Earlier I had gone to Hickory Hill for one of the quiet dinners Ethel gave after Bobby's death. I had gone upstairs to her dressing room where dozens of photographs of a smiling RFK in silver or plexiglass frames hung on every inch of wall space: Bobby sailing; Bobby with his kids; Bobby skiing; Bobby with his dog; Bobby's doodlings, notes, letters, clippings. More than any other part of the house, Ethel's dressing room was a shrine to her dead husband—a room filled with reminders of his vitality, his prolific achievements, both as a sire and as a politician.

Depressed, I returned to the living room and joined a group of men that included the former Secretary of the Interior under Kennedy and Johnson, Arizona's Stuart Udall; he was speaking rather profanely of Nixon's war policy and likening it to Lyndon Johnson's. I asked Udall heatedly why he had not mentioned all these things before, why he had not felt compelled to resign his cabinet post under Johnson to draw attention to Johnson's war tactics. Udall, replying that he had only been Secretary of Interior, would not agree with my statement that he should have cut ties with Johnson—especially in the last days of LBJ, when his old friend and frequent host, Robert Kennedy, was putting himself on the political line to oppose Johnson—if his conscience had so dictated.

I pointed out that, instead, Udall had been repeatedly photographed giving tacit support to the Johnson administration while accompanying Lady Bird down the Snake River, up the Smokies, across the wide Missouri, and through every tulip patch in America, holding a shovel while Mrs. Johnson planted trees, and his tongue while Mr. Johnson committed thousands of American boys to death. I suggested that if Mr. Udall had found it consciable to keep his silence then, I found it consciable that he keep his mouth shut now. My denunciation was met by shocked silence.

There were other places to go, other places to accompany Dr. Kissinger. We became friends, and I suppose this is as good a spot as any to interject that Henry Kissinger does not truly qualify as a sex symbol. A bachelor, yes; a love object, no. For all the nonsense of Danielle Huebelle in her book *Dear Henry*, for all the Jill St. Johns and the cadre of publicity-starved starlets with whom he linked his name, Henry Kissinger is a ladies' man in appearance only.

He is power- and ego-oriented, not sex-driven. To every woman who claimed Henry's nocturnal ministrations, I paraphrase Gloria Steinem in her public denial of an alleged romance with Kissinger: "These women are not now, and never have been, old girl friends of Henry Kissinger." Certainly not in the Biblical sense, and given Henry's rigid attention to duty, his tight schedule, and his long-time devotion to a splendid and publicity-shy lady named Nancy Maginnis, I question a lot of the unbiblical ones. Henry, you see, enjoys Henry and in so indulging his interest, he gravitates to women who share among themselves and with him an appreciation of his charms.

No one becomes a legend without penalties. Henry's have been to have his actions scrutinized, day and night, by a tut-tutting public that appears to enjoy the sexual shenanigans of famous men a good deal more than it enjoys their accomplishments. I have to credit Richard Nixon: unlike Kennedy and Johnson, who sought to control the private lives of their people, he hired Kissinger and turned him loose.

I think he understood that when Henry shouted to bring on the dancing girls, Henry's only interest was in dancing.

Occasionally, when the publicity of an X-rated starlet was particularly intense, Henry would shrug when I asked how his "stuffy Commander-in-Chief" viewed his dubious Don Juanism. Above all else, Kissinger understands the legend business, and my guess is that he has deliberately courted gossip and speculation about his private life. While I think Henry's constant presence in what Richard Nixon called "the liberal Georgetown cesspool" ultimately has come to annoy the President as much as the increasingly frequent references to "*Kissinger's* foreign policy," both he and Henry appear to enjoy the colorful image of the administration's number-one spokesman and bachelor.

Nixon and Kissinger are alike in their squareness; both are puritanical and moral men who believe a woman's place is three paces behind the politician. She is little more than the good wife, mother, friend—never the "shrewd little sounding board" that Democrats patronizingly termed their women. They are docile little followers without whom the politician could not be strutting victoriously before the cheering crowd in a freshly laundered shirt, lightly starched. My personal interpretation of Nixon's grand gesture of triumph—throwing both arms aloft in a "V for Victory" sign—is that he wanted us all to see that Miss Pat, a good wife, has tended to her real duties: there were buttons on his cuffs.

I often heard Henry praise Mrs. Nixon as a silent patriot—a loyal and uninterfering female in a man's world of politics, speaking only when spoken to, and not sullying the cigar smoke with her personal opinions. Conversely, Henry referred to his ex-wife as "too strong-minded," a possessor of souls, so to speak. I rarely explored Kissinger's distrust of dominating females because implicit in the damnation of them was the suggestion that I probably belonged on the side of the former Mrs. Kissinger rather than on the side of the present Mrs. Nixon.

Henry likes women. Conversation with them is not tiring; they neither bore nor challenge him. Kissinger likes intrigue rather than confrontation, and while few of his political adversaries do more than pander to his position, there is always the danger that one of them might openly take him to task in a conversation—an unforgivable gaffe to Henry, who believes all power begins in the White House. It is his firm belief that he and the President know what is best; the rest of us are to be patient and they will announce our destiny. Given that paternal attitude, Henry is annoyed if put to the task of explaining things to lesser lights.

Excepted, of course, are his encounters with reporters and columnists, whom he thoroughly enjoys and frequently uses to his best advantage. He has a ready quip for the press, a group he has thought more his peers than politicians. He does not like to fall from favor with a journalist. He would go to uncommon lengths to mend a rift if one occurred, because more than any other powerful Washington figure I have known, Henry Kissinger believes in what he does and is religious in his desire for endorsement.

Henry has been schizophrenic in dealing with the press. On the one hand, he has encouraged them to act in the public interest, and on the other, he is genuinely hurt and confused if they misuse or criticize him. This is especially apparent in his attitude toward social coverage. He likes to indulge the press in its fantasy about his being, as he confided to the *Washington Post*'s Sally Quinn at a party I had for Gloria Steinem early in the administration, "a secret swinger." But when society writers went too far in printing something he felt was not their business, he would assail them, often calling their editors or writing complaining letters about the item that displeased him. Like Ethel Kennedy, Kissinger takes poorly any printed mention of his private life that he himself has not divulged. Neither Henry nor Ethel ever seems to catch on to the facts of public life: when you ask for the public's ear, you must endure the public's mouth.

Police reporter Maxine Cheshire, who turned her magnifying glass on society when she came north from Kentucky to find that big city papers hired only male investigative reporters, once wrote in her nationally syndicated gossip column that Henry had taken up with a skin-flick Hollywood starlet whose screen credits, for the obvious reasons, never mentioned a wardrobe designer. Furious, Henry called Katherine Graham and demanded a retraction. On investigation, Kay found that Henry had indeed asked the starlet to put on some clothes and dine with him in a flashy Hollywood bistro. Kay conceded to Henry that she would rather have her paper carry a story of him eating with Clare Boothe Luce, but that the story was nonetheless true and she would stand by her reporter. Henry related the exchange to me and appeared incredulous of Kay, who had said to him: "Henry, as long as you actually make this kind of news, it's fair to print it." Her suggestion that Henry had asked for that kind of nonsense left him puzzled. It left me with the impression he felt Mrs. Graham guilty of some disloyalty.

He can take more teasing than one would have expected of a man of his temperament. As much to assuage my own guilt as to pinpoint his, I would attack Henry's war policies and ridicule the things he stood for and the man he served. But regardless of how pointed my antiwar remarks were,

Henry always chose to accept them as though issued from the mouth of an earnest, errant child, patting my head with a guttural, "Is my little friend, Barbara, picking on her old friend Henry?" My stand against his politics never extended to avoiding his company.

On the evening of the massive demonstration in Washington opposing Nixon's decision to invade Cambodia, Henry and I went to a dinner hosted by a columnist whose public and private dismay with the Vietnam war was well known. The guests included liberal politicians and journalists who comfortably dined with Henry that night while youthful demonstrators, some of whom were their own children, were being gassed and arrested. Henry showed no indication that he felt any responsibility for what was taking place in the city's streets. Nor did the assembled group. While not much more brazen than the others, I did accuse Henry of invading Asian countries alphabetically. To my statements of sympathy with the kids in the streets, Henry responded gravely that "this will all be over soon." He suggested that he had certain knowledge he was not at liberty to impart. The kids, he admitted, were good and well-intentioned youths, but "misguided and uninformed." After dinner, the host's young son and his friends came in to report on the rioting in front of the South Vietnamese Embassy and on police action toward them and the children of the other guests. The party dissolved in genuine concern. One young man sought to comfort Kay Graham. "Don't worry, Mrs. Graham, the kids are okay. It's the cops who are in trouble."

"But," responded Kay in her hasty exit, "my son Donnie *is* a cop."

Such was Washington during the first part of Nixon's "Bring Us Together" administration.

Everyone in that parlor felt disloyal chumming with Kissinger while their kids revolted against his policies. But we pretended we needed an association with Henry in order to know what was going on inside the White House. The rationale was, Henry might not be perfect, but we had to stick by him for fear that worse things would happen if Kissinger were not around and Richard Nixon were left to his own devices. We all knew Henry was Nixon's own device, but he was also Washington's only source of information, the solitary access to high power. It was not our finest hour.

For every public linking of my name with Henry's, there were disproportionate benefits. He was wont to boast that he did more to advance the women's movement than any public official. To some extent that was so, for any accessibility to Henry Kissinger gave a woman leverage within the male power structure of whatever publication or television medium she worked in. I could be disrespectful of Nixon, as opposed to the war as a Buddhist priest, and as disdainful of the "establishment" on the air as I wanted to be as long as there were photographs of me with Henry in magazines and reports in the newspaper of being seen with him.

I threatened to quit "Panorama" once when ordered to work the day of the first Vietnam Moratorium. I was sternly reminded that I was *working* press and had a professional obligation to fulfill. I countered with the suggestion that we turn the two hours of the show over to dealing solely with the Moratorium. That proposition was vetoed, and I was threatened with the probability that my chair would be then filled by a substitute hostess. I replied that "being antiwar is a religion with me and I'm entitled to a religious holiday." When that did not alter the station's adamant demand that I "show up or else," I told them they could fire me, but that I intended to bring a lawsuit against them for a breach of my civil liberties. At the very least such legal action would have resulted in publicity unflattering to the station. I stayed home that day and my chair remained empty, but, then, so did the questionable spot I had heretofore held in the hearts of the management. However, as long as I enjoyed the assumed patronage of the sovereign Dr. Kissinger, I could do no real damage. Instead, I was trotted out to advertisers and visiting station executives and chucked under the chin: "Well, how's your boy friend, Henry?"

But for all the rewards in associating with Henry, all the commercial spoils of being "in" with power, there were for me an increasing number of public incidents more annoying than gratifying. Being constantly asked about Dr. Kissinger was not everything I could desire. Magazine interviewers inevitably got around to the question: "Now, tell me, what is Henry Kissinger *really* like?"

I got sick of evading the subject, tired of appearing on talk shows to be asked about Henry as though he were the only topic on which I could possibly be articulate. Just as I wearied of being identified in print as the "sometime date of Dr. Henry A. Kissinger," I dreaded that moment in television conversations when the interviewer would turn to me with his inevitable query. On the Merv Griffin show, Henry was the main thing Mr. Griffin and the other guests cared to hear about Washington. I was not there to discuss Dr. Kissinger, and I resented capitalizing on him. It was a matter of professional pride. Eventually, I made a point of explaining this before accepting a guest appearance. Before appearing on the "Dick Cavett Show," I told the production people I would not discuss Dr. Kissinger, which was, of course the first question Cavett asked when we were on the air. Annoyed to have come so far and be identified as nothing more than a movable part of the Kissinger harem, I snapped to Cavett that Henry was a nice enough man, but that it was painful to have to constantly justify my liking of the man while deploring his war policies. "Henry," I said "is one of the Washington tragedies of the Vietnam war. It is hard to reconcile his charm with his actions. He's a jolly war criminal."

Ignoble, disloyal, all of that—but I was sick of being pumped about Henry Kissinger. Unhappily, and uncharacteristically, Henry was watching the Cavett show that night, and two evenings later, when I ran into him at a dinner party at the home of columnist Rowland Evans, Henry proceeded to lecture me severely on the limits of friendship, to remind me sternly that statements such as the one I had made on the air, and others in print, were constantly thrown up to him by his White House colleagues. His coolness was punctuated next day by a handwritten letter. "In these trying times," he said, "friends do not turn on old friends."

I was annoyed that Henry could not understand the strains our friendship placed on me professionally, that he could not take his turn with the double edge of our relationship. I never responded to the note, but eventually Henry chose to forget and actually sought me out to make amends. It was the first time I saw him vulnerable or understood that, for all his rigid control and discipline, Henry could not bear friction with anyone he had decided was a friend. It was a weakness I tried, often unsuccessfully, not to play upon.

Fascination with Henry in Nixon's first term was by no means limited to women. He was much the topic of men's conversation. Like the burning issue of whether Jackie should have married a man twice her age, Henry's sexual prowess or lack of it was a frequent subject of discussion among officials and journalists. "Would you like him if he were an insurance salesman?" was often asked. This was like asking Jackie if she would have married Ari if he were a shoe clerk.

Kissinger and Onassis deal in power, and if honest, any woman will admit to finding it intoxicating. Power is the magic that turns tiny, portly, egocentric, albeit personable, men into dashing, mysterious sex symbols. This is difficult for male minds to assimilate and tough for them to take without begrudging. It became something like masculine group therapy for Washington men to ponder, under the disguise of disdain and indifference, the great Kissinger question: "Do women actually go to bed with him?" The *Washington Post*'s expert on foreign affairs, Chalmers Roberts, once leaned across the table at a large dinner and asked quite directly if I had ever gone to bed with Henry Kissinger. My dinner partner, Bob Silvers, editor of the intellectual *New York Review of Books*, and several other gentlemen at the table, leaned in for my answer—just as many reporters and readers have leaned in for an answer from France's Danielle Huebelle, who alluded to a Kissinger liaison in *Dear Henry*.

Henry's love life was then, and would continue to be, a source of great curiosity and much jealousy. To Chal and Bob and all the fellows in Washington who have asked me about Kissinger on sex, I give the answer Henry gave me when I inquired about Miss Huebelle's insinuations: "My God, Barbara, absolutely *no*. I scarcely know this bitch. My relationship with her is not one-tenth as personal as yours and mine." Considering the absence of carnal knowledge between me and Henry, it would appear that Miss Huebelle could have profited from a course in primary sex education.

Whether or not Henry has chosen to exercise his sexual prerogatives, his attraction for women is genuine. Aside from power, intelligence, humor, and perfect courtesy, Henry *listens* to women, an extreme Washington rarity. He has a boyish need to make up to his parents for all the years of humiliation and poverty when, as refugees from Hitler's persecution of Jews, they came from Germany to America. Henry has long been driven as much by their needs as by his own, and his gentleness toward them is an endearing secret he shares only with women. He is thoughtful and acutely sensitive to human suffering on personal levels. At my mother's death, he made a point of getting me out of the house as much as possible. "Come, my little friend, your mother did not raise you to brood," is a strange and kind statement from the impersonal professional who looked upon Vietnam war deaths as statistics necessary to balance power.

This complicated man could negotiate with Hanoi, Peking, and Moscow, using utmost tact, but on the other hand, he devastated a much protesting Frank Sinatra one night when we were dining in a Washington restaurant, by blurting out: "My God, Frank, I always hoped you had Mafia connections. I need *somebody* to take care of my enemies."

Proud, intelligent, sensitive, and yet a professed megalomaniac, Kissinger deliberately trapped himself in the Washington web and learned to live with it and love it. He grew to depend on and demand still more attention and power, but his official portrait is not yet ready to be unveiled. Henry is too complex for that. And I would advise all those who have found Kissinger detestable not to damn the official man without first having the pleasure of being prejudiced by the inner man.

I have lost patience after many summer night discussions in the Long Island Hamptons with New York "intellectuals"—a word used loosely in the Big City—who, in judging Washington figures, tend to look for nonexistent integrity in politics and to ignore the ruthlessness of their own worlds of theater, art, publishing, even the food establishment. There simply is more to the political story than the front page of *The New York Times* or the pompous ramblings of a stern *Village Voice*; more to understanding government than the comfortable option of choosing one politician or policy and damning the rest. Change through revolt requires a good deal more than a Norman Mailer shuttling to Washington for an afternoon in jail as though one man could, by his incarceration, stop a war so complicated it has bloodied the administrations of three presidents. It is too easy to glance back at the three years of John Kennedy's presidency and announce that he and his Irish Mafia did us all in. There was also much to be praised in the Johnson years, and there are many fine aspects of Nixon's administration. Retrospective judgments of Washington by those not actually present at the time of decision are unfair and often incorrect. The struggles and anxieties and pressures of the times have to be considered.

Perhaps the man who has suffered most from a one-sided view of his actions and motivations is Eugene McCarthy, someone who should need no description, but given our poor memories for yesterday's household words, he is best recalled as Abigail's ex-husband, the Senator from Minnesota who fostered the greatest political schism of the mid-century.

I did not meet McCarthy until shortly after Jack Kennedy's death. He had aroused Kennedy's antagonism because of his moving nomination of Adlai Stevenson at the 1960 Democratic Convention, and was not often present socially during the early Kennedy years. A maverick even within his own party, McCarthy was not possessed of the absolute loyalty demanded by either President Kennedy or President Johnson. Even as Senate Majority Leader, Johnson could never place McCarthy in his hip pocket, and if a U. S. Senator could not be owned lock, stock, and vote by LBJ, he was a natural enemy. It came as no surprise that Johnson rejected McCarthy for the second place on the 1964 Democratic ticket.

The evening we met, a cool spring night, I was seated next to the Senator in the garden of F. Scott Fitzgerald's daughter, Scottie Lanahan. McCarthy had lost no position of power at the death of Kennedy, as had many of the other guests. Nor was he gearing up to bask in the glow of Lyndon Johnson, as were many of the others, myself included. Neither fish nor fowl in the political preserve, Gene McCarthy was a pale, retiring, and politically not very interesting man. In my smug assurance of better days ahead with LBJ, I was not highly complimented to be seated with him. He was without his wife Abigail, whom I was never to meet in all my encounters with Gene McCarthy. He would always be alone. But there was something about him that night that was straight and honest, even in a drab and sexless way. He was distracted and aloof—a far cry from the sharp-tongued tilter at windmills whose later foray into big-time politics would make him magnetic to women on precinct as well as social levels.

Over the ensuing years I would see him change from frog to political prince, from Plain Gene to Clean Gene to Mean Gene. At the Washington opening of "Man of La Mancha," the orchestra struck up "The Impossible Dream" as McCarthy entered his box to the thundering applause of a packed house. It was then that he took on the look of a man obsessed with power. As he gathered steam in his campaign to unseat Lyndon Johnson, he came to see himself as others insisted on seeing him: a knight in armor, the salvation of us all. I had not yet fully accepted the fact that no man rules this country wearing clean white robes, that he must first grub in the dirt before he is allowed to act on his eventually compromised principles. Before McCarthy took on the petty and narrow characteristics that he himself had loathed in other political figures, I, like many others, thought McCarthy was a better man than Lyndon Johnson, that he was possessed of all the high qualities I demanded he have. I too thought the cold Midwest had sent us a political Christ. I am suckered in every time.

After the 1968 Chicago Convention, McCarthy became a target for ridicule and abuse. It was uncanny to hear the men and women who had ridden his coattails turn against him so bitterly. Politically, Gene McCarthy was turned back into the colorless frog.

In the spring of 1972, I was once again at a dinner party with Eugene McCarthy. He was separated from his wife. The evening was not glamorous; there were few important guests and I wondered aloud to a very distinguished, silver-haired stranger: "Who are all these people?"

"Well, I'm not at all certain myself, but I am your host."

Under the circumstances it was to McCarthy that I gravitated.

We left together. Gene was driving an American sedan with an old McCarthy bumper sticker, and it was strange to watch the man who had spearheaded a political movement weave in and out of Georgetown's Saturday night traffic, roll up the windows, and lock the doors, much as any suburbanite with car payments still to make. We went to my house and talked until early morning. McCarthy was not easy to talk to; I felt that a wrong verbal movement would frighten him off. He had humor, a sharp acerbic wit that was seldom self-directed. The bulk of his conversations were too abstract and philosophical to be warm exchanges but he was not, nor would he ever be again, that retiring poet I had met half a dozen years earlier.

He was bitter about the coming political conventions. "George McGovern is foolish, he can't win. He'll destroy what's left of the Party . . .," and "Hubert is nothing but a nice guy . . . Johnson plucked his feathers . . . made Hubert more anxious to please than God did . . . I'm sorry for him but he knew what was happening." For Richard Nixon there was little wasted energy, but the actor in McCarthy allowed his brows to lift, his breath to expel at the proper moments, his hands to go up in exasperation—gestures that said more than he had the interest to articulate.

To my announcement that I thought there was still hope for the world, McCarthy smiled tolerantly, the wan smile of a man who takes for granted that all is doomed. But I sensed in him a peculiar peace, not the tormented resignation of the failed reformer, but an inner coming to terms with himself. When I asked what he felt about his past political life, was he sorry, did he miss it, he replied that it was never good to be sorry. He was content to be the figurehead history will record as voicing American objections to a senseless war. I asked, "Would you do things differently another time around?" He responded, "It wouldn't make any difference, Barbara." He went on to talk about his days in public office, telling me: "The Senate is not the *end*, not a comfortable cave in which to retire or even to be used as a springboard to bigger things. It's a job, Barbara, like any other job. It's not sacred, and I never thought of spending my life at it." He went on to say that politics had been only a part of his life and that staying in the Senate, "to die there as though it were my just desserts," had never been his aim. The political arena, he said, was merely one of many experiences he had had or expected to have.

Like the dissident priest who will not condemn or dissect the Church, McCarthy would not speak of his broken marriage. He was circumspect about his future ambitions, about anything in his personal world. I was curious about this man who was able to drink out of the cup and set it aside, and I could recall no other politician who calmly and deliberately cleared his Senate desk and walked away. But he had no interest in talking of these things, saying: "You get tired of yourself after a while." He seemed bored and unenthusiastic but he was not unhappy. When he left, I thought him less a cold man than a private one. Unlike him, I was not tired of Gene McCarthy.

Afterward, I sat looking at his vacant chair and thought of exchanges I had had with other controversial and misunderstood men, particularly two that had occurred out on the front steps on different warm nights: Adam Clayton Powell saying, "I make a difference, baby, a big difference." And George McGovern telling me haltingly of all the unrighted wrongs, all the failures and achievements of other men—and my never dreaming George could "make a difference" or that he even wanted to.

17

I had not realized in my conversations about Washington, both on and off the air, that I tended to dwell only on men. One afternoon, after being in town for two weeks and monitoring "Panorama" for twenty full hours, Mama asked me where all the local females were hidden: "Are there no interesting women now that Jackie has gone?"

Of course there were, but they had so little influence that there was a tendency to overlook them. Important Washington women are, by and large, widows. The only problem is that, given the protocol of Washington dinner parties, these ladies need, as I do, a single male to balance them off in the largely man/woman, man/woman seating scheme demanded by hostesses. Consequently one meets a lot of interesting widows in Washington, and a staggering number of obscure extra men whose greatest social or political assets appear to be dexterity with the knife and fork. The best of these are the socially sought-after homosexual or the between-marriages journalist. The rest are bureaucrats.

No one is more dull than a bureaucrat. He is part of that faceless legion that works the lower echelons of government on a career basis, that swarm of correct drones that keep mammoth government agencies functioning from administration to administration. Most are self-important, imbued with the foolish notion they are necessary government clutter. Actually they are like red ants clustered on a floating log, each certain he is controlling the log's direction.

By law, bureaucrats can express no political opinions. My secret surmise is that they actually know nothing and conveniently hide it behind their official silence. While silence could become a refreshing fad in Washington, bureaucrats are uninteresting and painfully unlively, as nonopinionated people tend to be. They can be excruciatingly boring in their attempts to insinuate "privileged knowledge" and to imply an uncelebrated prestige.

Other government minions—secretaries and administrative and legislative assistants—who run congressional offices for often absent Representatives and Senators, who draft bills, sign mail, and deal with issues and constituents while the Member is off making the speech they wrote for him, stick very closely to their own kind, forming an inner Washington society from which they rarely stray and to which they rarely admit outsiders. The bureaucrat, on the other hand, integrates as actively with official Washington as he is permitted to. Except for the fact that their gender stabilizes dinner tables for single women, I find them dispensable.

The widows are another matter. They are accorded respect seldom found in a sexist town. They played the female's role in the proper way and lost their husbands through an Act of God. Their independence cannot be helped and is therefore excusable. Seldom are they ambitious beyond a social level, and so they do not threaten male egos. Without certain of these moneyed dowagers, Washington might even sink into the cultureless pit it prefers.

Exceptions on the list of widows are Alice Roosevelt Longworth with her impeccable political lineage, prestige, and wit, and Katherine Graham, who has enormous power and the charm to use it discreetly.

Another powerful woman in Washington for many years, Mrs. Frank Wisner—whose husband was highly placed in the CIA back in the days when highly placed intelligence men were respected—draws good people together, feeds them well, and enjoys their minds. Polly Wisner operates a tasteful communications center. In her house one might meet informally three past Secretaries of Defense, each talking about his different decisions, each offering his different excuses. Conversing with guests that span several administrations could be Stewart Alsop, Clayton Fritchey, Flora Lewis, James Reston, young State Department men, fledgling congressmen, and the politically oriented friends of Polly's sons, who some day will replace the influential men they encounter in the Wisner house.

It was there in the early summer of 1972 that I sat next to Senator Thomas Eagleton and heard him tell me he had always hungered after high office, "because my dad wanted it so for me and I wanted to do it for him." Young and nationally obscure, Eagleton confided to me that his ambition, if he could fantasize, was to be the Vice President of the United States.

The year before, I had been seated at Polly Wisner's with the late Dean Acheson who, in our lengthy discussion of Lyndon Johnson, told me that Johnson had once complained to him that in spite of all the good things he, LBJ, had brought to the presidency, he was still unloved by the general public. Acheson had responded: "You are not a very likeable man."

Not to be overlooked as a visible Washington woman is

Anna Chennault, the highly scrutable Oriental widow of World War II's Flying Tiger, General Claire Chennault. She runs both her mouth and an airline to admirable advantage. As the Dragon Lady of the Nixon administration, she was rumored during the Nixon-Humphrey 1968 presidential race to have advised the Saigon regime to stall for time at the Paris peace talks, to underscore the Democrats' inability to settle the war by either negotiation or fighting. This, so the story went, was to handicap Humphrey and give the South Vietnamese more leverage with a triumphant Nixon. I always thought this rumor wishful thinking on Mrs. Chennault's part, although in an interview she once heavily alluded to my ignorance on such secret matters. But it remains my impression that the Saigon government had long known how to dawdle at the peace table and needed no liaison with the Widow Chennault to know when to hang onto a good thing.

Mrs. Chennault's political adventures with the China Lobby, a special interest group with commitments to Taiwan's Nationalist China, has added to her power legend. She was credited with maneuvering the White House and the Congress over several administrations to forestall recognition of Red China. While Mrs. Chennault is unquestionably a distinctive female personality on the Washington scene, my own opinion is that as a person of influence here or points East, she had a definite impact on popularizing Oriental couture.

The honest observer must include Senator Margaret Chase Smith, but so seldom did she use her high office to redress the grievances of women that men found her acceptable. Regardless of sex, Washington reserves respect for the seat she filled. There are also some fine congresswomen, but they are somewhat victimized by the general Washington snobbishness toward the House of Representatives and are doubly excluded from the higher plateaus of authority by their sex. Then there are those women, usually securely married, who hold rather insignificant jobs, minor agency jobs of little influence, in various administrations. They are on a plane with the ladies who occupy desks at the Republican or Democratic national headquarters and who are dusted off every four years to show the electorate that the party has women on the team. Each is allowed a little publicity, generally during an election year, when she is trotted over the pages of the Sunday supplements to discuss favored fund-raiser party recipes.

Occasionally a few ladies are hastily appointed to do something or other around the White House when the cry goes up for political equality for women. Others are allowed to sit out an administration as Ambassadress to Luxemburg or as arbiter of culture for the Fine Arts Commission. It is always a woman who housemothers the mint. I guess I have met all these ladies, but I cannot recall.

The women's press consists of Mary McGrory, Washington's only nationally syndicated, female political columnist who is printed in a local paper. Except for NBC's Barbara Walters, who lives in New York but often works in Washington, there are no national female television personalities. Barbara once told me, "I can get a better grasp of what is going on in the world from one good Washington dinner party than from all the background information NBC piles on my desk." At a party I gave for her, she glanced at the crowd, remarking, "I could be the most informed woman in television if I had access every night to all these minds."

Public Broadcasting featured Washington's Elizabeth

Drew of the *Atlantic Monthly*. She also found that social access to the men in power gave her equal footing with male interviewers.

Among the best female reporters in Washington are Helen Thomas of UPI, Frances Lewine of the AP, Nan Robertson of *The New York Times*, and Meg Greenfield and Marilyn Berger of the *Washington Post*. Bonnie Angelo of *Time*, forced to write anonymously under the magazine's "committee writing" policy, is one of Washington's most acute observers and sharpest journalists. Other women covering the lighter side of the news also do valid reporting of power-mongers in their social habitat, making it a necessity, as several presidents have acknowledged, to read the women's pages to really find out what is going on in government. These women understand that rumor on the social side of Washington generally becomes hard political fact.

These widows and newswomen, along with those who hold elective or appointive offices, comprise the small list of Washington females known on their own merit. The rest are wives. They come as part of a package with the politicians and journalists. They rarely seek or merit special attention. A notable exception outside the President's family is Lorraine Cooper, the stylish and free-spirited wife of Senator John Sherman Cooper of Kentucky. She says and does as she pleases. I once asked her advice about handling people on the receiving end of an outspoken statement. "When I'm contrite," she said, "I drop them a note in the mail before the incident is gossiped out of proportion." She added, "In your case, Barbara, you had better hand-deliver the apology."

There is also Marion Javits, the fun and zany wife of Republican Senator Jacob Javits of New York. Marion once incurred a certain amount of indignation by explaining to a national magazine that she chose to live in New York rather than the capital "because Washington is a factory town." Mrs. Cooper and Mrs. Javits are pleasant exceptions to the "official wife." No other Washington wives have ever garnered the blazing notice given the Kennedy women or Martha Mitchell.

I met Martha Mitchell during Nixon's first Inaugural in 1969, at the home of Gilbert Hahn, Nixon's chairman of the Washington City Council. The Hahns were host to out-of-town Republican dignitaries, Nixon's new cabinet, and other lesser GOP luminaries.

In order to meet flesh-and-blood Republicans, I persuaded the daring and liberal Margot Hahn to let me act as a cocktail waitress. In a black mini-dress, white lace cap and ruffled apron, I moved among the conservative crowd unrecognized or unnoticed, except by *The New York Times'* Charlotte Curtis, who thought me more amusing than did Gil Hahn, from whose irate grasp I was constantly slipping in order not to be tossed out. Republican seeress Jeane Dixon gave me the once-over and predicted I would go on to better things. Her forecast gave me personal courage, for I was learning first-hand that politicians are not very nice people to serve socially. Elbowed, stepped upon, ignored as a domestic robot, I was never once thanked for my ministrations with the hors d'oeuvre tray. One gentleman, upon whom I unceremoniously thrust a cocktail napkin when he wiped his greasy fingers on the upholstery, stared at me suspiciously and said loudly, "It's high time we got those Democrats out of office if *she's* any example of the work force in this country."

Martha Mitchell caught my eye immediately. Quite shy, and obviously hesitant to mingle with strangers, she was wearing the most incredible costume of pale blue; everything was matching except her yellow hair. As I passed her some smoked salmon, I remarked about her later-classic, pointed-toe, stiletto-heeled, sling-back shoes: "They must be killing your feet, dearie." It was the only time I saw Martha Mitchell speechless. Later, she found out who I was and accused me of eavesdropping on a conversation about her new apartment in the Watergate. She thought I had leaked to the press the outrageous figure printed as the purchase price. I told Martha I had not been the culprit—but only because I had missed the conversation. "I would have repeated it, sure as anything, but I simply didn't hear it to tell." She accepted the double confession. It was one of the reasons I liked her.

The sympathy I felt for Martha Mitchell derived from her complete naïveté and candor. I think she was the most uncalculating person I ever met in Washington. Like a precocious child, she had not yet learned she was exceptional and that she was able to create excitement simply by speaking the unspeakable. Martha was fun, and I was delighted with her outbursts, even though I disagreed with what she said. I never questioned her motives; it was enough that she, a Republican woman, broke the silence of official wives.

Mrs. Mitchell's opinions were not always taken as lightly as Washington would have you think. Her attention from the press was too formidable. I recall the night after her widely publicized phone call to the editor of the *Arkansas Gazette* demanding that Senator William Fulbright "be crucified" for his stand against Harold Carswell for appointment to the Supreme Court. I was sitting in the Georgetown living room of columnist Joe Kraft and his artist wife, Polly. Bill and Betty Fulbright were the last guests to arrive. The Senator had a pinched expression on his face, and it was apparent that the morning headlines recounting Mrs. Mitchell's phone call had troubled and embarrassed him. It was an awkward moment for everybody. To break the uncomfortable silence, I patted the empty space next to me on the couch and called to the Senator, "Sit here and tell me it's not true that you and Martha Mitchell have been having an affair."

In a town where few men are outspoken, an unabashed lady is a delight, but I am certain Martha Mitchell's innocence was lost somewhere in her scrapbook just as mine has been. As with Dr. Johnson's talking dog, the press was fascinated by her, encouraged and baited her, wrote her into a household word before they wearied and turned on her. It was a typical Washington story.

At the height of her notoriety, both *Time* and *Newsweek* were doing cover stories on her. *Time,* unable to relax her for complete public exposure, invited me to have lunch with her and several of their top New York writers in Washington, to explore the myth of Martha Mitchell. We met one early fall afternoon in a private dining room of the Madison Hotel. Over cocktails, we were turned loose on one another. Our exchanges were tape-recorded. There was at that time a pernicious rumor that Mrs. Mitchell drank when she did her telephoning; she was considered something of a lush by Democratic detractors.

Although she had high color, Mrs. Mitchell did not strike me as a heavy drinker. "Martha," I said, "tell me how you feel about the gossip that you have a weakness for whiskey." She said, "You tell me first about the gossip that you have a weakness for Henry Kissinger." "That particular passion is overestimated," I said. "So is mine for alcohol," she replied.

I seriously doubt our conversation was what *Time* had in mind when they pitted us, but I liked the way Martha handled herself, and I became protective of her throughout the interview. She would become almost pathetically excited, and in her dissertations on Nixon or John Lindsay would go too far in expressing her opinions of both men. Several times I found myself passing her that secret signal that, by a narrowing of the eyes or a lift of the mouth, is a warning to cool it. She began to glance toward me before speaking.

The last laugh was actually on *Time*, anyway. Their Japanese tape recorder was not electronically equipped to record Martha's Arkansas twang or my Carolina drawl. The tapes sounded like a garbled soundtrack from "Hee Haw"!

Rarely is a voice from the opposition missed when it fades from the Washington scene, but I missed Madame Mitchell. For all her nonsense, I admired her candor. She was both confused and impressed by the attention she caused, and she came to believe her publicity far too much.

The Mitchells' exposure to Washington was limited; she had no real friends, and Martha wanted to be accepted by the people her politics isolated her from. She once gave a small dinner for Katherine Graham and left the entire guest list to Mrs. Graham—her poignant plea to make new friends. Her many unpublicized telephone calls were discussed at Washington gatherings, and the more sensitive recipients were quick to sympathize with her. They came to understand that Martha Mitchell was lonely and often quite frightened.

Loneliness in politics, I hasten to add, is not peculiar to Mrs. Mitchell. Washington is a friendlier town than New York, courteous to connected newcomers, a place where good friendships are possible between transplanted smalltown people. But the pressures of ambition leave little time for befriending a Martha Mitchell.

Keeping the Kennedy women from being lonely was another matter. They had the magic glamour that draws helping hands. Kennedy women were also more sophisticated than Mrs. Mitchell, better company, full of flair, easier to endure and to like. Certainly it was more exciting and rewarding to cultivate Jackie, Ethel, or Joan; they had youth, money, connections, style, and energy. They were simply more interesting people, and they did not disappear from national prominence when their political day had passed.

I leave the exploration of Jackie to the fan magazines. The force of Ethel and Joan as Washington women was more personally compelling to me. Probably Ethel has had the happiest as well as the saddest life of all the sisters-in-law, but it was for Joan Kennedy I felt the most compassion. My association with her went back to younger days, times when I, like most American women, followed every move of the women married to Kennedys and envied them their positions. Later, I would be sorry for them as they became the perfect examples of the pitiable debris left in the wake of political ambition. Every woman who pays a dollar to buy a magazine with a Kennedy lady on its cover should understand the waste and heartbreak that is often the lot of women married to powerful men. It may appear glamorous on the surface, but these marriages to high-powered, sometimes ruthless men are seldom happy. I have met few who will admit this. Most of these wives spend lifetimes disguising their true feelings, neatly hiding their misery behind plucky, pleasant facades. The woman with the big-time politician is permitted no complaints. She dare not say even to her closest friends, "He's drinking too much. . . ." "He's running around with women. . . ." "We're over our heads in debt. . . ." "My kids are coming apart at the seams. . . ." "We really hate each other, you know." Instead they play the devoted couple for the sake of a career that inevitably takes the man away from home most of the time.

The Washington wife may not look bad, talk bad, or behave conspicuously at any time. She is always second to her husband, captive to his drives. She can express no contrary opinions, and she is rarely permitted interests that conflict with her husband's ambitions. She is always on display, and she dare not take a lover. She can never pack up her children for a life more suited to her temperament, unless, of course, she is prepared to destroy a political career. She survives on the glamour that surrounds the candidate's wife, the Senator's lady, the President's consort. She has no privacy. Her children may not dodge the draft, grow long hair, smoke pot, or live in sin.

In July of 1972, during the televised press conference from South Dakota when Tom Eagleton admitted to depression and shock treatment, while George McGovern stood by in temporary loyalty, both Eleanor McGovern and Barbara Eagleton sat on the sidelines, demurely dressed, discreetly tinted and coifed, their patient, loving faces expressing a bland passivity my personal encounters with them belied. The very picture of perfect political wives, they accepted a fate they had no real hand in shaping.

Washington wives are not blameless, but their culpability is outweighed by the sadness of the lives they have given over to the prize of power. They trade their individuality for a political title, which was how I thought of Joan Kennedy. As a bright-eyed, politically innocent Scarsdale bride, she probably knew little if anything about what was in store for her when she married into the ambitious Kennedy family. For that matter I doubt any political bride is aware of what will be asked or taken.

I met Joan shortly after she came to Washington as the wife of the new Senator from Massachusetts, the sister-in-law of the President. We were frequently mistaken for one another, being of an age, both leoninely blonde and given to faddish dressing. Ed and I even lived in the Georgetown house she and Teddy had rented their first year in the capital. Joan's daughter, Kara, was in Bader's class at the Beauvoir School; they played together on weekends and saw one another during holidays in Palm Beach. In the summer, the little girls and two friends belonged to a play group supervised by a young teacher from Beauvoir. They spent the hot June afternoons before each family left for vacation exploring the tourist attractions of Washington, visiting local dairies and commercial bakeries. They took overnight trips to the Hershey, Pennsylvania, chocolate factory or went down to Williamsburg. The late afternoons were passed in the Kennedys' swimming pool.

It is hard to describe the problems of children who go to school with the offspring of Kennedys. Though I gave the faculty of Beauvoir School the benefit of the doubt, it appeared that much bending over backward was done to accommodate Kennedy children; the other boys and girls bent, too. I question that any of the parents deliberately imposed their own awe of the Kennedys on their children, but it was always present and often blatant. Like the rest of the world that worshipped the Kennedys, the school did little to discourage it.

Joan Kennedy's children were the less aggressive Kennedys. Ethel's brood were schooled in Catholic institutions and traveled in swarms, while Joan's Kara and young Teddy went to Protestant schools and led a calmer family life, more isolated and less competitive. It was the custom for Bader and

Kara to spend Halloween night with several of their school friends, sometimes gathering at Hickory Hill with the Robert Kennedy children. There was always planned activity for the children at the Kennedys'—a Palm Beach boating excursion on old Joe Kennedy's yacht *Marlin* with the elder Teddy as captain, visits to the ballet; even Joan's benefit tea parties where the little girls deliberately dirtied themselves up before prancing among the ladies of the press.

During a second-grade Christmas pageant, shortly after the first assassination of one of her uncles, Kara Kennedy was the thumb-sucking Virgin Mary resting her chin on a rubber Baby Jesus while little Johnny Lindsay, bathrobed as St. Joseph, waved feverishly to his father, a Washington congressman just elected Mayor of New York City. Out of forty children in the grade, it seemed an unusual coincidence that Lindsays and Kennedys were cast in the major roles. Bader was a fairy dancing around the manger while Lyndon, the son of Mrs. Johnson's social secretary, Bess Abel, stalked about as a shepherd. It was, I think, the only children's nativity pageant ever covered by *Women's Wear Daily*, the only one where parents had to peer around the *Daily News* photographer to see their progeny perform. None of this attention was lost on the less famous children of Washington.

Kara, a pretty, likeable, and highly intelligent child, was unchallenged as the class leader during the years she and Bader were in the same school. Followed close on her heels by a very willing Bader, she caused such mischief that Mama would often remark that their behavior reminded her of my own childish pranks. By the afternoon the girls started the family cat through the sudsing cycle of the washing machine, the glamour of having a small Kennedy underfoot had grown thin for the luckless babysitter who policed them. My own children did quite nicely wreaking havoc on their own without the aid of an imaginative Kennedy leadership. It was enough to raise two children in a home where their divorced mother was away at work. We did not need a third child whose discipline was equally impaired by frequently absent parents.

This, of course, underlines the problem of mothers who do not fill their traditional role, and the last thing I choose to do is give unnecessary leverage to that theory. While my absences were necessary, even respites I enjoyed, I never felt Joan Kennedy liked her forced abdication as a parent. She once told me she wanted a large number of children because she liked them and because it was expected of her. Candidly she added: "With a lot of babies, Teddy would let me stay home." Joan never had the same enthusiasm for public life the other Kennedy women had. She was the youngest and newest to the energetic family, and she was insecure bearing the Kennedy name.

When she gave one of her rare large parties, a garden dance for the nineteenth wedding anniversary of Bobby and Ethel, she was anxious to carry it off with the gay aplomb so natural to Ethel. She worried that the decor would not be imaginative, or that she could not "mix people up and have fun like they did at Hickory Hill." She avoided any comparison with Ethel's bouncy casualness or Jackie's elegant sophistication; she feared the inevitable judgment that she could never, as she would admit, "look as good as Jackie no matter what I buy," or that she could not keep up with Ethel ". . . she's the best mother I know, she does anything Bobby wants." Nor did Joan have either sister-in-law's ability to make close friends. The day of her dance for Ethel and Bobby, she called to thank me for a hanging fern plant I had sent, telling me, "I'm a nervous wreck. Would you please see that no one is left just sitting around . . . grab strange men and *dance*, please."

Unlike Ethel, who had a legion of devoted women constantly surrounding her to keep things moving, or Jackie, who never lacked for ladies-in-waiting, Joan was something of a loner. Her few companions were less outgoing and jazzy, and they were rarely involved in her social life. She was easier to be around than Ethel, more tolerant of risqué humor—Ethel bordered on prudery—but Joan did not have Ethel's knack for putting people at their ease or making the thoughtful gesture. It was Ethel who would remember to send flowers to the hospitalized employee, or the funny card and special gift to indisposed friends or acquaintances. It was enough for Joan to be generous with her time, to be interested in what someone else was doing, thinking, or experiencing. Neither woman seemed to have a mean or vindictive moment, but Joan, in her insecurity, was the more approachable, the more eager to please, and the more vulnerable. Perhaps the lack of close friends to seal her off from new acquaintances made Joan seem accessible, while Ethel's friends, like characters from an Elizabethan court, were always standing guard, cautious that some new face might crowd them out of the domestic corridors of power.

To take Joan's friendship, though it might be easy to obtain, would have been time-consuming. There would be the constant need to protect her in her childlike honesty, the burden of listening as she confided more than was comfortable. Like a breathless little girl, Joan could embarrass her listener with information, family gossip, and personal admissions that were difficult secrets to keep. Occasionally given to having the one social drink more than she could handle,

Joan, because she was a Kennedy and because she was so endearing in an innocent, fawn-like manner, needed careful friendships. It was simpler to keep the relationship distant.

Returning from an afternoon of skiing near Washington with two other women, I was discussing my earlier experiences on the psychiatrist's couch and listened in surprise to Joan naïvely implying that she, too, might be seeking psychiatric counseling. It was one thing for Barbara Howar to admit needing help, but for the wife of Edward Kennedy, it was quite another matter. I recall being torn between wanting to hush Joan and protect her from the repercussions of a public admission, and wanting to hear every juicy word.

I admired her for stating in a national magazine that she had been to a psychiatrist. She may have pioneered a trail for other official wives. At the very least she shed some needed light into the darkness that surrounds the emotional problems of political personalities. She told a mutual friend it had taken years to persuade Teddy to let her go to a psychiatrist and that only after the Chappaquiddick tragedy had she dared to admit to it openly. She said that Kennedys had to be very careful of "skeletons" and that it was only Bobby who would finally admit that his sister, Pat Lawford, needed help for her much-publicized drinking problem.

The Kennedys, it would appear, were also caught in the trap of "what other people might think," a sad attitude considering the number of their public contributions and personal tragedies. Life dealt them every conceivable blow, and I for one was comforted to know that so much power had been concentrated on people with the sensitivity to feel deeply, to look over the edge and still come through it.

Joan Kennedy often appeared to be frightened of her public life, perhaps bored and unfulfilled by it. She was by no means unique. Money, fame, and power are no insurance against unhappiness. I once heard Joan's friend Mieke Tunney, before her separation from California Senator John Tunney, pour forth all the sadness and resentment she felt as a political wife; she had no life of her own, had lived half of the one she had, and had never done the things she truly wanted. She felt trapped and disappointed. The glamour was not enough. Six weeks later she went to California and filed for a divorce. I am sure it took great courage to put her individuality ahead of everything else; it always takes courage to walk away from a powerful man on his way up and face an uncertain life alone. But since Abigail McCarthy and Ellen Borden Stevenson shattered the tradition of placing public appearances above personal happiness, the number of political divorces has been growing. And while I by no means endorse wholesale divorce in big government, I cannot help admiring those women with the strength and daring to break the suffocating pattern of the political wife.

Any disregard for the strict rules that bind wives of politicians and business executives has got to be a healthy step. Gloria Steinem once asked if I would add my name to a list of prominent women admitting an illegal abortion. Pleased to be considered prominent, I felt I had let Gloria down by never having had an abortion, "In my case, Gloria, the supply has always been equal to the demand." Since it was too late to comply on that count, I asked if there was anything else I could do for the cause. Gloria suggested I compile a list of official Washington women who would publicly admit to having an abortion. I explained that the subject was so taboo in government circles that I probably could not get up a list of official wives who would even acknowledge participating in the act that necessitated the abortion in the first place.

This is not to say that many Washington women have not had abortions. A close friend of mine, the wife of a high government appointee, was pregnant with her fifth child. Already mired in an unhappy marriage and engaged in a desultory romance with a prominent elected official whose child she thought she was carrying, she burst into tears one day confessing that she had contemplated suicide rather than have an illegal, kitchen-table abortion at the hands of a back-alley butcher. Her husband, dreading scandal, would not give her money for a safe abortion, nor would he sign the necessary papers which, along with the required signature of two reputable psychiatrists, would allow her to have a therapeutic operation on the grounds of "emotional necessity." We went through the medical section of the public library and memorized the symptoms of German measles. She made an appointment with a new obstetrician and fabricated a bout with the disease considered so dangerous to pregnant women. The doctor put her in the hospital overnight and performed a simple D and C operation. She was back with her children the next day.

Gloria Steinem and I discussed abortion some years ago with George McGovern in a small restaurant on Connecticut Avenue, where the three of us were having dinner alone before a special screening Gloria had arranged of the movie Z. McGovern was the first truly sympathetic politician I had heard on the subject, and I recall a certain sadness that he was in no position to do anything about reform. During the movie, which dealt with a forced military take-over of a foreign democracy, I leaned over to ask George, "Could that happen in this country?" His answer was, "Yes. If laws are contorted to make it appear humane for women to bear children they don't want, laws can be twisted to permit thinly disguised dictatorships."

Some time later, Edmund Muskie and I were arguing about abortion, my temper matching his. Muskie, with all the decency he indeed has, stopped me short: "A woman's body is God's vessel." In a national television interview I had with George McGovern during his early and seemingly hopeless campaign for the 1972 Democratic presidential nomination, I brought up Senator Muskie's anti-abortion stand. Muskie at the time was the front-runner for the nomination. McGovern, though he later regretted doing so, stated publicly for the first time that, were he President, abortion would become a matter between a woman and her physician. But when George McGovern became the Democratic nominee, he softened his abortion stand, watering it down to the level of other candidates. A woman's body is the politician's vessel, to be used and regulated as the political climate demands.

18

It became increasingly apparent that only the *problems* of Washington women were making an impact on my thinking. The women themselves were seldom in any position to influence me. There was no lady on the Senate floor for me to watch champion the right to abortion; there were only those hundreds of welfare mothers with unwanted children. I was also having problems trying to make my own small influence felt.

After two years on local television, believing I had learned my trade, I asked the management for a raise. I explained that I earned less than half of what the men I worked with were paid, that they had the advantages of the tax structure, not to mention live-in wives to tend their children and do the housework. I needed, I argued, enough money to support myself and two children. For this I was prepared to work nights as the men did, to do Sunday specials and news inserts, and to change the towels in the ladies' room if need be.

"Barbara, women in television simply are not paid any more than you are," my superiors told me. I countered that the grocer and the phone company did not give me a fifty percent discount for being a woman; I would be better paid, or I would quit. They were not threatened. They warned me, "Dozens of women would give their eyeteeth for your job and do it for less money."

Since I was keeping less than $5,000 a year after taxes, wardrobe expenses, and paying a salary to someone to keep the children, I called their bluff. Actually, there were close to a hundred women who happily applied for my vacant job. In a four-year period, I had twice walked away empty-handed: no alimony from a husband, no pig-nonsense from television executives—two giant steps on principle and nothing in my pocket.

Divorcing a career is not unlike divorcing a husband; you have to find another meal ticket. This time I had a skill but no takers for it. Legally, under my separation agreement, I could not leave Washington with the children; there was no other opening in the city for me to work in television. I spent six months living off what money Mama could send me and worrying about doing nothing. Deals came up and fell through. Eventually I sank into another confidence crisis. Again I was terrified I would lose my children because I did not have what it took to stand alone. For a woman who had believed all her life that she could fly if she flapped her arms long enough, I felt completely impotent.

It never occurred to me to seek a more humble life. I missed my platform and the public attention; I had no forum for my views, and I was not being so quickly seated at the restaurants' best tables. Drop from view in Washington and you are forgotten before you have gone. A lady in the supermarket stopped me one day with: "I beg your pardon, aren't you the *former* Barbara Howar?"

Small Edmond unearthed the four-year-old addressed, stamped invitations to the dance for Luci Johnson and Pat

Nugent and mailed them one fine afternoon. Not one recipient made mention of it.

The worst part of being a has-been is that you give off the aroma of failure—a deadly smell, particularly lethal in Washington where people are afraid to be seen in the company of a loser. Rejection breeds rejection. It also breeds creditors, which is how I came to be the first non-staff woman columnist in the style section of the *Washington Post*, a female allowed to write her own opinions rather than someone else's gossip. Ben Bradlee, the editor of the *Post*, let me file seven hundred and fifty words each week on any subject. He persuaded his Sunday magazine editor to ask me to write a long article on "How to Give a Christmas Party No One Will Ever Forget." "Why," I arrogantly asked, "would I do something like that?"

"For $500, kiddo. I hear you need the money," was his accurate rejoinder.

It was the same question I asked an editor at *Esquire* who suggested I write what I thought might be in my imaginary FBI file. He gave the same answer and I wrote both articles.

One of the reasons I never became the truly irate women's liberationist is Ben Bradlee. He picked me up when I was down, gave me space in the *Post*, worked on my copy, and smiled when the going was rough. It was he who asked me to review Lady Bird Johnson's *White House Diary* and he who took the criticism that I, an unpolished writer, was handed such an assignment. I tried in every way to be fair to Lady Bird, and not to let my personal feelings get in the way of an objective review. Alas, objectivity bores me; I do not believe in it.

As a text for historians, Mrs. Johnson's diary, nearly two thousand days of tape-recorded recollections macheted down to one thousand pages, had too many rationalizations, too many unstrung names of people whose only connection with the Johnsons was that they altered Mrs. Johnson's clothes at Nieman-Marcus or taught Bible to Luci Baines at Camp Mystic. There were too many incomplete vignettes about incidents of national impact, far too many defensive arguments for her husband's policies, and too few personal revelations. There were no real insights, no commentaries on the troubled times that characterized the Johnson years. While it was understandable and even admirable that the loyal Lady Bird was dedicated to the man whose political career she shared for twenty-five years, her diary was a one-sided, often blatantly slanted version of a highly complex period. For the Johnsons, people deeply concerned with history, it was a pedestrian and biased book.

It was with irony that I saw Mrs. Johnson peddle her expensively commissioned book in a flurry of commercialism surpassed only by Jackie Susann, appearing on pop talk shows and being crowded for autographs at a Brentano's counter. The former First Lady used the same tasteless tactics to capitalize on her high office that she found deplorable in others. With no financial need to jeopardize the dignity of a First Lady, one can only wonder what motivated a chatty, self-serving book only two years after her husband had left office. One could also wonder the same thing about Lyndon Johnson's million-dollar *Vantage Point*. Neither book would accurately serve future students of history nor, for that matter, were they monetarily rewarding to their publisher. The books, like the era they recalled, were not popular.

Three weeks of conscientious reading and research went into reviewing Mrs. Johnson's mammoth manuscript. I carried it with me everywhere and had a recurring nightmare that I was Fay Wray carrying around King Kong. That the book was lighter in content than weight was something I was obliged to say in my review. Bradlee personally edited the copy, earning gratitude from me and a cactus plant from Mrs. Johnson's old staff chief, Liz Carpenter, who was monumentally affronted that I had reviewed the diary. Later, one of the book's editors confided that my critique was, unhappily for his bookkeeper, an accurate accounting. The *New York Times Book Review* carried a glowing piece on Mrs. Johnson's book by Marya Mannes, whom I later asked why she had praised it so highly. To my acute disappointment, the brilliant Mrs. Mannes responded cryptically: "As you get older, Barbara, it is often easier not to be controversial." I hope some day to acquire Mrs. Mannes' comfortable wisdom or, at the very least, have her review a book of mine.

Columns are part of what is wrong with journalism; it just is not possible to write something worth reading every two days. If a columnist has one good article a week, he is better than average. The other two are generally space-fillers. My weekly column hung over my head constantly. If I actually had something to say, it did not always stretch or confine itself to a block of seven-hundred-and-fifty words. One column took me days, and I no sooner finished than I was faced with the whole ordeal again. Someone told me it took Mary McGrory six hours to write one column, and while I think the bearer of this information sought to comfort me, my response was one of awe: "Only six?"

No matter how many opportunities Ben Bradlee gave me, no matter how often Jack Chancellor would think up "a great story for you to do for *Look* on Billy Graham," there was not enough money to live on. Art Buchwald sat me down in the Sans Souci restaurant one day and suggested I had a talent for running my mouth, adding, "You may as well get paid for it." He convinced me to go on the lecture circuit and set me up with the New York agency that handled his schedule. He gave them a couple of flattering quotes about me for use in their brochures and explained carefully to me the hazards of lunching and lecturing in a roomful of women. Art, a resourceful speechmaker, told me what women's groups wanted to hear about Washington and helped me think up four snappy titles. He explained that one uses the same speech for each title. At the top of the list was "The Washington Nobody Talks About," dubious lure considering that my version of secret Washington conversation dealt mostly with women's rights, and women in television and politics.

Fully launched, I flew on more obscure airlines and stayed in more remote hostelries than Duncan Hines ever dreamed of recommending. From Madison to Pittsburgh, I ate chicken—salad, croquettes, creamed, à la king, baked, broiled, fried, or curried—with thousands of "involved ladies," Junior Leaguers, Town Hall groups, afternoon literary societies, and women's clubs. I addressed school teachers in North Dakota and homemakers in Minneapolis, any luckless group with time and money to hear me out. I appeared on dozens of television shows. I was interviewed by reporters and questioned by the audience, all of them apparently consumed by one overwhelming question about their national capital: What is Henry Kissinger really like? Nothing else seemed to matter, and with the exception of a very knowledgeable crowd of young women in Cleveland, the ladies appeared to enjoy their own conversations a good deal more than mine.

In Denver, a handsomely dressed matron told me her nineteen-year-old daughter, with no narcotics record and not traveling with suspected possessors, had been subjected to a random gynecological examination by a customs woman on returning home from a vacation in Jamaica. This complaisant mother, who knew little and cared less about civil and personal liberties, thought her daughter's reproductive organs fair game in the war against crime: "If it will halt marijuana smuggling, then it's my child's *duty*." The apathy was overwhelming.

I do not know where Mesdames Friedan, Steinem, Millett, and Greer got their idea of a grassroots women's movement in America—surely not from my crowd on the lecture circuit. The impassioned plea that women can make a difference usually fell on indifferent ears. The women's issue was not a burning one in suburban America. They were comfortable and financially secure matrons, generally distrustful of successful career women and frightened that a real change in the role of women would force them into a job market they were unskilled to enter. They equated emancipation with a loss of femininity and feared that it would turn them into man-hating lesbians.

Many of these women would nod in agreement on the principle of equal pay for equal work, but shrug indifferently over the inequities in the education of women and the discrimination in employment and advancement on the basis of sex. Any discussion of problems beyond these would be met with fearful or hostile stares.

To a stunned crowd in Grand Rapids, I elaborated on the evils of illegal abortion only to have it slowly dawn on me that most of my audience was well past menopause and could not have cared less. But I learned a valuable lesson from these women all over the United States: what heated up New York and Washington merely wilted the hinterlands. The

East Coast was neither the beginning nor the end and our personal furies were not currently theirs.

I despised the lecture world—that unfathomable sea of solid faces under flowered hats, and those talcumed bosoms that heaved indignantly at any suggestion that all was not well everywhere else. Only occasionally would there be someone like the Akron widow who stood up and told the audience that, qualified by her training, she applied to a rubber factory for a bookkeeping job, only to be told, "Madam, with six children to care for, you cannot afford to work."

She replied, "With six dependents, I can't afford not to work."

After a lecture I would fly back to Washington, stop at the supermarket, go home and cook dinner for my children, who had been left all day with a baby sitter. I would worry about the direction of my life, depressed that I had just spent an entire day with two thousand women without once leaving them with any new thought that did not involve Henry Kissinger. Weighing my time and energy against the small personal and financial returns, I retired my speech to a bureau drawer and put an end to my career as lady lecturer. The lot of the call girl is better. Never facing an unenthusiastic audience, sure of her talents, and working mostly at home, she gets a higher fee and manages to avoid both the Internal Revenue Service and an overnight stay in Fargo, North Dakota.

19

Although I thought nothing could be worse than lecturing, I had not yet run up against the David Susskinds. Robert Bennett, the Washington station manager who first put me in front of a television camera, had been promoted to Metromedia's New York station, WNEW. He had long tried to package a syndicated nighttime talk show with women as hosts, a unique attempt to use females on prime-time television in a capacity other than singer, dancer, clown, or dramatic actress. Bennett's idea of a feminine Cavett, Carson, or Frost was so radical that he ran into untold programming complications. Originally, he had hoped to pair me and Gloria Steinem to show that women had something more to sell than detergents, deodorants, or helpful hints on how to use yesterday's leftovers in a thrifty casserole. Unfortunately, Metromedia had been hit by a financially crippling strike which lasted five months, only to be settled in the middle of Mr. Nixon's 1970 recession. There was no money for an experimental show, which was how David Susskind came into my life.

I had been on his show twice and had interviewed him on "Panorama." He was apparently professional, certainly commercially successful, and it seemed a splendid solution that his Talent Associates should take over Metromedia's plans for Gloria and me. Susskind would produce the show, package it with a sponsor, and sell it nationally; we were all to live happily ever after collecting residuals. Susskind insisted that the format be expanded to include a third woman, his wife Joyce, who had been on Canadian television before marrying him. She wanted something to do, and, in her words, she turned to David one day and said, "Daddy, buy me a show." Daddy did.

After unsuccessful meetings in New York, Gloria Steinem turned to me one afternoon and said she could not work with Susskind, that he was incapable of seeing women in any role other than sexual, that Mrs. Susskind had reached her intellectual peak doing a Maxwell House Coffee commercial, that she, Gloria, was walking out the door and that I would be a stupid ass not to do likewise.

Stupid Ass and Joyce Susskind did the pilot for the "Joyce and Barbara Show" in Philadelphia in November of 1970, but not before adequate indication of things to come. I was in New York auditioning for CBS' "Sixty Minutes" with Mike Wallace when Mr. Susskind tracked me down, demanding I sign and return my "Joyce and Barbara" contract. "David, I can't sign a five-year contract; I could hardly stay married that long." He suggested I cross out the five-year clause and write in a three-year one. When I told him I could not sign away that much of my life either, Susskind flew into a rage, referring to me over and over with the pool-hall slang for women's sexual organs, adding that I was "stupid and ignorant," undeserving of the big break he was giving me, permitting me "to work with a *star* like Joyce." Further, he could "push a button and get twenty women more qualified than you who would fall on their backs for the chance to work for me. I can make a star out of you or anybody else . . . I don't take this shit from *anyone*."

"I don't either, David," I said. "It may be the one thing we have in common. If you want to play Henry Higgins, you get yourself a nice waitress from Howard Johnson's. Make her a star, but count me out."

I got on a shuttle and came home. Washington might be a conniving town, I figured, but it was a place of some civility. I was at least accustomed to being addressed by my given name.

Money reunited us: Susskind, because he had sold the show to the William Estey Ad Agency for a sizeable sum with me as part of the package, and me, because I was stone, cold broke and needed work more than endearing names. Mama, with her cat-like intuition, cautioned me not to become involved again: "Something good will happen for you, Barbara. Don't tie yourself up with those people."

Actually, Mama was still disappointed that Jackie Kennedy had gotten to Aristotle Onassis before me; she was convinced he would some day meet me and realize his grave mistake. In the meantime, she preferred I bone up on my Greek unless I could have my own show, which she was convinced I could handle alone. It had never struck her as proper that the show should bill Joyce above me. "You even come first alphabetically," she said. "Working with Joyce on her husband's payroll is a mistake, Barbara. The only way to work a husband and wife team is for *you* to be the wife."

But then the phone was cut off and the fuel company notified me they could make no winter delivery until their bill was paid. Mama gamely wrote a check from her next month's household allowance, sent me to Elizabeth Arden for a complete overhaul, and drove me to Philadelphia.

George C. Scott, bearded and remote, was our guest for the pilot show, owing, I think, to a longtime obligation to Susskind. It was one he grimly discharged. There had been no real preparation for the show. It was taped in a rented Philadelphia television studio to cut New York costs, and none of us seemed to have any idea of a format. Susskind's major concern, other than the cost of the set—clear plastic chairs backed up by hundreds of twinkling little Japanese lights that gave us the look of Park Avenue at Christmas—was to console, convince, and placate what seemed to be the entire office force of the William Estey Advertising Agency. The ad company's boss clapped my back every time we passed, urging me to call him "Duke." He had brought all his gang to Philadelphia, their wives, relatives, and neighbors. Old Duke's wife had been an army nurse before signing on with him, and while there was no encouragement to call her Big Nurse, it was how I thought of her as she gave me untold advice on the intricacies of television. Too late, I learned that she ran Duke and Joyce ran David.

George Scott was sport enough to make some ten or twenty entrances to the set by a rather impossible circular ramp down which he would bound in his front-zippered jump suit. Between theatrical successes, Scott tends to gain weight, and in his electric-blue coveralls he looked more like a healthy Eastern Air Lines ground crewman than the highly talented actor he is. He also has an admitted and publicized affinity for alcohol which he indulged that night, in some hope, I suppose, of dimming his sensitivities to the chaos and confusion that accompanies a pilot show.

We started and stopped the tape dozens of times, with

Susskind popping onto the set with the wild regularity of Groucho Marx's famed rubber duck which appeared whenever someone said the "magic word." For Susskind, any reference to politics or women's rights was the magic word. He would bounce in from the control room, raging, "Talk like that won't sell this show, Barbara. Now start again and keep it *light*."

It took six hours to tape a thirty-minute pilot. Susskind took me aside several times. "This show has got to have *sex* to sell. Quit being so heavy, Barbara. Get back out there and *be feminine*. Give this show some *sex*."

"But David, I thought we agreed this would be an opportunity for women to really *say* something."

"Look, Barbara, you can say something, or you can talk on subjects that won't alienate men. The things you think are important won't sell. Stay off serious subjects, or I'll replace you tonight." Then he softened, "Barbara, just let Joyce set the pace of the interview; follow her lead. This pilot is only to be shown to simple-minded station managers around the country and they want *femininity*. The Scott show will never run as a part of the series. It's just for selling purposes. No one will ever see it once we've sold the package."

And so we stumbled through an evening of unrelieved tripe, starting and stopping, ending the session only before the audience and the performers passed out from fatigue and Scott from something else.

We adjourned to one of the big hotels that help make Philadelphia a questionable Eastern Seaboard stop. The suite was full of admen, Duke, Big Nurse, the whole Madison Avenue group. Everyone called me "Barbara, baby," and said I was "a smash." That they were smashed was more accurate.

It was a lousy pilot. I thought so; the beleaguered producer, impotent working under Susskind, thought so; George Scott thought so. I had been particularly bad, overly cute with Scott—chatty, giggly, talking "big star sex appeal," silly, gushy, and full of double meanings. The final tape showed me cooing over George while I ran the jumpsuit's zipper up and down his stomach. The pilot screamed that women should stay in the bedroom where they belonged.

Nevertheless, the buyers were anxious to air the "Joyce and Barbara Show" immediately. We opened in San Francisco with the only available tape, the Scott pilot. The reviews were ruthless, but accurate. We were shredded by those critics with enough sense to see the production as a silly, sex-oriented commercial exploitation of women. The pilot that was never to be aired was the show that set the pace in city after city. In the aggressive role, I came in for the lion's share of the viewers' disaffection. I was stigmatized as sex-oriented and acid-tongued, adept at banalities and zippers.

Joyce, a genuine candy-box beauty and a camera man's delight, fell happily into the demure, kind, sweet, and gentle hostess stereotype, hands crossed primly in her lap, smiling serenely, the loving wife and dedicated mother. The more bovine she became, the more bored with it I was. Eager to do anything to quicken the pace, I would create a controversy by saying something outrageous, and dropping sexual double entendres until, finally, I worked myself into a twenty-six-week rut that I was incapable of escaping. I would do anything to liven up that show, and it came to be expected of me. Often we would stop the cameras, and I would be told to "hit harder," while Joyce would smile gracefully through it all. She began making on-camera remarks about my "preoccupation with sex," until one night, interviewing Dick

[284]

Cavett, she gratuitously said to Cavett on the air that he should be tolerant of me: "Barbara is our sex authority, Dick."

Dick replied, "And just what is it you are an authority on, Mrs. Susskind?", making me a life-long Cavett fan.

We settled into a working schedule. I would fly into New York, spend the afternoon in a production meeting in Susskind's office, and tape the show that evening. There were many such evenings of confusion and clutter, of living out of a suitcase and never having everything with me I needed, while Joyce arrived with her personal maid, her wardrobe carried by a liveried chauffeur, and a personal hairdresser hovering over her as she expertly applied make-up. I detested make-up and refused to wear any until ordered to do so: "Your paleness makes Joyce look over-painted."

Scaasi, a New York designer, was signed on to do the show's wardrobe. His creations were lovely on the diminutive Joyce but impossible on me. I looked like a woman in a magazine advertisement lamenting that she had "forgotten to look for the Sanforized label." I bought my wardrobe in Ohrbach's and Alexander's. I recall coming out of Bloomingdale's late one day, loaded with paper shopping bags, to find it dark and sleeting with no sign of a vacant cab. I sat on the curb hugging my packages, chin on knees, tears streaming down my cheeks—and laughing. It was, I said aloud to Lexington Avenue, not one bit different in the big time than it was on Washington television.

20

Three weeks before beginning production on the show, I had brought Mama to New York from a hospital in North Carolina where she was suffering increasingly from osteomyelitis, a slow disintegration of the spinal bones. She was in constant agony and needed increased sedation. We decided to do something about it before, as she told me, "I die from an overdose of pain killers."

She was examined by a Park Avenue specialist, who told her the chances were better than four to one that she had cancer of the spine. She should undergo surgery immediately. It was, however, three weeks before she could be scheduled into the operating room in Manhattan's St. Luke's Hospital.

Overcome with fear, we returned to Washington to wait. Mama and I passed those three weeks joined in an unusual love, even compared to an adult lifetime of extreme closeness. Together night and day, we took long walks and never stopped talking. My friends came to dinner often, diverting Mama, talking politics and Washington personalities far into the night. Other friends would take her to lunch to spell my vigil and give me time to prepare for the "Joyce and Barbara Show," which would begin taping the day of Mama's operation.

Once in the grip of alcoholism, Mama had stopped drinking years before, but I convinced her to try some wine; it relaxed her. She was a product of a bourbon society, but she managed to acquire a taste for vintage Bordeaux, telling friends how much she liked it, how different it was than she had imagined. "I always thought," she said, "that wine was something people drank when they couldn't afford whiskey."

She was violently opposed to narcotics, even those medically dispensed, and had always sent me early-morning special-delivery letters filled with local newspaper clippings warning of the evils of marijuana. I told her that Alice Longworth had declared it was silly to worry about dope addiction at her age and that she had tried smoking some pot. I bought Mama a plastic bag of unrefined marijuana and gave her a tea strainer, tweezers, and three plastic pill bottles. She would strain out the twigs and put them in one vial. In the other she would drop the tweezed seeds which she planned to plant in her garden back home to "turn on the bridge club." In the third bottle she stored the smokable product. She boiled the twigs to make tea. She said it helped her sleep.

Clumsy at first, Mama became expert at rolling cigarettes, later doing it with one hand, licking the cigarette papers and talking at the same time. Words like "pot" and "stuff" became an easy part of her vocabulary. I was the "pusher" and she would "roll a joint" to "turn on." I was far from being the old dope peddler, but introducing my silver-haired southern mother to the suburban joys of pot was one of the best things I did for her. It gave her more peace and comfort, she said, than "any of those needles they shot me full of in the hospital." Unfortunately, my mother, the junkie, feared being "busted" and took to hiding her "stash" in so many different places that she actually spent more time searching for marijuana than smoking it.

On the day she was to check into the hospital, we arrived in New York by train in the midst of a snowstorm, Mama and I hailing cabs and dragging suitcases, then riding silently into the city's slum area to the gloomy St. Luke's Hospital. Mama sat looking out the window, as if it were her last glimpse of city streets, and holding in her lap a giant bottle of Elizabeth Arden lotion the children had bought and decorated with purple yarn and funny handmade cards telling her to get well before she got sick. With more bravado than we felt, she and I spent four days in the hospital before the operation. This period, we were told, was for the residents to work up Mama's charts, run tests, and do all the mysterious things hospitals find necessary and patients find expensive. In truth, other than an occasional sleeping pill or thermometer, no one from the hospital came into her room except to bring flowers or food.

We were beyond fear. We sat watching television, alternately silent, then bursting into hysterical conversations. Somehow we laughed a great deal, Mama pausing to remind me of things I should do if she did not come out of the operating room: "See that all my plants are given to people who will water them . . . Make sure your father does this . . . Tell your sisters that . . ." I never loved that courageous lady more than the day before the operation. She put her closed fist over my hand as I was leaving for the night and pressed $740 into my palm. "This is some money I've been saving to have my face lifted," she said, "but you need it more. You buy whatever you need. I don't want you looking like Joyce Susskind's poor relation."

[288]

My sister Charlsie arrived from South Carolina the night before the operation. We were at the hospital the next morning at five to spend an hour with Mama before they took her away on a rolling stretcher. I was to begin taping "Joyce and Barbara" that night—the Susskinds' schedule required that it not be postponed—and Mama's main concern was that I be rested for the show. "You are to get in this bed," she said as they lifted her out of it, "and sleep while I'm downstairs. And you, Miss Charlsie, are to take my Saks credit card and buy yourself something nice to wear to Barbara's show. She'll need you."

Puddin, my older sister in Connecticut, was commanded to wait out the operation in her office. "You can't afford to hang around the hospital," Mama said. "You come into the city after work. I need to know you're with Barbara tonight. That's the best thing you can do for me; there's nothing for you to do here, and you know how to organize your sisters. You see to them for me." Her last words as they wheeled her into the elevator were: "You be your own sweet self tonight, honey, and you'll be just fine." To Charlsie: "Stay by your sister. Don't let those Susskinds run over her. Remember everything that happens, so you can tell me tomorrow." She told us both how proud she was of all of us, that she loved us more than we knew. She was giving us the thumbs-up sign when they closed the elevator doors.

Charlsie and I went back to the empty room. From six-thirty until four in the afternoon, we sat. Our only diversions were the constant phone calls from Puddin in Connecticut. At four Charlsie put me in a cab for Kenneth's Hairdresser —a twenty-minute crosstown drive I do not recall. I was completely surprised when the driver slid back the glass partition: "Hey, lady, I said we're here. You okay?"

Charlsie phoned to tell me the frozen section had come back from the pathologist, there was no cancer; they were operating, doing a spinal fusion. Exhausted, I went off to the television studio, to the Susskinds, to our first guests, Truman Capote and David Frost. I was the first of two females to break into nighttime television, and I looked more like the last woman to get out of Buchenwald.

I remember little of the taping. My hands trembled so that the director told me he would have to keep the camera off me as much as possible. I was impatient with David Frost as he answered all conversation with pointless anecdotes. I was full of relief and affection for my own mother, and I asked Frost about his publicized closeness with his mother in England who flew to the States often to visit him. Frost mistook the interest as a suggestion of something unnatural, asking off-camera if I were implying some Oedipal-homosexual disturbance.

Things were no better with Truman. Susskind had persuaded him to parade about in a white linen suit, spats, and a broad-brimmed 1930s Panama hat—the costume he wore in his portrait that was currently on display at the Metropolitan Museum.

I had put my foot down at Susskind's suggestion that Joyce and I query Frost about his interracial romance with Diahann Carroll or question Capote about Princess Lee Radziwill and all the beautiful jet-setters whose prominent places in Truman's life often made it necessary for me to remind myself that Capote is a splendid and serious writer. It fell to me, as the conscientious objector, to think up other questions that would make a good interview. Frankly, I was incapable of inquiring about their views on the weather intelligently: both shows were bad. Neither man gave of himself because he was not asked to do so. The Frost interview was nothing but more Frost. The Capote half-hour was so silly and simpering that old Duke at the ad agency kept it from being aired for months on the grounds that the sponsor, the Chesebrough Pond Company, was pushing Q-tips, cold cream, and petroleum jelly. Capote, he thought, was projecting the wrong type of femininity for beauty products.

The next day Joyce and I met the press. Columnist Eugenia Sheppard asked how our interviewing techniques differed. Joyce volunteered that there were two ways of getting a guest to open up: "One method is like the weather; if the interviewer blows hard, shrill air, the guest draws his cloak of personalness tightly around him; but if the interviewer is like the warming, gentle sun, the guest will remove his protective covering of his own accord." That Joyce considered herself the Sally Sunshine of our duo became more apparent when she told another writer, "Interviewers are like interrogating cops; one officer pushes the victim around threatening mayhem if he does not confess his deeds. The other cop is good, kind, and gentle, telling the victim to 'come on, you can trust me, tell me you did it.'" "I," she added sweetly, "am the good cop."

"And I," I recall thinking, "am going to have to do some fancy stepping to get around this clever little sunbeam."

Some time later we were guests on the "Dick Cavett Show." I was in the make-up room with Joe Colombo, who was publicizing his stand against the linking of Italians with organized crime. Some weeks afterward he would be gunned down at an Italo-American street rally, but that night he was in fine form and quite likeable. From the adjoining make-up chair I asked: "Where is your gang with machine guns in their violin cases?"

"Just outside this door, dolly, so don't try anything."

"Certainly not," I said. "I'd hate to wind up floating face down in the East River!" He told me they used the Hudson.

Mr. Colombo, his friends, and I, spent quite a while together chatting and watching the TV monitor in the Green Room while Joyce was on camera with Cavett. Probably because of my experience with organized government, the Mafia never seemed any more formidable to me than the power gangs of Washington; we got along famously. Out on the stage, Cavett asked Joyce the inevitable question about our differing interviewing techniques. Joyce told him that she went straight to the "heart and soul of the guest . . . while my partner approaches from a more *southerly* direction." Backstage, Colombo grabbed my arm saying, "You see what it's like, don'tcha, dolly: someone doing you dirt and you can't do nothing about it?"

In introduction Cavett called my name three times; pronouncing Howar to sound like "whore." By the time I came out to the stage, I was not amused. I managed in the small space of time between my introduction and the thousandth commercial break to let Mr. Cavett and Mrs. Susskind know that my indignation at their cavalier twisting of my name and mention of my professional techniques sat as poorly with me as the word "Mafia" did with the Colombo gang backstage. I told Cavett that women in general were constantly defamed and abused on television, that we were tired of being projected on the air as stupid idiots whose level of intelligence is judged by the amount of soap powder we are suckered into buying, that it was asinine for women in television to be depicted as genies in bottles, flying nuns, and nose-twitching witches who, when cleverer than men, had the excuse of magic powers.

I do not think anyone listened except Mr. Colombo, who came up to me afterward and gave me his business card which, among others, stated his profession as florist, undertaker, and haberdasher. He told me, "We gotta keep in touch, dolly, we might be able to work something out together some day."

Faster than the actual televised show went downhill, the relationship between Joyce and Barbara disintegrated. When *The New York Times* hinted that I might be bearable if I worked alone, and *Newsweek* said I was sprinkled with stardust, morale fell apart. Rupert Hitzig, the show's producer, managed to keep Susskind off the set during the taping; but when things did not go to her liking, Joyce reported fully to Susskind, who stepped in to make matters worse. No one trusted anyone; no one liked anyone. I was despondent over the largely poor acceptance of the show, disgusted to be one of the first women on night air and not be good enough to open the industry to more women. I was more than a little concerned at the prospect of being unemployed again.

Hitzig and his assistant producer, a wonderfully level and talented woman named Phyllis Adams, became so powerless that all they could do was grit their teeth and hope to make it through the season with professional reputations and sanity intact. While I was certainly no paragon of wisdom, I became enraged when Joyce asked of Hubert Humphrey, "How does Muriel feel when you dance with pretty girls?" or of George McGovern in discussing abortion versus religion, "I thought Jack Kennedy cleared up all that Catholic thing." When Joyce was not embarrassing me with her questions, I was traumatizing her and the sponsor by discussing sex in politics with Barry Goldwater, urging Tony Bennett to expose the Mafia hold over nightclub performers, James Michener to explode the fraud of the best-seller list, or badgering Walter Matthau into agreeing that women ranked sociologically lower than Spanish-speaking prizefighters. Often Phyllis and Rupert would take me to lunch and console me: "Something good will come out of this for you, Barbara, just don't lose your temper. Ride it out."

One afternoon, Susskind stopped Phyllis and me in the hall, calling us "castrating bitches." I turned on him. "Sorry you don't have anything we can work on, David." So much for temper control.

After the first taping, I went to Washington to get my children organized for the rest of the television season. Resentful of my absence, Edmond, whose illness had left him with a hearing loss, was becoming abusive of authority, using language bizarre in a seven-year-old and blaming the obscenities on "my hearing aid. It told me to say that." The hearing aid had quite a vocabulary.

Mama was still in St. Luke's Hospital, convalescing from her spinal fusion. It was necessary that she spend the two weeks after the operation on her stomach, not moving, and that she be attended around the clock by nurses. I had been in Washington only two days when her morale began to deteriorate. I was told she was suffering from a common affliction of people immobilized so long. Called "hospital fever," it is a form of depression in which the patient loses hope of recovering, of ever leaving his room.

I talked by phone to her or her nurse a half-dozen times a day. I pleaded with her, "Hold on now, I'll be back in a couple of days and I won't leave again until I take you with me." On the Saturday night before the Monday of my proposed return, Mama's voice on the phone had a peculiar resignation that had passed beyond the panic of lying face down in a hospital bed. I decided to leave the children with a friend and go to New York the next morning. At 3:00 A.M., ten days after a successful operation, the telephone rang, and before I picked up the receiver, I knew my mother was dead.

I could not talk or cry or scream; I could only walk around in shock. I would go to the phone to call Mama, to tell her something terrible had happened, that, as always, she had better come to Washington, that I needed her. Several times I went so far as to dial her number before I realized that the terrible thing I needed her to help me through was the fact that she was gone. I waited the hours until the earliest plane left for New York.

The plane had no through space to New York. I took a seat as far as Baltimore, strapped myself to it, and when the plane landed there and filled up, I told the shocked stewardess that I would not get off, that my mother was dead in the basement of a strange hospital and she needed me. I told her she would have to get the police to get me off. Without another word, I flew into New York and went directly to the hospital, straight to her empty room. The mattress was rolled up. Cards and letters, clippings about my show, funny Valentines the children had made her, were all in the trashcan. They were the only sign she had ever been in that room. I picked them out of the basket, walked out to the nurses' station and asked where my mother was. The nurse called to an orderly, "Which morgue floor is 1102 on?"

On her desk was Mama's bottle of Elizabeth Arden lotion, the purple bow exactly as the children had fixed it two weeks before. I picked up the bottle, that indisputable evidence of the callous looting of the dead that prevails in hospitals, and for the most horrifying moment, I considered bludgeoning the nurse with it.

At the morgue desk, I asked a Puerto Rican attendant for my mother. In Spanish-English he told me I could not have the body unless I had a written release from the deceased's husband. I lied, telling him my mother was divorced. He argued that his records showed otherwise, then told me I needed the signatures of both my sisters to remove the corpse. I told him they were in the hall, took the release papers out of his hand and into the ladies' room where I forged both names. I collected her suitcase and signed the necessary papers for the undertaker to prepare Mama for the flight south. I was desperate to get my mother home.

An autopsy was done. Death was caused by massive blood clots in the lung: suffocation. Though the surgeon never communicated with us other than to submit his bill, I learned that, by some hospital mishap, the medication to thin Mama's blood had been administered only several hours prior to death. I could never locate the private nurse who was on duty; she had been out of the room most of the evening. A hospital resident told me that my mother had defied medical science in her will to live and had gotten up out of bed dragging with her the apparatus of two intravenous feedings. She died in the hospital corridor. Even in death, Mama imparted to me some of her enormous love of life.

Puddin and Charlsie went directly to Raleigh to begin funeral arrangements. I stayed the night in New York and brought the body home by plane. The knowledge that it was Mama's and my final adventure together took something out of me that would never return. Mama had told me that she never wanted her body dressed and waxed for public display. She was to be wrapped in a linen cloth, placed in a simple closed coffin, and put into an above-ground mausoleum. There would be no elaborate funeral.

Then began the whispered inquiries from the funeral home: "Do you want the waterproof, worm-proof, grave lining or the *cheap* one?" "Do you really wish your mother to rest eternally in a *wooden* coffin?" "It is *highly unusual* to have no pallbearers." People I had known all my life found it peculiar that the body was not on view and thought it strange that no casket was at the service. My sisters stood by me in honoring Mama's wishes, but we could not sway my father on the subject of the mausoleum. A rich business associate had built himself an expensive tomb in anticipation of his yet unrealized death, and it had become something of a provincial joke around Raleigh. Daddy would have no part of a burial process he had ridiculed. Mama was put into the ground.

The night before the funeral, Rupert Hitzig called to tell me that two segments of "Joyce and Barbara" would be filmed as scheduled on the day of Mama's funeral. David Susskind was to sit in for me. We taped only every two weeks, but it was inconvenient for Susskind to rearrange his schedule. Rupert was embarrassed and promised he would do everything he could to see that I was paid for the shows. Along with the rest of the staff, he and Phyllis sent flowers and notes. From Joyce and David Susskind I never received a card, flower, or call. Susskind refused to pay me for the missed performance.

21

There were many feelings and emotions that surrounded me then, thoughts I succeeded in suppressing for a long time. Everywhere were painful reminders of a woman I loved with a closeness I cherished and missed deeply. There were terrible nightmares, sweat-filled morning hours when I cried until my throat glands swelled, funny daytime fantasies when I pretended it was all a bad dream, that Mama was alive down South, waiting for me, loving me, and needing me. I learned to blot out thoughts of her under six feet of red clay. I could not stand to think of her in the ground. Often I would see things, eat something, hear a snatch of television dialogue, listen to the children talk about her, even watch the changing of Washington's trees in the spring—and I would be reminded of her great zest for life, her ambitions for me, her love of things and people dear to her.

I hated her loss of freedom. More selfishly, I missed her—her humor, her loyalty, her courage, all the things she did for me. Death had left a raw emptiness and for a long time I was not sure I had any spirit without her. A part of what I was belonged to Mama—much of what I did, how I had used my life. I scarcely knew what part of me had been buried with her, what part was validly my own to piece back together. I was overcome with paranoia, the feeling that someone was out to get me, to take from me whatever I had left to love. My old fear of losing the children came back and it was becoming harder for me to leave them to go to New York and finish up the "Joyce and Barbara Show." I felt I had no friend any more, only my sisters whose individual griefs were similar to my own. I could not come to terms with the feeling that I was no longer anyone's little girl, that I was *it*, the buck now stopped with me.

I completed taping my television series, happy that it was over and not to be renewed. While I knew I had failed in the big leagues, I was not sorry to let it all slip away. Not only did television seem an unnecessary evil, but I had, in my own neurotic grief, come to think of the mammoth eye of the camera as evil—if allowed to focus on me, it would suck out whatever life was left. What the camera took, it would not give back.

At the end of the season, May of 1971, a close friend and I went to Paris where we rented a car and drove through France to the Riviera. I harbored a plan to bundle up my children and move them abroad. But the land of Scott and Zelda Fitzgerald was no comfort to me. I brooded through the French countryside, looking deeply into myself; I found the richness of the Riviera cloying, and was dissatisfied with French customs and food. I learned about myself in those weeks. I was deeply and irrevocably North American—southern above all else. I needed the tackiness of American life—cheeseburgers, television, Miss America, Doris Day, all the honkytonk clutter of things familiar. I could never be the expatriate. I came home to Washington, the only place where I belonged. I needed to feel at one with my surroundings, needed the security of southern life that Washington gave me. I wanted my children; they seemed to be all I had.

But I had friends. They were all there, ready and warm in a sense I had never imagined. They gathered me up and held me until I could take care of myself again. Despite the poor ratings, Kay Graham began running "Joyce and Barbara" in a nighttime slot on her station and gave an opening party to which all the people who understood my grief came and said the right things. I was rarely left alone, and although I knew my friends were taking turns keeping me occupied and that it was an imposition in a fast-moving society such as Washington, I was grateful. I needed them, and they did not let me down. Completely lost in sorrow, I stayed mostly in a dark room until Sarah, a wonderful Negro woman who had loved Mama too, came in one day with a broom, telling me, "If you aren't out of this bed today, I'm gonna broom you out. Yo' mama was too proud of you to let her down this way. You got to like life enough for her now."

There were days when a close friend, pregnant with her own fourth child, would take time out of her hectic personal and social life to collect my children and take them to play, to the ballet, to dinner. There were days when women I had taken for granted for many years would bring busy-work and sit with me through the afternoon—wives of city officials, television correspondents, newspaper columnists, and politicians, all of them anxious to get me through a bad time. They showed no exasperation with my prolonged grief, and when things got better, they were genuinely glad for me. Being private people, they would be embarrassed to be named, but the Joans, Margots, Sallys, Anns, Pollys, Ediths, and Muffies poured energy into me in a way that is not expected from women whose lives are filled with the activities of an ambitious, power-oriented town.

Each of their husbands, together with my unmarried male friends—all of them integral parts of Washington—took care of me at social gatherings, calling to offer help, encouragement, legal assistance, money. There was Joe Alsop telling me one night that he did not have vast wealth, but he would do whatever he could if I needed anything; David Brinkley not offering to lend me money, but saying: "Hell, Barbara, you can *have* it—that's what it's for"; Henry Kissinger taking me out to dinner, sometimes with friends, sometimes alone, calling long distance to make sure I was all right—all of them touching base to let me know they cared, that they were ready if I needed them, that in some very sweet way, I was a part of them, and that they were loyal, even anxious to give to me the kind of love that is not associated with Washington.

They got me through. Those complicated people that make Washington the mysterious jungle it is, those famous men and women who to the rest of the world are glamorous and powerful, even ruthless, public figures, have in them a specialness that is inconsistent with the city's official image —a combination of worldly involvement and personal commitment that makes Washington genuine despite its reach for power. It seemed I had to find depth in myself to see it in others.

When I look back at the two years since my mother died, I am enormously saddened to understand that I would not be on my way to real peace if my mother were still alive. I feel guilty that this is so. I also feel anger and frustration that a complex woman like my mother was forced to seek her fulfillment through me and that only through her needless death could I be free to arrange my life to bring me happiness. I waste no time regretting, but sometimes I wish Mama and I had channeled all the energy we spent making me noticed and publicized into something meaningful and lasting, something from which we both would have derived contentment. Such is her grip on me, even from the grave, that I wonder if Mama would approve of my life now, if she would have gone along with my changing needs, encouraged my efforts for privacy, understood that I needed more for myself than my picture on a television screen, my name in print—and that she did too.

She only wanted me to be special. It was I who chose the method. She encouraged me because it seemed to be what I wanted. Many years back, she and I crossed that line where she relinquished command of our relationship and passed the upper hand to me. She became the daughter, I the mother. I made the decisions and set the pace; she kept me honest. Mama would have mellowed with me; together, we would have matured from *enfants terribles* to *anciennes terribles* and had a fine time doing it.

There is great irony that after Mama's death, I would come to love deeply the city that had frustrated and influenced me the most, the city Mama and I had always thought the place I should conquer. We are all victims of the past. Ed Howar reacted to his upbringing; Mama to hers; I to mine and so on down the line. I love them all, often wishing I had been wiser in dealing with each force, that I had stormed the citadel with more kindness than enthusiasm, that I had been a better daughter, wife, mother, friend, citizen, and woman. When Mama died I lost the need to prove myself to Washington, and strangely, the relationship between me and the city assumed a new meaning, not the passionate possessiveness of my youth and maturing, but a comfortable, gentle friendship.

This is not to say that I will not continue to observe and participate and comment in the town where I have spent my youth, a town where I will perhaps spend the next half of my life doing many of those things I have done all along, but I believe I may take it all with a lighter heart, with less madness and a different enthusiasm. My greed for the city has been replaced by a more delicate, maybe even wiser, affection. It amuses me to know I am emotionally ready to handle power and I no longer want it.

28 Q